STARTING UP

DO YOU HAVE WHAT IT TAKES TO MAKE IT IN YOUR OWN BUSINESS?

DAVID E. RYE

CRAIG R. HICKMAN

PRENTICE HALL PRESS

Library of Congress Cataloging-in-Publication Data

Rye, David E.
    Starting up : an interactive adventure that challenges your entrepeneurial
skills / David E. Rye, Craig R. Hickman.
        p.   cm.
    ISBN 0-13-312240-9   ISBN 0-7352-0028-9 (PBK)
    1. New business enterprises—Management.   I. Small business—Management.
3. Entrepeneurship.   I. Hickman, Craig R.   II. Title.
HD62.5.R927   1997   97-19720
658.1'141—dc21   CIP

Printed in the United States of America

10 9 8 7 6 5 4 3 2 1   10 9 8 7 6 5 4 3 2 1

ISBN 0-13-312240-9   ISBN 0-7352-0028-9 (PBK)

ATTENTION: CORPORATIONS AND SCHOOLS

Prentice Hall books are available at quantity discounts with bulk purchase for
educational, business, or sales promotional use. For information, please write
to: Prentice Hall Special Sales, 240 Frisch Court, Paramus, NJ 07652. Please
supply: title of book, ISBN, quantity, how the book will be used, date needed.

PRENTICE HALL PRESS
Paramus, NJ 07652

A Simon & Schuster Company

On the World Wide Web at http://www.phdirect.com

Prentice Hall International (UK) Limited, *London*
Prentice Hall of Australia Pty. Limited, *Sydney*
Prentice Hall Canada, Inc., *Toronto*
Prentice Hall Hispanoamericana, S.A., *Mexico*
Prentice Hall of India Private Limited, *New Delhi*
Prentice Hall of Japan, Inc., *Tokyo*
Simon & Schuster Asia Pte. Ltd., *Singapore*
Editora Prentice Hall do Brasil, Ltda., *Rio de Janeiro*

Contents

III

Contents

INTRODUCTION

You've just made one of the most dramatic decisions of your life. You have decided to leave the corporate world of downsizing and build your own business where your entrepreneurial skills are about to be put to the test. Your goal: find a business venture that will replace your lost corporate income and provide for your future retirement expectations.

If you succeed, your new start-up could emerge as a huge success where you would stand to gain a great deal of job satisfaction for the first time in your working life and wealth beyond your wildest expectations. If you fail, your limited personal funds will be exhausted and you may have to go back to a dreaded corporate job.

So begins *Starting-Up*, the book that gives you a fascinating way to sharpen your practical knowledge by entering one of today's most challenging and exciting opportunities: Starting-up and running your own business.

Starting-up challenges your insight and entrepreneurial judgment as you hammer out tough business alternatives that you must consider to get started. Each decision brings about a different situation filled with opportunities, pitfalls, and a new set of decisions you must make that will lead to your success or failure. Whatever decisions you make, there will be consequences that demand further analysis and action. You'll be required to make tough choices involving finance, the competition, market share, your own personal desires, and much more. Each decision can take you one step closer to triumphant success or catastrophic failure.

From the outset, *Starting-Up* introduces you to a colorful cast of characters and challenging situations, which will immerse you in the energy and drama of setting up your own business. You'll meet adversaries who are determined to rip you off, as well as legitimate people who can help you make it in a setting that will influence your every move as you grapple with real-life situations. In the process, you'll learn about the author's proven techniques for building a successful start-up business.

Whether you succeed or fail in your first attempt at becoming an entrepreneur, the best is yet to come. *Starting-Up*'s unique "you make the decision" approach lets you replay your choices again and again to explore the outcome of different decisions. In all, the book covers 76 decisions and 26 different outcomes for hours of exciting reading.

Combining the suspense of an adventure novel with the expert insight of a seasoned entrepreneur, *Starting-Up* lets you experience firsthand what you need to do to take advantage of the fastest growing segment of America's economy: the small business. It's the most enjoyable and provocative way to sharpen your decision-making skills and your innovative thinking. Good luck!

CHAPTER 1

YOUR CURRENT SITUATION

Some days it pays to stay in bed.

You wake up at 6:00 A.M. to the sound of running water that turns out not to be your spouse taking a shower, but a steady stream of rainwater pouring from the ceiling of your recently rebuilt Victorian house in Lincolnwood, Illinois. The day goes downhill from there. The contractor who put the new roof on the house has gone out of business, and you can't find anyone else to look at the problem for two days. Traffic to your office is the worst you've ever seen, and as you sit there fuming you spill a cup of hot herbal tea in your lap. When you finally pull into the parking lot at Candela Resins, your executive parking slot is blocked by an electrician's van. At least you brought an umbrella, but that doesn't keep your shoes from getting soaked as you run two hundred yards across the parking lot. Finally seated at your desk staring at your laptop computer, you discover why the electrician had been called to corporate headquarters: the electricity was out for several hours during the night, and the lightning bolt that struck a nearby power line fried your laptop's hard drive since you had failed to plug it into the power-surge bar behind your credenza. The fifty hours of work you had done on that crucial market-positioning report due on the CEO's desk this morning was wiped out with no back-up.

1

That's when a ray of sunshine finally breaks through on your day. When you call CEO Martin Candela to explain why you will not be able to give him that report on time, he laughs and says, "Don't worry about it. Come on over anyway. I've got some big news for you!"

Visions of a promotion and a handsome raise dance in your head as you sit across from the CEO, still slightly damp around the edges but feeling optimistic for the first time all day. That's when lightning strikes again.

"I see a real opportunity for you, given your talents," announces Candela. "Since the merger will eliminate your position as Director of Market Research and Analysis, you can do what I did at your age; strike out on your own. Of course, we'll be giving you a small fortune in severance pay to help you get started."

"What merger?" you gasp.

"Late last week," Candela prattles on, "Hoerst-Brandt, the $30 billion German chemical company, made a surprise offer to our major shareholders. After a lot of soul searching, we agreed to the deal." He drones on about how the merger will bring needed synergies to Candela Resins over the long term, all the while apologizing profusely about the elimination of your job, but insisting that it represents an opportunity rather than a problem. Of course, he never mentions the enormous wealth the sell-out will bestow on a small group of Candela Resin shareholders in the short term. Just when you thought things couldn't get worse, you're not only out of a job, but Martin Candela's promise six months earlier to raise your position to Vice President status within the year means nothing anymore. The only silver lining in this otherwise ugly storm cloud appears to be your severance package, eighteen month's salary without bonuses, $144,000 paid out over the next year and a half. Unfortunately, at this point in life (you just turned 45 a month ago) you estimate it will take almost that long and that much money to find another job. Later in the day an outplacement specialist suggests you should anticipate one month of job searching for every $10,000 in expected compensation. With bonuses, you made just over $120,000 last year and would have approached $135,000 this year had the merger not changed everything. According to your outplacement counselor, then, you should look for a total compensation package in the $140,000 to $160,000 range, which boils down to 14 to 16 months of job hunting.

A few days later, walking back to your office after a brief good-bye party with your seven-person staff, only two of whom will remain after the merger, you feel a depressing mixture of fear and uncertainty growing inside you. "Corporations are like politicians," you think to yourself, "always around when they need you, but conveniently indisposed when you need them." You chide yourself for that negative attitude which sounds suspiciously like your steelworker father, the only man in America who still openly praises Senator Joseph McCarthy. You remind yourself that Martin Candela, despite his selfish reasons for accepting the merger, did give you some good advice. As your father also used to say, "If life hands you lemons, make lemonade." You pack your briefcase with a few personal items and leave Candela Resins forever at the end of the day, beginning on June 10 what you jokingly call an extended summer vacation.

"Good riddance," you exclaim as you climb into your new Range Rover 4.0 SE, price-tag $54,000, purchased only a month ago. Oh, how you wish you had held on to your 1982 Toyota Celica just a little longer. But you wipe that thought away, too, telling yourself, "No matter, what's done is done. Look on the bright side." At least your spouse has a good job working as Midwest Regional Budget Director for the Environmental Protection Agency at $52,000 a year plus benefits. If it weren't for your two children, both in college (price tag, $54,000 per year), you could probably stay home and do nothing: take up painting, write a novel, enjoy life. Up to now you and your spouse have paid for all your children's expenses at Bowdoin and Swarthmore, because your income and assets have proved too high to qualify for financial aid. If you can't find another job in the next 18 months, that will certainly change. With patience and perseverance and a lot of luck, you can keep your promise to fund your children's undergraduate education. By the time all the severance money runs out, son Jack will still have two years to go at Bowdoin, but daughter Stacey will have graduated from Swarthmore. Thank God.

You spend the afternoon in a little "authentic" Mexican cafe with your brother-in-law, an awfully dull fellow for an astute CPA, to review your financial situation: two life-insurance policies with a combined cash value of $69,000; stocks with a current market value of approximately $42,000; a fully vested pension plan currently worth $58,000; IRAs and an old Keogh with a current value of $26,000; two weeks of Marriott time-shares worth around $20,000; a home in suburban Chicago worth $400,000, you hope; three cars worth about $78,000; and a Harley-Davidson Sportster worth maybe $8,000. On the liability side, you list: a $350,000 home mortgage; $54,000 in annual college obligations; $62,000 in car loans, and miscellaneous consumer debt of approximately $17,000. Your current net worth amounts to approximately $210,000. For the next 18 months your family's combined income will average approximately $10,000 per month, after taxes. Monthly expenses averaged $13,000 per month last year, including monthly payments for college. You had prepared yourself for going in the hole each month for a couple of years, drawing upon savings, when Jack entered Bowdoin, but you also hoped salary and bonus increases would stop the bleeding when you became Vice President. That brings to mind another of Dad's favorite clichés: "Never count your chickens before they hatch." You could always sell the house and move into a condominium. Corporations are downsizing, why can't families? Your brother-in-law says he has to run to meet a client. With a smear of refried beans in his beard, he quickly departs, leaving you the unpaid check. You smile at the irony, glad that you took some cash out of the ATM before meeting him for lunch.

Over the next several weeks you work diligently, reviving your neglected network of friends and associates, scouring the newspapers, writing letters, following-up by telephone, contacting headhunters, and keeping yourself as busy as possible. By mid-August you've gone through two interviews, both of which proved fruitless, and you've scheduled a third for next week with a toy-making company that looks even less promising. The outplacement counselor warned you about discouragement, but you had no idea it would get this bad. You've ignored your spouse for weeks and hardly spoken to your two children who are home for the summer, both working two jobs in an effort to defray their expenses. You feel a strange sort of numbing misery encroaching upon you daily, and you must fight hard to keep from thinking of yourself as a complete failure.

After your third job interview, where the 26-year-old CEO of TechToys suggests you're overqualified, your spouse suggests a camping trip to the Black Hills before the kids go back to school. At first you object, saying you'd only put a damper on the fun, but your spouse persists.

"It would do you good. We need to find a few moments of peace this summer, and we can't do that if you just sit around the house feeling sorry for yourself."

"I'm not feeling sorry for myself."

"Face it. You haven't smiled at me in a month."

That stings you. "I'm worried about our future."

"You need to stop living for tomorrow for a few days. Enjoy the moment. Stop the worrying. It's only been two months. This summer will never come again. Spend some time with those you love most, even if that means forcing yourself to forget for a few days. Maybe a break from it all will help you put your life back into perspective."

"It's not just the lousy job search, I feel like I'm going through the motions. It's dehumanizing. What's worse, I get sick to my stomach thinking about going to work for another corporation where I have no control over my destiny. Working hard and performing well just doesn't cut it anymore. Candela proved that. I actually dread another job."

"How many times have I suggested starting your own business?"

"Easy to say. Tough to do."

"So get tough."

With that, your spouse turns and walks away, leaving you to ponder the conversation. You have gone soft, you conclude. Ten years ago you would have handled this setback differently. Can you muster the courage, the toughness, to heed Martin Candela's parting advice and strike out on your own? With a new sense of possibilities opening up in front of you, you agree to join the family on the Black Hills outing.

Five days into this year's downsized family vacation (last year you spent three weeks in Italy, the year before that two weeks in Australia) you finally feel new stirrings of life. You share some of your deepest fears and hopes with your family around a midnight campfire only to rediscover the sweet joy and peace of family love. Your spouse was right, strength does come most from those who love you most.

Then, on the sixth day of your vacation, the miracle of rejuvenation stuns you as you stare at the emerging image of Crazy Horse carved into the side of Thunderhead Mountain. The sheer audacity of sculptor Korczak Ziolkowski's vision and ambition mesmerizes you as you think of the five decades of back-breaking work and millions of tons of removed rock that have only begun to shape the 600-foot monolith into a memorial to the Native American spirit. But that's not all; Korczak's vision not only includes the mountain carving but also an Indian Museum of North America, a University, and a Medical Training Center as part of this North American Indian humanitarian project.

And, even though Korczak died in 1982 at the age of 74, his vision and ambition live on in the Black Hills. You can feel it, touch it, smell it. For the next four hours you immerse yourself in learning everything you can about Korczak and the Crazy Horse Memorial, relishing tantalizing bits of information, such as the 176 gallons of paint it took to outline Crazy Horse on the side of the mountain; the 741-step staircase to the mountain top built by volunteers; the 9 million tons of rock blasted away; the erection of a 26-ton scaffold on tracks to carve Crazy Horse's face; the 2,000 miles of rock surface in the carving; the hundreds of Native American scholarships already awarded as part of the larger humanitarian project; the reality that the Crazy Horse Memorial is not a Federal or state project but privately funded, and, finally, how Korczak himself carried on relentlessly through numerous serious injuries on Thunderhead Mountain, including four spinal operations, two heart attacks, quadruple bypass surgery, and worsening diabetes and arthritis to ensure that his dream would find eventual fulfillment. Later that night, long after your family has returned to the campsite a few miles away, you continue gazing at the now flood-lighted sculpture in progress with one thought on your mind: with enough vision and ambition, one individual human being can accomplish anything.

As you reluctantly return to your campsite sometime after midnight, you realize that today's experience has changed you somehow. It's not that you've never experienced awe at the accomplishments of great men and women or that you've never contemplated the matchless power of the human spirit, but never before in your life has all your experience, learning, insight, and inspiration come together in a single moment of personal need to illuminate the pathway ahead. Thanks to Crazy Horse and Korczak Ziolkowski, you lie down under the stars not thinking about carving a mountain memorial but about starting a company. For a brief moment you wonder what Crazy Horse and Korczak would think of your dream, then you remember one of Korczak's quotes from the exhibit: "Work is one of our greatest blessings. Everyone should have an honest occupation, a job they believe in, so they can give it their best. Of course, first they must believe in themselves. I believe in myself, and I believe I can do this job."

During the last three days of the vacation you savor every moment with your family, even tourist-infested Mt. Rushmore, sharing your new-found enthusiasm for life at each opportunity. By the time you return to Chicago and spend the weekend helping Stacey and Jack pack up for college, you can't wait to get going on your new venture. Having already purchased several magazines and books about starting your own company, you launch into an intense reading marathon to orient yourself to the task ahead.

You read about Steve and Andi Rosenstein, who started their highly successful *Fitigues* clothing line with only $20,000 and grew it to $20 million in revenues in seven years; Mary Naylor, who started a business offering hotel-style concierge services to office buildings with only $2,000, and after eight years built her business into a $7 million enterprise; David Uible, who began publishing Russian medical journals with $15,000 in start-up costs and five years later enjoys sales of $7 million; Beth Stewart who started, without any up-front costs, a business turning mass-transit buses into traveling commercials by painting the entire outside of the bus, until, after nine years, she's racking up $3 million in sales; Chuck Crary, who spent $30,000 in start-up costs to launch a farm and lawn manufacturing company that makes stump grinders and *The Weed Roller*, a machine that cleans weeds out of lake swimming areas, and who after fifteen years has created a $10 million company; Gail Lozoff, who started a bagel business seven years ago with $250,000 and now owns seven stores with over $10 million in sales; Laverne Woock, who began a business that designs and manufactures three-dimensional archery targets and decoys with only $3,500 ten years ago, and now sells over $6 million worth of products a year.

In addition, you read dozens of reports on the hottest businesses for entrepreneurs, including such ventures as Family Entertainment Centers, Specialty Plants & Flowers, Long-Distance Reselling, Multimedia Services, Music Lessons, Aerial Photography, 900 Numbers, Ice Cream/Yogurt Shops, Desktop Publishing, Tea Salons, Specialized Staffing Services, Telemarketing, Maid Service, Bulletin Board Services (smaller versions of major on-line services like CompuServe), Pretzel Shops, Picture Framing, Children's Learning Centers, Bed & Breakfast Inns, Medical Billing Services, Herb Gardens, Exporting, Catering, Specialty Travel, Delivery Service, Home Health Care, Environmental Services, Sports & Recreational Rentals, Brewpubs, and Computer Training Centers. After countless hours of research, you begin to feel slightly overwhelmed by the number of "business opportunity" publications on the market. One evening at dinner, you ask your spouse, "Did you know that over 30 percent of the GNP comes from entrepreneurial ventures, and that over 40 million Americans work in small businesses?" Without waiting for a response, you bolt from the dinner table and return to your reading. You haven't felt this excited in years.

Your spouse brings you a bowl of chocolate ice cream as you continue your search. You spend the rest of the evening studying the top ten franchise opportunities in America today, as updated in *Entrepreneur* magazine: Subway, McDonald's, Burger King, Hardee's, 7-Eleven, Dunkin' Donuts, Mail Boxes Etc., Choice Hotels International, Snap-On Inc., and Dairy Queen. By midnight you're so emotionally pumped up you can't go to sleep. Your head buzzing with all the possibilities, you spend the next three hours mulling over one business venture after another. You finally fall asleep around 4:00 A.M., with a biography of Korczak Ziolkowski perched on your nose.

The next morning you wake up at 10:00 A.M. with a sore throat and headache, and you realize that you can't continue letting your emotions run out of control. It's time to make a move. Fortunately, an *Inc.* magazine cover story, "4 Steps to Start-Up Success," puts things in perspective for you. The article summarizes Norm Brodsky's advice to husband and wife entrepreneurs Bobby and Helene Stone who are trying to build a computer supply business. Brodsky, a confirmed entrepreneur who has made and lost millions of dollars over the years, is the founder and former CEO of Perfect Courier, a three-time *Inc.* 500 company. Currently working on another start-up, Brodsky became a reluctant consultant to the Stones as they struggled to get their little business off the ground. You jot down the essence of his advice:

4 STEPS TO START-UP SUCCESS

1. *Get a Grip on Your Emotions and Decide on Your Goal*: By identifying the goal, you can get your extreme emotions out of the way.

2. *Make Sure You Understand What Cash Flow Is and Where It's Going to Come From*: You don't need an elaborate business plan, just your best guess of how you're going to get your business to generate the cash it needs to pay its bills. Construct simple yet realistic income and cash-flow statements.

3. *Recognize the Sales Mentality Before It's Too Late*: Just having a sales mentality does not guarantee success. You must also develop a business mentality, and that means insuring healthy margins.

4. *Learn to Anticipate and Recognize the Changes in Your Business*: Look at your business as a living organism. Living things constantly change.

Feeling subdued and sobered by Norm Brodsky's advice, you quickly move from an emotional frame of mind to an intellectual mind-set, spending the rest of the day and early evening at the Northwestern University library. You read some recent research in entrepreneurship that shows how education in leadership and management, the kind of stuff you learned twenty years ago in business school, contributes little if anything to an entrepreneurial education. One researcher, Allan Gibb from Durham University and author of *Recent Research in Entrepreneurship*, contrasts the elements of a traditional management education with the realities of an entrepreneurial focus:

Management Education Focus	*Entrepreneurial Experience Focus*
The past	The future
Critical analysis	Creativity
Knowledge	Insight
Passive understanding	Active understanding
Absolute detachment	Emotional involvement
Manipulation of symbols	Manipulation of events
Written communication and neutrality	Personal communication and influence
Concept	Problem or opportunity

Stimulated by these insights, you peruse numerous other books on entrepreneurship with lofty titles such as *International Perspectives on Entrepreneurship Research, Entrepreneurship and the Outlook for America, Entrepreneurs in Cultural Context, Entrepreneurship and Social Change, Frontiers of Entrepreneurship Research, The Environment for Entrepreneurship,* and *New Findings and Perspectives in Entrepreneurship*. At the end of the day you realize that your internal pendulum has swung from one extreme to the other. Yesterday you were an emotional basket case, today you're an intellectual egghead. Neither extreme, you tell yourself, will get you where you want to go. As you leave the library, you take heart in the words of techno-futurist George Gilder, author of *Recapturing The Spirit of Enterprise*: "The spirit of enterprise . . . is best embodied not in the theory of a writer but in the life of an entrepreneur."

With every fiber of your being, you want to live such a life.

Over the next several days you begin realistically evaluating the business start-up alternatives that seem most appropriate for you. With the help of *Prentice Hall's Vest-Pocket Entrepreneur* and *The McGraw-Hill 36-Hour Course on Entrepreneurship*, you assess your entrepreneurial aptitude as sufficiently strong to fuel the start-up of your new venture. On a page from your son's 20 × 28-inch artist sketchbook, you then begin wrestling with the following questions:

1. What really matters to me in terms of personal satisfaction?

2. What minimum income level do I need to meet my current obligations, and what income level do I hope to reach in the future?

3. What will I do if I do not achieve my income expectations?

4. What type of work really turns me on?

5. What lifestyle considerations mean the most to me?

6. What are my personal talents?

7. What are my financial capabilities?

8. What level of risk can I handle?

9. What amount of money will I need to start-up my business, and where will the money come from?

10. What does my family think of my new business idea and are they prepared to make the necessary sacrifices to help me get started?

To help answer these questions you spend two weeks networking with friends, former business associates, local entrepreneurs, and a couple of small-business consultants. While their input proves helpful, you realize that only you and your family can come up with the answers because only you will end up living with the consequences of your decisions. All the questions begin to numb your mind, but then even your spouse gets tired of your endless questioning and tells you during dinner at the local Red Lobster restaurant to pick something and "just do it."

"I'm not sure I'm ready yet," you say.

"Look. I know in my heart you'll succeed in whatever you do. I'm behind you 100 percent. But I don't think your success depends as much on picking the right business as it does on making whatever you pick work."

After a long silence, you look deep into the eyes of the person who knows you better than any other human being on the earth, "You're right. I could waste a lot of time trying to find the perfect business when what we really want is financial independence and freedom."

"Don't go to the other extreme. I'm not saying stop looking for a business that fits you. You'll do best at something you love. Remember Gail Sheehy's advice in *New Passages*. The difference between a successful and less successful passage from your 40s into your 50s lies in finding and following your passion. Find a business you love, but don't fool yourself into thinking there's only one kind of business that will make you happy. I'm just saying you can analyze this thing to death."

"Who, me?" you say with a broad smile, appreciating once again your spouse's insights.

The next day you begin narrowing your list of possible ventures to those that best fit your capabilities, expectations, and resources. After writing yourself a note to buy Jack a new sketchbook, since you have covered this one with notes, you finalize your list of best start-up options and pin it to the wall.

SIX BEST OPTIONS

1. *Management Consulting and Training*: Provide consulting and training services to small and medium-size companies located in the Great Lakes region, specializing in market research, analysis, and strategy development.

2. *Real-Estate Development*: Acquire property for residential, recreational, and commercial development in the North Chicago area.

3. *Mail Boxes Etc. Franchise*: Purchase several Mail Boxes Etc. franchises in areas throughout the Midwest as the basis for offering customers a variety of superior packaging and mailing services.

4. *Auto-Accessories Manufacturing*: Manufacture innovative, low-cost car and truck accessories for distribution through auto wholesalers and retailers such as NAPA, Big A, Auto Zone, and Checker Auto Parts.

5. *Software and Multimedia Development*: Develop software and multimedia entertainment and educational products for distribution through software outlets such as Egghead, Software Etc., and Babbages.

6. *Lodge/Restaurant/Conference Center in Montana*: Lease to own a mountain retreat on Flathead Lake near Kalispell, Montana to capitalize on that region's growing attraction as a family vacation, management retreat, and personal sabbatical destination.

To summarize the strengths, weaknesses, costs, returns, and timing of each of these potential business ventures, you create an evaluation grid that highlights the essential facts.

EVALUATING YOUR OPTIONS

Business Venture Alternatives	Major Strength	Major Weakness	Start-Up Costs	Income/Profit/ Net Worth Goal	Time to Reach Goal	Key to Success	Risk Rating*
Management Consulting & Training	Ease of Entry	Intense Competition	$30,000	Income of $150,000 per year	3 years	Professional Competence	2
Real-Estate Development	Wealth Creation Potential	Debt Exposure	$100,000	Net Worth of $5 million	5 years	Property Selection	6
Mail Boxes Etc. Franchises	Franchise Support	Heavy Marketing Expenses	$150,000	Profit of $200,000 per year	6 years	Customer Service	4
Auto- Accessories Manufacturing	Opportunities for Innovation	High Capital Investment	$500,000	Net Worth of $10 million	10 years	Product Innovation	7
Software & Multimedia Development	Explosive Demand for Products	Dominance of Large Competitors such as Microsoft	$300,000	Profit of $300,000 per year	7 years	Distribution and Sales	8
Lodge/ Restaurant/ Conference Center in Montana	Lifestyle	Extent of Personal/ Family Change	$200,000	Income of $200,000 per year	5 years	Marketing	10

* On a 1 to 10 scale, 1 represents the lowest risk, 10 the highest.

After three days and nights of nonstop contemplation, you realize it's time to make a decision, but you're still plagued by the trade-off between taking action or doing more analysis. Your spouse provides little help at this point, continuing to express ambivalence about the possible choices and leaving the final decision to you, even if that means moving to Montana. Now you must decide, but first you must resolve your "action vs. analysis" dilemma by choosing one of the two options below:

1. If you want to take action now by selecting one of the six best options, turn to Chapter 2.

2. If you prefer conducting more analysis of each option to further inform and narrow your decision making, turn to Chapter 3.

CHAPTER 2

TAKING ACTION NOW

You have left the corporate domain and decided to become an entrepreneur. Congratulations! You want to be your own boss, run your own business and you're sure you have the right qualifications to be an entrepreneur. Self-confidence is something that you are not lacking. You read somewhere that until recently, entrepreneurs were not widely understood. There was a general lack of knowledge and information about what made them successful and how they operated. The recent interest in America's small businesses has revitalized your interest in entrepreneurs.

Armed with a copy of Prentice Hall's book, *The Vest-Pocket Entrepreneur,* you are drawn to the first chapter that includes a profile of a successful entrepreneur. It even includes a good definition of an entrepreneur: one who organizes and directs a new business undertaking and assumes the risks that are associated with a start-up business. Some of the qualities that are typical of successful entrepreneurs are also discussed:

1. High achievers. Over the past 25 years, studies have shown that entrepreneurs are characterized by their high need for achievement. Because of their need for achievement, they prefer to work with experts when confronted with challenging problems. They tend to be long-range thinkers and will often focus on the vision for their businesses rather than on immediate problems. This attribute can prove to be frustrating for anyone working with entrepreneurs who are attempting to get their attention to help resolve near-term problems.

2. Risk takers. Entrepreneurs are not afraid to take on tasks that are accompanied by risks. However, they are not high risk takers. They prefer to take on intermediate risk and will avoid high risk whenever possible. Entrepreneurs recognize that higher levels of achievement are possible only if they are willing to accept risks to accomplish their goals.

3. Problem solvers. Entrepreneurs are natural leaders and are usually the first to identify problems to be overcome. If it is pointed out to them that their solution to a problem will not work for some valid reason, they will quickly identify an alternate problem-solving solution.

4. High energy levels. Entrepreneurs are physically resilient and in good health. They can work for extended periods of time when building their businesses. They almost refuse to get sick when they are in a "business-building" mode.

5. Self-confidence. Entrepreneurs are highly confident individuals who believe in their skills and abilities. They think their actions can change events and they refuse to believe that outside events can decisively influence their drive for achievement.

6. Emotional attachments. Entrepreneurs frequently have difficulty forming close emotional attachments with people. As a result, they will often become deeply involved in their work, and in the process transfer their feelings for others into their businesses. Some will subsequently treat their business as a living being and become emotionally involved with it.

7. Personal satisfaction. Because entrepreneurs are motivated by a need for personal achievement, they have little interest in any kind of organizational structure. They treat most of the traditional organizational activities of management with disdain and have a difficult time working for large corporations.

8. Controlling their work. Entrepreneurs are self-confident when they are in control of what they're doing. They tackle problems immediately with confidence and are persistent in the pursuit of their objectives. They're at their best in the face of adversity because they thrive on their own self-confidence.

9. *Getting things done.* Entrepreneurs have a never-ending sense of urgency to develop their ideas. Inactivity makes them impatient, tense, and uneasy. They thrive on activity and are not likely to be found sitting on a bank fishing, unless the fish are biting. When they are in the entrepreneurial mode, they are more likely to be found getting things done instead of fishing.

10. *Self-directed.* Entrepreneurs prefer individual sports such as golf, skiing, or tennis over team sports. They prefer games in which their brawn and brain can directly influence the outcome of the game. They have drive, display high energy levels, are achievement-oriented, and are tireless in the pursuit of their goals.

11. *Manage by objectives.* Entrepreneurs can comprehend complex situations that may include planning, making strategic decisions and working on multiple business ideas simultaneously. They are always aware of important details and will continuously review all possibilities to achieve their business objectives. They believe in the management by objective (MBO) principles.

12. *Opportunity analyzers.* Entrepreneurs will carefully analyze opportunities before they commit themselves. They act only after they are convinced that little risk remains in the endeavor. These are traits that carry them on to success where others fail.

13. *Objective thinkers.* When entrepreneurs find a solution to a problem, they will brainstorm the solution with as many qualified people as they can find to avoid judging their own answers. They accept solution modifications that make sense and are willing to replace their own solution with a better alternative. Entrepreneurs refuse to allow their egos to override their objectivity.

Entrepreneurs are achievement-oriented, believe they are masters of their own destiny, they are not dependent upon others for emotional support, and are highly self-directed individuals. They tend to concentrate on the long-term vision of their businesses and ignore daily organizational problems.

You ask yourself: Does the entrepreneurial profile fit me? You know your success as an entrepreneur and a business owner doesn't depend on any one factor, such as having a perfect business location or an adequate source of capital to get started. It depends on your ability to provide excellent general-management capabilities to your business. You recall what Malcolm Baldrige once said: "In the race for excellence, there is no finish line." As an entrepreneur, you plan to continue to develop excellence in everything you do to assure your success. You have some tough choices to make as you contemplate which one of six different business opportunities you want to start-up. Before making your final decision, you review the advantages and disadvantages in the lists that follow:

Consulting and Training

Advantages
1. Lucrative hourly rates
2. Variety of assignments

3. Low start-up cost

4. Relatively easy to change strategic direction
5. Creativity and independence

Disadvantages
1. Requires time to build client base
2. Extensive travel and long hours required
3. May require high-end educational degree (CPA, MBA, Ph.D., etc.)
4. First budget to be cut in tight times
5. Difficult to find qualified employees

Real-Estate Development Company

Advantages
1. High profit potential
2. Somewhat inflation proof
3. Relatively low down payments for property
4. Financing relatively easy to obtain
5. Market comes to you via ads

Disadvantages
1. High start-up cost
2. Long project completion time
3. Heavy dependency on subcontractors and vendors
4. Cash-flow-intensive business
5. Excessive government regulations

Purchasing a Mail Boxes Etc. Franchise

Advantages
1. Purchasing discount on supplies
2. Expert advice available
3. National advertising
4. Proven business plan

5. Association with other owners

Disadvantages
1. Franchise fees
2. Franchiser controls part of business
3. Must follow defined structure
4. Can't add products and services at will
5. More paper work

Creating an Auto-Accessories Manufacturing Company

Advantages	*Disadvantages*
1. Huge market	1. High start-up cost
2. Demand for variety of products	2. Major competition
3. High retail price mark-up	3. May require national distribution
4. Relatively stable market	4. Inventory required
5. Large average customer orders	5. Constant car model/accessory changes

Launching a Software and Multimedia Development Company

Advantages	*Disadvantages*
1. Low start-up costs	1. Very competitive
2. Can be run with small staff	2. Constantly changing technology
3. High retail mark-up	3. Good technical employees hard to find
4. Location of business not important	4. Industry dominated by big companies
5. Multimedia relatively new market	5. Long product development lead time

Finding a Lodge in Montana

Advantages	*Disadvantages*
1. Living in the outdoors	1. Seasonal
2. No commuting to work	2. High staff turnover
3. Cash business	3. Seven day a week operation
4. High tax write-off	4. High maintenance
5. Property appreciates with inflation	5. Very competitive

What type of business do you want to start-up? As you contemplate this crucial, future-shaping decision, you find yourself talking to anybody who will listen to you in a futile attempt to solicit meaningful advice. Your friends all tell you: "Oh what a great idea and be sure to let me know how it all works out!" You know you have a lot of great ideas but they can't all be great. You're convinced that all you are getting from your friends is lip-service. After several sleepless nights, you realize you can wait no longer to make a decision. It's time to get on the train before it leaves the station.

1. If you decide to start a consulting and training business, turn to Chapter 4.

2. If you decide to start a real-estate development company, turn to Chapter 5.

3. If you decide to purchase a Mail Boxes Etc. franchise, turn to Chapter 6.

4. If you decide to create an auto-accessories manufacturing company, turn to Chapter 7.

5. If you decide to start a software and multimedia development company, turn to Chapter 8.

6. If you decide to find a lodge in Montana, turn to Chapter 9.

CHAPTER 3

CONDUCTING MORE

ANALYSIS

Your search for advice about starting a business with your close friends and associates was somewhat successful. Lots of great ideas were generated, but the sessions were missing something. They lacked enthusiasm and elements of real creativity. You're still left with that nagging question: "How do I get started and what can I do to assure my success?" You pick up a bright red brochure that's on your desk entitled *Thinking Like a Start-Up: The wave of the future.* It's an advertisement for a one-day seminar that takes place tomorrow in Boulder, Colorado. The seminar should offer answers and insights about how to apply entrepreneurial principles to start-up your business. Why not attend? A simple 1-800 call, a Visa card and you're registered.

Boulder is a beautiful Colorado city located at the foot of the mighty Rocky Mountains. You pull your rental car into the parking lot of the historic Boulderado Hotel, the host location for the seminar. The registration is a delightfully efficient process that is obviously organized by a market-driven seminar company. You settle down in your seat as the guest speaker approaches the podium.

"Good morning, ladies and gentlemen. My name is Jack Washburn. Over the next eight hours I will show you how to analyze any business opportunity to make sure it's right for you. I'll also show you how to apply the principles of business administration to assure the success of your start-up. First, let's define the core principles that we will be discussing:"

1. Creating, qualifying, and implementing viable ideas

2. Establishing and maintaining competitive advantages

3. Implementing pricing and marketing strategies that work

4. Growing your business in adverse and good times as well

5. Applying technology to get ahead even if you are not a technical person

6. Taking ownership in everything you do with goals, goals, and more goals

"You will notice that I did not list management in the core list of business principles that we will be discussing. That is because the principles listed are nothing more than the tools entrepreneurs apply to complete the management process. All of the business principles that I cover are interlocking. That is to say, each principle relies on support from the other principles to complete the management process. Jack continues with his presentation for the next six hours. You're intrigued and stimulated by what you hear. You begin to understand how to organize your ideas into a viable action plan, one that matches your strengths with what you want to do. At the end of the seminar, Jack passes out what he refers to as an *Entrepreneurial Qualification Questionnaire.* You anxiously answer the questions to see how you stack up as an entrepreneur.

ENTREPRENEURIAL QUALIFICATION QUESTIONNAIRE (ANSWER "YES" OR "NO." NO "MAYBE" ANSWERS ARE ALLOWED.)

1. Do you like to take charge of a given situation and make your own decisions?

2. Do you enjoy competing in competitive business environments?

3. Are you a self-directed individual with strong self-discipline?

4. Do you like to plan ahead and do you consistently meet your goals and objectives?

5. Are you good at time management and do you consistently get things done on time?

6. After you start your business, are you prepared to lower your standard of living until the business produces a solid income?

7. Are you in good health and do you have the physical stamina to consistently work long hours?

8. Can you admit when you are wrong and take advice from others?

9. If your business fails, are you prepared to lose everything you own?

10. Do you have the stability to withstand stress and strain?

11. Can you quickly adapt to changing situations and implement changes when necessary?

12. Are you a self-starter who can work on your own, independently of others?

13. Can you make decisions quickly and not regret bad decisions that you may make?

14. Do you trust people and do they trust you?

15. Do you know how to solve problems quickly, effectively, and with confidence?

16. Can you maintain a positive attitude even in the face of adversity?

17. Are you a good communicator and can you explain your ideas to others in words that they can understand?

18. Can you acquire the skills or find people that have the skills and expertise that you need for your business?

19. Do you know what your personal income expectations are and when you expect to achieve your desired income?

20. Do you know what will you do if you do not achieve your income expectations?

21. Do you know how much money you need to start-up your business and where the money will come from?

22. Will you make more money in your own business than you could working for someone else?

23. Does your family support your new business idea and are they prepared to make the necessary sacrifices to help you get started?

You answer "yes" to all 23 questions and it feels good; you know you're ready to get started! As a result of today's seminar, you realize that business owners are a new breed of entrepreneur capable of dealing with a variety of obstacles to achieve success. Many start their own business as a way to get out of the corporate world. Others start their own businesses under the belief that if their ideas are properly exploited, they'll be catapulted into instant success. Let's face it, you already know the odds of succeeding in a start-up are against you, but you are committed to success and are willing to learn how to avoid failure.

You return home from the seminar and start thinking about some of the businesses you have patronized in the past that no longer exist. Why did they go out of business? According to the *Forbes* magazine you read, most new businesses fail within the first year of operation. And yet, despite tough economic conditions and high business-failure rates, more people are pursuing self-employment opportunities today than ever before. Among the most common reasons given are: self-satisfaction, desire for independence, limited job opportunities, corporate downsizing, reductions in work forces, and lay-off threats.

Many businesses fail because there is not an adequate market for their products or services. You know you've got to be careful not to enter a market that is contracting or changing so quickly that your business cannot establish a sufficient share of the market. A thorough competitive examination and market analysis will be one of your start-up prerequisites.

Your friends at the Chamber of Commerce meetings are constantly telling you that the lack of management skills is a major cause for high business failure rates. You tell yourself this issue doesn't apply to you since you're a great manager. Then you wonder how good you really are! Some people try to beat the odds by buying an established business or a franchise. Although this makes sense, you believe that the long-term success of a purchased business may not be much better than for a start-up business, particularly if you lack management skills. The lack of momentum is another thing that concerns you about start-ups. Start-up businesses have momentum problems that must be overcome. They start off with zero momentum in new markets, momentum that must be established if they are to survive. Adequate financing must be found, supplier relationships must be established, employees must be hired and trained. You're the one who must coordinate all these elements at the same time and you realize it's not going to be easy.

You remind yourself that the failure to obtain the capital needed by start-ups is another common mistake to avoid. Businesses that lack sufficient cash to carry them through at least the first twelve months of operation or until the business starts making money generally don't make it. Undercapitalizing a start-up is much like sending someone across a thousand miles of the Sahara Desert on foot with a cup of water, a blessing, and a hope that they will make it. Without capital or water, you won't make it! Poor budgeting practices will compound the undercapitalization problem. The shortage of capital can become a vicious cycle. If you attempt to solve the problem by borrowing, lenders will shy away from your poorly capitalized business or charge exorbitant interest rates, which further compounds the need for capital.

"What about the competitive analysis?" you ask yourself. Joe Kary, one of your closest business associates, failed to properly appraise the competition and market environment for his new desktop-publishing business. He went out of business in six months. You vow to find the answer to the most fundamental start-up questions: Does a market exist for your products or services? Who are your competitors and how will you successfully compete against them? What are their strengths and weaknesses?

Based upon your reading and discussions, you realize it's not uncommon for an entrepreneur to enter a new market that looks moderately competitive, only to find that his or her new entry causes pricing or promotional wars. You plan to conduct a comprehensive examination to determine if the existing consumer demand can support all competitors currently serving the market and your new business entry before you get started.

When you first heard about Gloria Rickle, you thought you would love to have her problems, but then you learned the rest of the story. She started a graphics service business and encountered too much success during the early start-up stages of the business. Demands for her services skyrocketed and she subsequently expanded too quickly. She strained her financial resources to the point where she was forced to sell the business prematurely at a loss. Even large corporations can go bankrupt by expanding beyond their resources. When profitability begins to decline in a fast-growing business, your creditors will be the first to back away. You make a mental note to control your growth throughout the business development cycle.

Your mind continues to mull over the endless tips and pieces of information you have absorbed. For example, "Location, location, location:" the well-known "what sells in real estate" slogan. For some businesses, like a retail store, location can be more important than what it sells. Finding the right location can be a difficult task even for an experienced business analyst. You plan to analyze and investigate all potential sites for your start-up and list several questions you need to answer relative to location:

1. If you are considering an existing retail location, how many businesses have moved out of that location in the past 10 years?

2. What kind of businesses were they and why did they leave?

3. Is the business area or neighborhood changing?

4. If so, why is it changing and are the changes good or bad for your business?

5. Are parking facilities an important factor to your business? Will you lose customers if parking facilities are inadequate?

After several days of going through all the analytical questions and answers you can think of, you still come back to your original nagging question. How can you be assured that your start-up will be a success? You remember what Peter Drucker once said: "One way to succeed is to work hard at not failing by always anticipating problems before they occur." You promise yourself to take a proactive posture toward everything you do to run your business, every second, minute and hour of the day.

You are aware of several small businesses that have succeeded, such as your favorite restaurant. It has been in business forever. You begin thinking of all the reasons you can about why they are successful. These insights help you think about success factors you can immediately begin applying to your start-up.

A final question comes to mind. How do you determine which business is right for you? You're considering two basic types of businesses: a product business and a service business. A product business could include products you make or buy from another source for resale. Service businesses fall into three broad categories. You may provide a service that is performed at your business location, outside of your business location, or both.

The business you select could be a combined product and service business. You know the basic principles of running a business apply equally to a product or service business. Based upon the options that are in front of you, you are considering joining a consulting firm, creating a personal coaching business, or moving to Montana to find a vacation lodge.

1. If you want to start a consulting/training business, turn to Chapter 4.

2. If you want to create a personal coaching business, turn to Chapter 12.

3. If you want to relocate to Montana to search for a vacation lodge, turn to Chapter 11.

4. If you would like to consider other start-up options, turn to Chapter 2.

CHAPTER 4

STARTING A

CONSULTING/TRAINING

BUSINESS

You have decided to start a consulting and training business in the Great Lakes region. The focus of your business will be on market consulting and training in three primary areas: (1) Market Research, (2) Market Analysis, and (3) Market Strategy. At this point in your start-up development cycle, you are not sure if training or consulting will be the main thrust of your business. You have arbitrarily decided to let the market make that call for you. If the market demands more training than consulting services, then that is the direction you will head. Either way, you believe you will win in the long term. A good training program will feed your consulting business and good consulting services will feed your training business. You believe you would be better off concentrating your marketing efforts on small to medium-size businesses before you move up to larger corporate clients. Your rationale is simple: It is typically easier to gain access to the CEO or decision maker of a small rather than a large company.

Roy Gordon, who is fondly called "Flash Gordon" within the consulting and training circles, is a short, stocky man who's always bristling with enthusiasm. Over the past year, you have gotten to know Roy quite well and trust his judgment. Roy was hired away from CareerTrac, a major provider of corporate training programs by IBM to head up its western region training program. Why he took this "revolving door" assignment with IBM is anybody's guess. It will be interesting to hear what he has to say about the question you posed to him now that you have decided to start a consulting and training business. "Should I chase big clients or small clients for consulting and training contracts?" You have an appointment to meet with Roy in his office this afternoon.

As you enter Roy's office, he greets you with an energetic "Welcome, my friend, and I hope you are having a good day." You are not having a good day, but you manage to smile anyway. The dilemma of whether or not you should chase small or large clients has given you a splitting headache. Roy invites you to sit down before he begins. "You ask me to share my thoughts with you as to whether you would be better off chasing big versus small clients. In my opinion, both options offer you the same number of advantages and disadvantages, which I have listed on the board."

Chasing Big Clients

Advantages

1. More stable than small clients

2. Can often afford to pay more

3. Faster interdepartment word-of-mouth exposure in larger organizations

4. Longer and more complex assignments

5. More opportunities for additional work with multiple locations and subsidiary companies

Disadvantages

1. Difficult to make executive appointments

2. More competitive if already using consultants

3. Contracts delays due to multi-department approval requirements

4. Staffing requirements difficult to meet

5. May require extensive travel

Chasing Small Clients

Advantages

1. Easier to see decision maker

2. May not require large consulting staff

3. Loss of one small account not as significant as loss of large account

4. Less travel required

5. Quicker approval of contracts

Disadvantages

1. May not be able to afford fees

2. Shorter assignments

3. Lower fees

4. Less stability than larger clients

5. Less diversity in assignment

You interrupt Roy's presentation with a question that has been nagging at you. "Roy, do you involve any of the other departments in the consulting/training selection process? For example, does IBM's purchasing department review your proposals before they are approved? Is any background check done to determine the qualifications of the consulting company under consideration?"

Roy gives you one of those "yes and no" answers that you hate. "They can if they want to, but my department has all of those areas covered. We know cost as well or better than any of the bean counters. My people have been in this business for a long time and they know who is and who is not qualified. No offense to our administrative departments, but quite frankly, they don't have the technical background to understand which consulting and training services we really need." You hope Roy is right. If you decide to chase contracts with big clients, you can't afford to justify your existence to every department in the company just to get one contract.

On the other hand, small clients are typically controlled by one person, the president or CEO. You sell the CEO and you've got the deal. And, small businesses are the fastest growing segment of the domestic economy. According to the U.S. Department of Commerce, by the year 2000, sixty percent of the population will be working for small businesses. Maybe chasing small clients is the way to go. You thank Roy for his time and head out to face the evening rush-hour traffic.

Later that evening, you stumble into the sanctuary of your office where the moment of reality comes to you. Your wall clock is moving toward ten as you stare at the incredible mass of unopened mail stacked on your desk. To your delight, there are three letters from firms you had previously contacted, authorizing you to proceed with one consulting and two training programs. You had initially allocated $30,000 to start-up your consulting and training business. Over the past year, you have worked long, hard hours to get this business started. Before you contemplate your next strategic move, you turn on your personal computer to review where you are financially on the spreadsheet you prepared for this purpose:

FIRST YEAR FINANCIAL SUMMARY

Revenue/Expense Item Description	Budget	Actual	Variance
Revenue From Training	$23,000	$22,500	($500)
Revenue From Consulting	$16,000	$17,300	$1,300
Total Revenue	$39,000	$39,800	$800
Travel and Entertainment Expense	$16,700	$23,950	($7,250)
Postage and Office Supplies	$2,700	$3,400	($700)
Professional Fees (Legal and Accounting)	$7,200	$5,975	$1,225
Other Expenses	$3,400	$1,400	$2,000
Total Expenses	$30,000	$34,725	($4,725)
Total Gross Profit (Loss)	$9,000	$5,075	($3,925)

Although your actual revenues exceeded your estimates by $800, your expense projections were off by $4,725. However, with the new contracts in today's mail, you feel confident you'll be well ahead of your revenue estimate by the end of the year when you review your financial statement.

First Year Financial Summary

Beginning Year Net Worth	$210,000
Plus: First Year Revenues	$39,000
Less: Business Expense	$30,000
First Year Net Worth	$219,000

Exhausted, you find yourself muttering: "Do I want to chase big or small clients?" You reach for your binder and run your eyes through the meeting notes you took today to collect your thoughts. As the smoke begins to clear from your mind, you begin to understand the underlying problems and challenges of the decision you are about to make.

1. If you believe you can accelerate the growth of your business by chasing big clients, turn to Chapter 13.

2. If you believe that beginning with small companies makes more sense, turn to Chapter 14.

CHAPTER 5

STARTING A REAL-ESTATE

DEVELOPMENT

COMPANY

Andrew Carnegie once said that "Ninety percent of all millionaires became so through owning real estate. More money has been made in real estate than in all industrial investments combined." You believe Carnegie was right because real-estate values do not depend upon emotions but upon the economic laws of supply and demand.

By comparison, buyers and sellers of common stock and commodities are at the mercy of the marketplace, which may or may not reflect the owner's opinion of the asset's value. In fact, you just proved this point when you sold common stock last week for less than the corporation's per-share book value. It was another one of those lessons learned in your financial life that reinforces your convictions that real estate is the place to invest your money.

Unlike the stock and commodity markets, which in your opinion, are a form of legalized gambling, the owners of real estate control its value. If an owner thinks a property is worth a certain amount, he or she will set the price and wait until a buyer pays the asking price. It is one of the primary reasons why you have decided to start a real-estate development company in the North Chicago area. You want to specialize in residential, recreational, and commercial property.

Every person you know who has invested in well-selected real estate in a growing section of the country has never lost money and in fact, they have all done quite well. Some made it by investing in homes and apartments, while others made a fortune in raw land investments. What route should you choose? You know you don't have the resources to chase after both residential properties and raw land. It's a tough decision you have to make.

A trip to the local library helps you find the information you need to make informed decisions. As you sit in front of a personal computer that's networked into the library's comprehensive database of available books, periodicals, videos, CDs, and reference materials, you enter search words "Real-Estate Investing" at the subject prompt on the screen. Instantly, over seventy-five book titles covering real-estate investing appear on your screen. As you browse through the options, one of the titles catches your eye: *Why Real Estate Is the Best Investment in the World.* You check it out!

Later that evening, in the sanctuary of your home office, you pore over all 675 pages of the book. You are particularly interested in the chapter entitled *Successful Real-Estate Investing* since it addresses exactly what you want to do. Again that nagging question comes to the forefront of your mind. Should I invest in land or residential property? Along these subject lines, the book talks about two key factors in real-estate investing: (1) You need to understand the inherent value of land and the added value of improvements constructed on land, and (2) The dynamic tax consequences of owning real estate can lead to profit.

In your personal vocabulary, profit is not a dirty word. You'll take all the profits you can get your hands on. As you read on, one way to make a profit in real estate is from the inflationary increase in property values. You know this intuitively since every house you have owned and sold was at a price that exceeded the inflation rate. The book also talks about real-estate wealth creators. These are people who improve real property at a cost that is less than what the market will pay for the increased value of the improvements.

Your next-door neighbor Fred is a classic example of a wealth creator. Fred is a highly regarded senior programmer for Allied Signal, but he also knows how to fix and upgrade anything that is attached to a home. You name it and he knows how to do it—from plumbing, electrical fixtures, to tearing down walls for whatever reason. He is a classic example of a guy who loves to buy "fixer uppers" in his spare time, fix them up and sell them for a nice profit.

You don't have Fred's "fixer upper" talent so you know you'll have to rely on your ability to subcontract any needed improvements. That begs the question, if you decide to invest in residential property, will you be able to find subcontractors who are honest and charge reasonable rates? You won't have that problem if you decide to invest in raw land. However, you can rent residential property to defray your carrying cost prior to the sale, which is difficult to do with land. If the land has agricultural attributes for cattle grazing or to grow corps, it too can generate an income to offset your carrying costs.

You have asked your real-estate broker Susan Jones to assist you in determining the best approach to take to start-up your real-estate development corporation. You're keenly aware that every decision you make must be based on information and facts since you have limited personal funds to invest. Tomorrow arrives and your meeting with Susan begins on time.

Susan tells you about three properties that she feels might interest you. "Residential properties on the North end of Chicago are selling at a premium and for good reason. The bumper-to-bumper commute out of the suburbs like Evanston into Chicago is encouraging people to consider moving into the inner-city areas. High crime, which used to be a real detriment in the greater Chicago area, has decreased substantially as a result of the city's 10 P.M. teenage curfew. Suburbanites want to rent either private dwellings or apartments first, before they commit to buying a home in the city. And, they're willing to pay top dollar for the privilege. Many of my clients are willing to sign a "lease with options to purchase clause" if that is acceptable to the landlord. The North Chicago residential properties are hot commodities right now that can be quickly turned for a profit in one to two years."

"You ask me to investigate recreational and commercial properties as well in the North Chicago area. Before I proceed, do you have any questions regarding residential properties?" You tell Susan you want to hear everything she has to say before you ask any questions. "North Chicago recreational and commercial properties are going the same direction as residential properties. Recreational property along the lake front is shaping up to become one giant marina. The significant clean up of Lake Michigan has dramatically opened the sports-fishing and water-sports industries. Everybody is buying a boat and they need a place to keep it. They can't build marinas fast enough. Unless you have access to several millions of dollars, you can't as a private investor afford to become a major player in the marinas. However, there are a number of limited partnerships in new marinas that you can invest in for around $50,000 a share."

You ask Susan to tell you what she has found out about commercial property. "More and more office buildings are being constructed in the North end to take advantage of the influx of highly qualified professional residents. Just last week, Allstate Insurance announced plans to construct a 250,000 square foot office building to house its midwestern claims processing center. The scenario for investing in commercial properties is similar to what I said about recreational properties. It takes millions but there are a number of excellent limited partnerships available."

"There are some opportunities to invest in raw land, if you are willing to take the risk. Several sections of North Chicago are classified as tenement land. Most of this is land where condemned tenement buildings are still standing. They are unoccupied since they cannot be rented in their condemned condition. I am not suggesting that these are anything close to "fixer-upper" buildings. Over time, I believe they will be replaced with high-rise apartments and office buildings. The only question is when. If you can afford to buy the land and hang onto it, you could make a lot of money."

You're impressed with the manner in which Susan is handling her presentation. She presented a viable set of alternatives that, when implemented, will allow you to realize an attractive profit out of your real-estate venture. After reading a number of books and periodicals on real-estate investing, you are convinced that no other investment offers you the flexibility of real estate to meet your financial goals. If this program goes the way you think it will, you plan to get your own real-estate license.

Before the year is over, you purchase a fixer-upper duplex in a North Chicago area. The duplex was purchased from a couple who were going through a divorce and wanted to unload the property as quickly as possible. Susan believes you purchased the property for $20,000 below market value. You reflect the true market value in your latest financial statement:

First Year Financial Summary

Beginning Year Net Worth	$210,000
Plus: Equity in Investments	$90,000
Less: Business Expenses	$75,000
First Year Net Worth	$225,000

You close out the year by completing a series of real-estate cours-es and getting your real-estate license. You are poised to make your second year in real-estate development a very good year. The vacant land in the North Chicago area is directly in the path of the ensuing growth. On the other hand, buying houses and apartment buildings offers you an immediate opportunity to earn rental income on your investment. You can't afford to pursue both options.

1. If you believe that acquiring land would be the best way to start your real-estate development corporation, turn to Chapter 15.

2. If you believe that buying houses and apartment buildings would be the best way to start your real-estate development corporation, turn to Chapter 16.

CHAPTER 6

PURCHASING A

MAIL BOXES ETC.

FRANCHISE

Going to the National Franchise Exposition in Cleveland was well worth your while. You had no idea that franchising has grown into a multibillion dollar annual industry. There were over 3,000 companies represented at the show offering every conceivable type of business opportunity. However, some of the well-established franchise companies want a fortune to buy into one of their franchises.

Initially, you were discouraged. It appeared as though there was no chance for a newcomer to find a viable and affordable franchise opportunity. You discovered that apart from all the familiar franchise names, smaller companies are continually turning to franchising as a means to expand their businesses. One of the exhibitors told you that a complete list of every franchise company in the country and world for that matter is available at the research desk of any good public library. He tells you to check out the national or international Franchise Directory. You obtain the names and addresses of several hundred relatively new franchise companies at the show. You've written to several of them including Mail Boxes Etc., and asked for their start-up information package.

The conference lasted two days and when you get home, a package from Mail Boxes Etc. is waiting for you. You can't believe the speedy response. You just talked to the sales representative at the conference two days ago. Since it's in the mailing business, the company should know better than anybody else how to get packages through the mail. You are impressed with the promptness and the cover letter says it all:

Congratulations! You've taken the first step toward building a better future for yourself and your family by examining franchising. Today, franchises account for more than one-half trillion dollars of retail sales in the U.S. By the year 2000, over fifty percent of all retail sales will be made through franchises.

Once you decide franchising is right for you, there is only one decision left to be made: Which franchise is right for you?

At Mail Boxes Etc. (MBE), we think the time has never been better to join our worldwide network of over 3,000 retail service centers. The MBE network has more centers, more strategic alliances with major national companies and retail stores than ever before. During MBE's recent fiscal year, average store sales increased 20%, pushing MBE's retail sales to over a billion dollars. And best of all, MBE franchise owners accomplished this working in a professional environment, without cooking hamburgers or making submarine sandwiches.

It's no wonder that *Entrepreneur Magazine* named Mail Boxes Etc. the #1 Business Service Franchise in the world. Enclosed is our basic information package. To assist us in evaluating your interests and goals, we need to know more about you. After you've read the enclosed material, please complete and return the confidential questionnaire so we can give you meaningful input as to your qualifications to become a Mail Boxes Etc. franchise owner.

You complete the questionnaire and fax it out that afternoon. Two week later, Janette Harrison, MBE's Regional Director, calls you. She wants to meet with you in an hour to discuss your application for one of their franchises. Your meeting with Janette proves to be very informative. You learn that franchises offer you a way to buy into a part of an existing business to minimize many of the trial-and-error steps that are an inherent part of starting a business from scratch, and cover nearly every type of business imaginable. Franchises have consistently grown over the past ten years and currently dominate mail-service retail sales in the United States.

Janette tells you, "There are two basic types of franchises for you to consider. Trade-name franchises cover the auto dealerships, gasoline service stations, and soft-drink dealerships. Franchise holders typically have the right to sell brand-name products by using their own marketing and selling techniques."

"The second type of franchise is referred to as a business format franchise. The franchiser establishes a fully integrated relationship with the franchise owner by providing all marketing, operating manuals, training, and quality-control standards. MBE is a business format franchise and enjoys a much lower failure rate than independent small business. Less than 5 percent of new franchises fail in their first year as compared to 40 percent of independent start-ups. This is due to the fact that most franchises like MBE have already been subjected to the test of durability. We have an established track record that is a testimonial to our survival. Additional advantages of MBE franchises are summarized as follows:

FRANCHISE ADVANTAGES

1. MBE offers a proven formula for success.

2. MBE provides training programs and other forms of management assistance for new business owners.

3. MBE offers expert assistance in starting the business.

4. MBE offers volume discounts on group and national purchases.

5. Accounting systems are pretested and established.

6. Advertising and promotional programs are initiated by MBE.

7. MBE brand and trade names are already established."

Janette continues with her presentation. "Most name-brand franchises cost a considerable amount of money to start. If you buy a MBE franchise, you must abide by our rules and regulations. This can present a difficult adjustment for some entrepreneurs. Disadvantages of opening a franchises include:

FRANCHISE DISADVANTAGES

1. Most franchises charge an 'up front' franchise fee and annual fees.

2. The start-up cost for a franchise is usually higher than it is for a start-up business.

3. Franchise owners must abide by the operating restrictions mandated by the franchise.

4. Some franchises require a renewal fee after a specified period of time.

5. The growth of your franchise may be limited if you want to expand into an area that is already controlled by another franchiser."

You thank Janette for her thorough presentation and tell her you'll make your decision about acquiring an MBE franchise in the next couple of days. That afternoon, you talk to your attorney, Judy Crawford. She tells you: "One of the legal advantages of buying a franchise as opposed to buying an existing business is that state and federal laws require franchisers to provide disclosure statements to franchisees. A disclosure statement must contain information about the franchiser such as the names of the officers and principal owner along with a description of their business experience. In addition, the statement must describe the terms of the licensing agreement, all fees to be paid, the types of assistance the franchiser will provide, and the territory covered by the franchise. An audited copy of the franchiser's income statement and balance sheet must be included in the disclosure statement. Some states like ours require the franchiser to provide prospective buyers with additional information."

You review the sales and profit figures in MBE's disclosure statement and are satisfied with the performance of the company. Next, you select a group of MBE franchisees that reside in the section of the country that you are interested in and pay them a visit. They are all more than willing to meet with you to discuss different aspects of their operation. Only by asking the right questions will you get the facts you need to make an informed decision. Questions you ask are summarized as follows:

1. Knowing what you now know, are you pleased with your decision to buy a MBE franchise?

2. If a second MBE franchise became available in your area, would you buy it?

3. Has the franchiser been responsive to the needs of your business?

4. What is your opinion of MBE's training program?

5. Were there any surprises in your first year of operation?

6. Do the MBE franchise owners have an association and is it helpful?

7. How long are your average work days and do you take vacations?

8. Are the sales seasonal?

9. What were your annual sales over the past three years?

10. Do you believe MBE has a strong future?

You decide to buy an MBE franchise and select a store location in a busy convenience mall anchored by an Albertson's food store. Your demographic research really helped. The chamber of commerce, city planning commission, economic development agency, and local office of the U.S. Census Bureau all provided you with valuable demographic data such as average family income, length of residence, and average age. Most of the information was available free or at a nominal cost.

First Year Financial Summary

Beginning Year Net Worth	$210,000
Plus: MBE Sales	$90,000
Less: Business Expenses	$75,000
First Year Net Worth	$225,000

When you review your financial statement at the end of the year, you're pleased with the progress you have made. However, you believe that if you can expand the scope of services you currently offer, you can dramatically increase your income and net worth in the coming years. Two alternatives intrigue you. If you add new MBE locations, you could dramatically increase your annual revenue. On the other hand, if you just expand the scope of your existing services, you could accomplish the same thing without running the risk of opening new locations.

1. If you believe that adding new locations would be the best way to increase your annual revenue, turn to Chapter 17.

2. If you believe that expanding the scope of your existing services would be the best way to increase your annual revenues, turn to Chapter 18.

CHAPTER 7

CREATING AN

AUTO-ACCESSORIES

MANUFACTURING COMPANY

Deep down inside, you love to make things. Maybe that is what led you to select manufacturing auto accessories as the thrust for your new business venture.

The market is huge and it begs the questions: Where do you start? How do you get started? As you make the daily trek down to the mailbox, you find yourself simultaneously experiencing both excitement and frustration. You're excited about the prospects of the auto-accessory industry but you are also frustrated by the sheer vastness of the industry. It's so big, you literally don't know where to start.

You'll think about it later because this is the weekend you're going to the Jeep Jamboree at Pikes Peak, Colorado. It's your opportunity to leave the paved world behind and enter the world most people never see. As you pull into the Jamboree registration center, you are taken back by the sheer number of Jeep owners from all over the country who have come to this event. The Jamboree includes experienced guides to help guests put their Jeeps through their paces, tackling hairpin turns, traversing rolling hills and granite-strewn trails.

Two days later, you arrive home and begin extracting the mail from your mailbox when a bright orange legal-size envelope catches your eye. It's the current catalog for Jeep Wranglers that you ordered when you were at the jamboree. What a story the Jeep could tell if only it could talk. The vehicle dates back to World War II, and it has-

n't changed all that much. Maybe that's the sign you have been waiting for. Why not build auto accessories for Jeeps?

- Point out the array of accessories available and how easy they
  are to install.

- Utilize high-traffic areas in new-car showrooms and retail-
  store accessory areas to sell your products.

- Find dealers that will let you display your accessories on their
  showroom vehicles.

- Don't bog a showroom-floor vehicle down with accessories.
  Keep it simple so that it is easy to see how your products add
  value to the vehicle.

- Get ideas from your local parts dealers on how to set up an
  effective display. Most of the veterans know what sells and
  what does not sell.

- Make all of your aftermarket accessories enticing, attractive,
  and accessible to your customers.

Many of these ideas came together when you attended the
Automotive Aftermarket Industry convention in Cleveland, which
dealers consider to be the can't-miss show for aftermarket parts.
Sponsored by the Automobile Aftermarket Trade Association, this
show is the Octoberfest of the aftermarket industry. As one of the
vendors tells you, "The motivation for any car dealer to attend the
show is simple. They can see accessory items that can be added to a
vehicle to increase dealer profits, move inventory that's hard to move,
and differentiate their inventory from competitors down the street.
Dealers can take plain-Jane cars and turn them into merchandisable
product. If the average profit on a new car is $500, you can triple that
profit on one set of aftermarket wheels. Aftermarket can be a real
profit maker."

You learned at the Jamboree that Chrysler Corporation needs
plastic light grids for the front head lamps of its Jeep Wranglers. They
are soliciting bids by sending would-be suppliers all of the specifications and information they need on a computer disk. You write
Chrysler and ask to be included on its bidders list. Two weeks later, you
receive a copy of their solicitation. Initially, you thought the request
was a bit odd since there are dozens of companies who make and sell
light grids to enhance light styling while providing lamp protection.

You then learned that the head lamps on Jeep Wranglers are square, rather than the traditional circular shape. You respond to Chrysler's request for square light grids with a formal proposal that exceeds all of its submission requirements. Three weeks later, you receive a registered letter from Chrysler and a purchase order for 150,000 square light grids, the first 25,000 of which are to be delivered in 90 days. All of a sudden, you find yourself catapulted into the auto aftermarket for the vehicle of your choice: the American Jeep! You estimate your first year revenue and start-up cost for your new venture:

Estimated Start-Up Revenues and Costs for Jeep Head Lamps

Description	Actual Cost
Total First Year Revenue	$300,000
Estimate of Costs	
Tooling and Material Costs	$150,000
Labor and Payroll Taxes	$76,000
Rental Space and Utilities	$39,500
Estimated Total Costs	$265,500
Estimated Gross Profit	$34,500

You purchase a pneumatic plastic injection machine and custom dies to produce square light grids for Jeep Wranglers. Location is not important for your manufacturing business, so you rent space ten miles outside of town at a very reasonable rate. You meet your first-order commitment to Chrysler within the allotted 90 days when you ship 25,000 light grids to its Oak Creek, Illinois plant. A follow-up order of an additional 125,000 lamp grids is faxed to you within the week. The excitement mounts as you watch your auto-aftermarket business begin to take off in the right direction.

However, the headline in this morning's paper caused your heart to skip a beat. "September Auto Sales Down 20%: Annual Forecast Revised." It only gets worse than this as you read the rest of the article. "In case there was any doubt, September put the last nail in the coffin for record sales this year. In fact, with three quarters of the year gone, it will be a stretch to top last year's 14 million light-vehicle sales, let alone the 18 million peak set two years ago. It's clear that if there's any improvement in sales at all this year, it will be thinner and will cost more incentive money than analysts expected at the beginning of the year."

To top it all off, your current issue of *Four Wheeler* magazine has a feature article about the new Jeep Wrangler, which will feature circular rather than square head lamps. Most of your tooling and molds will have to be replaced to accommodate the new model, which will cost you $150,000. After reviewing your financial statement, you abruptly realize you can't afford to be in a business that can abruptly change with a devastating impact on your operating costs. A review of your financial statement shows you made money this year but the added tooling costs will throw you into a loss next year. You decide to "pack it in" and try something else.

First Year Financial Summary

Beginning Year Net Worth	$210,000
Plus: First Year Revenues	$300,000
Less: Business Expenses	$265,000
First Year Net Worth	$245,000

Looking back on where you have been, would you alter your decisions in order to create a different future for yourself?

1. If you would like to select another business venture to start-up, return to Chapter 2.

2. If you would like to conduct more analysis before you start-up another business, turn to Chapter 3.

If you're still feeling the sting of defeat and believe you could have made your last strategic choice work in real life, you may be right. After all, this is just a game. However, if you select one of the other start-up alternatives, you will learn why the authors consider them a better choice.

CHAPTER 8

LAUNCHING A SOFTWARE

AND MULTIMEDIA

COMPANY

It's Monday morning and you're enjoying the peace and solitude of your hotel patio as you sip hot coffee and canvas the pool area twelve stories below. The idea of launching a software and multimedia company has captured your imagination. In the interest of starting out on the right track, you flew into Tucson, Arizona last night to attend a multimedia forum sponsored by Microsoft.

As you settle into your seat for the morning session, John Evans, a former executive at Rupert News Corp., walks up to the podium, looks out at the crowd of multimedia wannabes and proceeds to tell it like it is. "Few businesses can match the intellectual pretensions of the computer business. Its leaders are not satisfied just to make money and move product. They also must attend interminable conferences where they debate the future of the industry. They write books and articles outlining their vision of a world in which every business action will be supported by a microchip in the next 5 years."

He goes on to say, "After spawning scores of millionaires and making every family without a PC worry about accusations of child abuse, the business has been invaded by a certain smugness. The 'hipness' of multimedia has added to this sense of arrogance. Multimedia entrepreneurs see the media transforming the universe, putting information, voice, and video at everyone's fingertips in the form of CD-ROMs. While the not so minor matter of making money on multimedia still eludes most of these players, they believe it's just a matter of time until the world beats a path to their door. And, it will happen if you have the right multimedia products and can hang onto whatever market share you establish. Make no mistake about it, if you are successful, the competition will come after your business!"

Patrick's comments remind you of your good friend, Jim Barksdale, a 52-year-old Mississippian who finds himself performing the functions of a field general, fighting in a virtual battlefield to protect his market niche. His company is Netscape, Silicon Valley's youthful flagship of the Internet boom, boasting annual sales in the $100 million range and a market valuation close to a billion. His prime weapon is a program known as Browser that allows users to cruise the World Wide Web to find whatever they're looking for. Netscape's market position is enviable: 45 percent of all Web riders use Browser.

Microsoft, the current champion and undisputed Gibraltar of software, wants a piece of Netscape's market. The trade journals claim that Microsoft won't be satisfied until it gets it all. Can a two-year-old start-up company populated by a bunch of software nerds who wear shorts to work win the battle against a company like Microsoft? By all indications, Netscape is not only winning the battle, it's winning the war with Microsoft and remains the dominant provider of search-and-find software for the Internet. As you pursue your own software-development ideas, it's refreshing to know that Jim and his start-up company have survived against the enormous odds of competing against an industry leader.

You vow that when you enter the market, you will be the market leader in whatever you do. Why take on competition when you don't have to? You decide to focus your attention on the college and university application software market, a virtually untouched market niche. Your good friend, Dr. Mark Sayers, who teaches at the University of Colorado, tells you the traditional "never change" attitude of American universities and colleges is about to change. He explains, "Competition for students is becoming fierce as students demand quality education. Universities have suddenly realized that students are their customers and the university is nothing more than a retail store where they can shop and buy the educational products they need. Students are in fact shopping for the best prices and quality they can find. Quite honestly, it is scaring the heck out of my colleagues."

When you probed Mark to find out what students are specifically looking for, he tells you reality: "They are tired of listening to some professor lecture for an hour or two about nothing. The National

Education Association has proven, through countless studies, that the traditional lecture is one of the least effective ways to teach anything to anyone. You have to show them what it is you are teaching them if you really want to add value to the educational process."

Following Mark's suggestion, you develop a business application that runs on a personal computer simulating what a student needs to do to start-up a business. You show them how to set up an accounting system, how to interpret economic projections to establish a sales plan, and how to run the operations of their start-up company to make a profit. The application software is combined to run on a CD-ROM with multimedia to add sound, video and graphics to the program to lend an element of reality to the courseware. When you demonstrate the courseware to Mark, he solicits and gets approval to use your courseware in the University's School of Business Administration curriculum.

In the fall, you introduce your multimedia start-up program into the three state universities and six junior colleges who initially plan to use the program to supplement their introduction to business undergraduate classes. You work closely with each of the schools to assist in developing training and test materials. To your delight, your first multimedia application program for higher education is an outstanding success. You receive several calls from colleges and universities all over the country who order copies of your CD-ROMs for their students. As you review your personal financial position, you realize you did not make a lot of money in your first year, but that is to be expected. Most of your time was spent developing the application and marketing the product.

First Year Financial Summary

Beginning Year Net Worth	$210,000
Plus: First Year Revenues	$90,000
Less: Business Expenses	$85,000
First Year Net Worth	$215,000

You are intrigued by the idea of continuing to develop your own software applications. Since you can run the entire operation out of your home office, you are contemplating keeping your operation small and developing additional software applications. However, you also like marketing and have been actively considering working with software developers who need marketing support.

1. If you believe your personal and financial interest would be better served by searching for software developers needing marketing help, turn to Chapter 19.

2. If you believe your personal and financial interest would be better served by developing your own software products, turn to Chapter 20.

CHAPTER 9

The smell of smog is wafting in the subtle breeze that brushes past your hair. You know you have reached the perimeter of the city as you roll up the car windows to keep the smog out and slowly come to a stop in bumper-to-bumper traffic. All the cars around you are beeping, as an ambulance with sirens blaring roars past you toward the demolished vehicles a mile ahead. One-half hour later and you're still not moving, which gives you little hope of making this morning's job interview appointment. You realize the only savior in this situation is to find a humorous radio program to cheer you up.

Flipping through the channels, you instinctively stop at the word Montana on one of the radio talk shows. "Montana is a beautiful place, Bob. I moved there about a year ago and I'm telling you, I sure like the great outdoors."

"But, tell us honestly Steve," demands the DJ, "Aren't you all really just a bunch of hicks and hillbillies out that way?" Laughter is shared by all in the studio.

"Now, now," adds Steve, in between his laughs. "Don't let my flannel shirt and chew-spitting fool you. I'm just like all the other people in your big city . . . rude and obnoxious when they get into traffic jams. In Montana, a traffic jam to us is when two cars are backed up at a stop sign."

You suddenly realize how much you hate your present life and want a change. Maybe you're fed up with the traffic, smog, big buildings, impersonal people, or the fast pace of life. You pick up your cellular phone, punch in Chandler Phillip's number, and wait for Chandler to come on the line. Chandler is the Executive Vice President of General Motors' research division and the one you had an interview with this morning. "Hey Chandler, it's me!"

"Where the heck are you? I waited two hours for you before going into the next interview session. If you want this job, this better be the best darn excuse I've heard in years."

"Well, to tell you the truth Chandler, I'm not interested in any position General Motors has to offer."

"You what? You can't do this to us. You're our number-one candidate. Can't you wait until we have at least had a chance to get together for a formal interview before you make a decision like that? We're so close."

"Sorry Chandler, but I've had enough of this city life and I am moving to Montana to buy a lodge in the mountains."

"But. . . ." Click. That was easy, and now it's done! It was a great relief, but at the same time, scary. You've been saving all your money for this point in your life when you can afford to tell all of your city-slicker friends goodbye. You just didn't realize it would be so soon. As you switch lanes, turn around and head out of the city, you want to stop and thank God for giving you the courage to go through with this Montana move, and maybe ask for a financial hand in seeing you through the move.

Upon reaching your small apartment, you pack everything in record time, load the car, and head North out of town. The excitement of wondering who else could just drop it all and go for their ultimate life's dream lingers in your mind. The idea of ultimately moving to Montana was why you have been saving so much and why you bought a four-wheel-drive Jeep Wrangler. Everyone called you crazy for having a Jeep Wrangler for city driving, but you knew in the back of your mind that one day, you would make it out to "God's Country." And that's just where this highway is heading.

The long drive gives you time to think. You're the type of person who when you get an idea, you work out how to implement it in detail. That is precisely what you did with your Montana lodge idea. Initially, your friend Chris and you wanted to open a lodge together. You were roommates in college several years ago and you both liked Montana. You even talked about where to build a lodge, if you couldn't find one to buy, how to finance it, and what style would be best. The only problem was Chris got married, quit school, and moved to Montana to become a carpenter. You graduated and got the big job in the city like you were supposed to do. You've kept in touch with Chris over the years and now your visit with Chris is only hours away as your car speeds north past Sheridan, Wyoming, on Interstate 25.

You haven't yet decided if you want to build or buy a lodge and wonder if your savings will be adequate to start-up a lodge. If you buy a fixer-upper, perhaps Chris would still be interested in helping you put everything together. Chris could be the handyman and you could be the business person. As you enter the city limits of Billings, Montana, it takes you no time at all to find the exit for Sweetwater Road. In a matter of minutes, your car is in Chris's driveway. As you climb out of the car, the porch door opens as Chris runs out to meet you. After a few "you've gotten uglier as you have gotten older" exchanges, the two of you go into the house where you enjoy a quiet dinner with Chris's family.

Later that evening, you tell Chris about your continued interest in finding a lodge to buy and quickly realize that Chris has changed. He's not even remotely interested in teaming with you on a lodge. During the course of the conversation, he tells you some things you were not aware of. "Since I knew you were coming to Montana, I contacted a real-estate friend of mine to find out if there are any lodges for sale in Montana. Would you believe it if I told you there's not a single lodge that is available for sale in the entire state? She told me only a couple will come on the market each year. You may have no other choice but to build a lodge. However, I did learn that there are a number of motels available for sale throughout the state. That might be an option that's worth considering. You could get your feet wet by running a motel first, and buy a lodge later if and when one comes on the market."

The next morning, as you leave Chris's house to strike out on your own, you wonder what you should do next. You had counted on Chris's support and in your haste to get to Montana, you didn't think about the possibility that no lodges would be for sale. You check into a motel in Billings and decide to review your financial position before you make your next decision:

First Year Financial Summary

Beginning Year Net Worth	$210,000
Plus: First Year Revenues	$90,000
Less: Business and Living Expenses	$110,000
First Year Net Worth	$190,000

The idea of buying a motel first, before you buy a lodge, intrigues you. It would afford you the opportunity to learn more about the hospitality industry before you stepped up to a more complex lodge venture. The fact that there are motels for sale and no lodges for sale is influencing your decision. However, the idea of building your own lodge has an appeal all of its own. Why wait if you can build a lodge and eliminate the risk of running a motel?

1. If you believe your personal and financial interest would be better served by buying an existing motel, turn to Chapter 21.

2. If you believe your personal and financial interest would be better served by building a new lodge, turn to Chapter 22.

CHAPTER 10

AFFILIATING WITH A

CONSULTING FIRM

In your living room that evening, you listen to your friend Craig Hickman, the author of *The Organizational Game*, talk about the ins and outs of joining a consulting firm. "It is not uncommon for entrepreneurs to become affiliated with a consulting firm first, before they strike out on their own, which has a number of advantages. The generally good consulting fees can be used to finance the initial stages of a start-up business and the experience can prove to be invaluable. No two assignments are ever the same and each assignment is always a challenge. Most of the time, you have to dig deep into your arsenal of past experiences to understand the problem you have invariably been hired as a consultant to solve. If that's the kind of job you're looking for, I'll introduce you to Steve Stein, Organizational Dynamics' Senior Vice President, tomorrow." You tell Craig this is exactly what you want to do and he calls Steve at his home. When he hangs up the phone, he tells you the meeting with Steve is set for 10 A.M. the next day.

The next morning you meet Steve Stein. He's aggressive, supremely confident, and you feel comfortable with him. More importantly, you know he likes you when he tells you: "I have been surveying a field of possible candidates, from large international consulting firms such as McKinsey to smaller niche specialists, and quite honestly, I like you the best. If you want the job, you can start tomorrow because I need somebody to take on an assignment with CyTech, one of our major clients." You stand up, shake Steve's hand and ask him what time you should show up tomorrow.

As your consulting engagement begins at CyTech, you find yourself working closely with seven senior CyTech managers assigned to develop an automated materials requirements planning (MRP) system for the company. The data-gathering phase moves so slowly that you wonder if this project will ever get off the ground. By definition, MRP touches every department in the company, starting with manufacturing's need for materials based upon marketing's sales projections, to accounting's confirmation of projected material costs and procurement's requisition of the required materials. In a manual environment, everything happens on a "handshake" and the accountability for costly miscalculations are therefore easy to hide. Once you automate MRP, which requires a finite paper trail, instant accountability is created. Subsequently, nobody on the MRP team with the exception of yourself wants to see MRP automated.

Six months later and the MRP team is still gathering data. George Harding, CyTech's Senior Vice President, whom you met once when he first introduced you to his MRP team, abruptly calls you into his office. "What the heck is going on with our MRP project? I'm paying Organizational Dynamics big bucks to help implement this system and when I talk to my people, I'm told we're still gathering data. What's data? I don't need any data. I want information and facts, and if I don't get what I want soon, your consulting assignment at CyTech is over. What's going on?"

You admire executives who tell it like it is! At the risk of betraying the confidence you have developed with the MRP team, you tell George why nobody wants the accountability that is inherent in automated MRP systems. "The project will never get out of the data-gathering phase without some type of external stimulus." George thanks you for your candid opinion and tells you to assemble the MRP team in his conference room tomorrow morning. "You make sure everyone is there and I will provide the necessary external stimulus."

The morning meeting is a memorable event. After a lot of polite, politically motivated how are you George, can I get you a cup of coffee or polish your shoes acknowledgments, the meeting gets down to business. Standing tall at the head of the table, George begins the session with what is obviously a prepared statement. "It has recently been brought to my attention that you, the MRP team members, are having difficulty implementing my MRP system." Susan Redding, one of the team members, quickly raises her hand, anxious to provide an explanation. One glare from George and her hand goes down as fast as it went up.

"Let me explain how you and I are going to solve our mutual problem. Effective immediately, our consultant will head up the team effort to complete this project six months from today. I will know if it is in fact completed on time because you will demonstrate all phases of the MRP system to me exactly six months and one day from now. If the project is not completed within the allotted time frame, nobody in this room with the exception of myself will be working for CyTech. Now, Susan, or any of the rest of you, I will be happy to answer any of your questions." Nobody raises a question. George concludes with a remark. "Well, if there are no questions, then you all must know exactly what needs to be done. Let's get back to work and make it all happen for your own sake."

George abruptly exits the conference room leaving the MRP team with glazed looks on their faces. A silent minute passes before you break the silence. You offer to quickly develop a six-month implementation schedule, which could be ready in draft form by tomorrow morning, if that would be acceptable to everyone. Nobody objects and in the schedule review meeting the next morning, they all accept your schedule without any major modifications. It gives you cause for concern because you don't want to risk implementing a "rubber-stamped" schedule. To your surprise, however, now that all of the team members suddenly want an automated MRP system, every major deadline of the schedule is met. If one department encounters problems meeting its schedule, the other departments all jump in to help. You have heard about "jelled teams" but this team has turned jelly into cement. Joint ownership of every milestone and task on the schedule becomes an absolute reality.

The automated MRP system is implemented in six months and the system is demonstrated to George to his complete satisfaction. Everybody keeps their jobs. You become an instant hero at Organizational Dynamics, receive a bonus for your efforts and an offer to start another challenging assignment.

As you contemplate your next move, you find yourself inundated with calls from consulting firms. Word about your success at CyTech travels quickly and at the risk of swelling your ego beyond the bounds of control, you've received more job offers in the past two weeks than you have in the past two years. Two offers intrigue you.

Arthur Andersen wants you to join its consulting division. It promises to put you on its "fast track" to a partnership position within five years. That's where the big bucks are but, as you review your current financial position, you can't complain about Organizational Dynamics.

First Year Financial Summary

Beginning Year Net Worth	$210,000
Plus: First Year Salary and Bonus	$90,000
Less: Living Expenses	$75,000
First Year Net Worth	$225,000

At the other end of the spectrum, you have an opportunity to join a group of five independent consultants who are starting up an independent consulting firm called Computech. They are anxious to capitalize on the surge of corporate interest in the Internet by offering long-term functional consulting roles in areas such as webpage design, Internet security, and virus filtering.

Arthur Andersen offers you an opportunity to join one of the largest and most stable consulting companies in the world. If you join Computech, you will become a partner in one year and will be directly involved in building a start-up. Both opportunities will demand long hours, and extensive national and international travel.

You promised to let Organizational Dynamics know if you will accept its new assignment tomorrow. You've already made the decision to resign from Organizational Dynamics. You want to make sure you have a position with either Arthur Andersen or Computech locked down today, before your meeting tomorrow. As you pick up the telephone, you're not sure which number to dial, Computech's or Arthur Andersen's.

1. If you believe your career would be better served by joining a Big-6 accounting firm in the consulting area, turn to Chapter 23.

2. If you believe your career would be better served by linking-up with a group of independent consultants, turn to Chapter 24.

CHAPTER 11

RELOCATING TO

MONTANA

"Come on, why are you moving to Montana? No one wants to live in that God-forsaken state."

Your best friend, Pam Harris, was on your case and clearly did not want to see you leave the big city. You owe her an answer: "It's simple. I can't stand city life any longer, I hate my job and I am not going to commute to work for two hours a day anymore. I'm going to buy a lodge in Montana and become an entrepreneur."

"That's a bunch of stuff." The anger was slowly building in Pam's voice as she began to realize the reality of your situation. "You know darn well it's just a chance for you to leave all your real problems behind. Besides, you don't know anything about Montana."

On the defensive, you tell Pam, "The wonderful part about going to Montana is I'll learn everything there is to know." This is definitely the words of a converted pioneer talking and you know it. The only thing left for Pam to do now was go with the flow. Based on your current financial situation, you have saved enough money to move to Montana and make a down payment on a lodge. Just to make sure, you preview your projected year-end financial statement:

First Year Financial Summary

Beginning Year Net Worth	$210,000
Plus: First Year Revenues	$90,000
Less: Business and Living Expenses	$75,000
Less: Supplemental Living Expenses	$35,000
First Year Net Worth	$190,000

You're off to Montana in less than a week. The movers came and packed all your furniture. You already sold your house at a nice profit, which you'll use to augment your lodge purchasing fund. The move was sudden, but with the exception of Pam, you had no tie-downs.

As you drive north on Interstate 25 bound for Montana, you're excited about the opportunities that lie ahead of you. You can finally go fishing in some of the best trout streams in the country and take on outdoor hobbies, such as horseback riding, that you had to push aside when you lived in the city. As you think of the positive side of moving, you're excited to have a new experience. After all, you were born and raised in the fast pace of city life. It's all you know and what you have been accustomed to before you decided to look for a slower lifestyle. Montana will work for you.

As your lengthy drive continues, several thoughts and ideas roll through your mind. You wonder if you're psychologically fit and ready to tackle the unknown new life you are about to inherit. You pull into the small gas station at the Montana border that's complete with two old-fashioned pumps and a tiny market, fill your tank, grab a candy bar, and ask the gray-haired toothless man how to get to the Mahogany Lodge. This is where you plan to stay for at least the first week you are in Montana.

His directions are, simply, take a right at the old farm house, cross over the old wooden bridge that takes you over the Rocky River, take a left at the red barn, and then follow the signs that say Mahogany Lodge. You thank him and with a wave, are off down the road, thankful that he had drawn up a map since his words were hard to understand.

The dirt road leading to the lodge was lined with huge pine trees towering over your Jeep. The moon is beginning to brighten the darkened sky, emphasizing the beauty and clarity of the stars. Tired and exhausted, the lodge is sounding better and better as you picture yourself sitting in a huge chair in front of a moss-encrusted rock fireplace with a cold drink in one hand and a large steak delivered to you by room service on the table in front of you. With this thought in mind, you press down on the accelerator and reach the lodge 20 minutes earlier than planned.

The wooden engraved sign with "Mahogany Lodge" written on it at the end of the road is a welcome sight. The lodge is larger than you had pictured, a typical dark, wooden structure with large windows lining the front and a perfect habitat for hikers, hunters, or skiers. The setting is gorgeous, with huge boulders and pine trees everywhere. As you step out of your car, you hear the therapeutic sounds of nature and realize you have made the right decision to move to Montana.

"Welcome," comes a friendly voice from the balcony that lines the entire second story of the lodge. "Did it take you a long time to find this old place?"

"Oh, it wasn't too bad. The man at the gas station gave me super directions."

"Well then I see you've met toothless Joe. He's often coming up here for a drink and often stays the night because it turns into a few too many drinks. But, he's a real nice guy. Can I help you with your stuff?"

As you settle into the luxury of a hot shower, you begin to think about the business strategies you outlined in your mind during the trip. One strategy is to immediately start looking for a part-time job so that you will not have to live off your savings. You could look for a lodge on a part-time basis when you are not working. However, if you devoted your full effort to finding a lodge, you would stand a better chance of finding a lodge that would be right for you than you would if you're conducting a part-time search.

1. If you believe that obtaining temporary jobs would be your best strategy, then turn to Chapter 25.

2. If you believe that intensifying your search for an appropriate lodge would be your best strategy, then turn to Chapter 26.

CHAPTER 12

CREATING A

PERSONAL COACHING

BUSINESS

Most people go through their lives trying to avoid conflict. You thrive on it. People who are willing to perpetually learn, Peter Senge, author of *The Fifth Discipline,* says, define what they need to do to become successful at whatever they do. Their personal growth and development become a state of mind, a culture that values continuous learning. Solving problems, making the right decision most of the time, expanding product lines, and entering into new markets depend on one's ability to contribute to the business all of the time, rather than just some of the time. The individual who fails to invest in training and development will quickly fall behind those in the organization who do. People who engage in continuous learning improve their skills, upgrade their quality of performance, and provide exemplary service in everything they do.

As you think through the personal coaching process, you realize that by their very nature, educational institutes can't provide the personal tools one needs to immediately respond to today's dynamic and constantly changing environment. All they can do is show, from a historical perspective, the events that cause the change to ultimately occur. This is your opportunity to take a leading position in the new and emerging industry of personal coaching to teach, train, coach, and counsel self-motivated individuals.

You have decided to start a personal coaching business where you will show perspective clients how to confront problems and take corrective action that is basic to any coaching assignment. Every professional tennis player and golfer has a personal coach to help him or her play what is basically a simple game. Very few, if any, executives have a coach to help them play a significantly more complex corporate game. That's because until now, it was not fashionable for an outsider to appraise an executive's performance, a prerequisite to the coaching process, if improvements are to be made. In your mind, personal coaching is basic to the learning environment insofar as it:

- Facilitates the learning experience

- Involves the problem-solving processes

- Provides decision-making opportunities

- Ends with a planning session

The executive coaching program you plan to offer will help executives improve their work, upgrade their skills, learn how to solve problems more effectively, and improve their decision-making capability. Your primary role will be to facilitate self-discovery and guide executives to change the conditions under which they work. In short, your coaching program will stress corrective and improved action. Your success will depend upon your ability to manage the discussion with your executive clientele. Most of them are used to doing all the talking and very little listening. You can offer your opinion, but you have to stage the words so that the solution comes from their head. In this sense, coaching is really guiding based on listening, probing, encouraging, exchanging information or opinions, resolving disagreements, and ultimately, designing a game plan to accomplish specific objectives.

After numerous phone calls, reams of correspondence, and countless revisions to your personal coaching brochure, you finally land an interview with Bob Reynolds, the president of Cycore Inc. Cycore is a national distributor of floor tiles used in commercial office buildings. With the exception of Cycore, your executive coaching service was soundly rejected by the other executives you talked to when they said, "Why do I need you when I am the coach?" Most of the time, all you heard was the click of the phone before you could even respond to the question. For some reason, Bob is very interested in your personal coaching concept and has granted you a two-hour time slot tomorrow morning to "sell him on the idea."

At 10 A.M. sharp the next day, you appear in front of Bob's office and introduce yourself to his attractive secretary. She tells you that Bob is running a little late, delivers you a cup of coffee and escorts you to the executive lounge. An hour later Bob lumbers into the lounge and tells you he thought the meeting was at 11 A.M. When he asks you what was it that you wanted to discuss, you begin to wonder if you are at the right place. You may have a real coaching challenge with this man.

Things settle down when you get to Bob's office and begin explaining the principles that are behind your personal coaching service. You ask Bob if he has any questions. "Throughout your explanation of the objective of your program, you seemed to say that I should ask a whole lot of questions before I make a decision. Since I'm the President, why not just tell people what to do and when to do it?"

"Do you also tell them how high to jump?" You can tell you have irritated the man but you've got his attention and continue. "Management in the past did just that. We called it command-and-control management. It worked for most managers in another industrial era with employees who were used to taking orders. Today, employees expect and demand much better treatment from senior management."

Bob asks you to explain what you mean by better treatment. "They want stimulating work and control over their work. The buzz word today is empowerment."

"Your approach seems pretty extreme. Do you really think I need to take Cycore apart and put it back together from scratch?" You respond by saying, "Bob, I want to see you and Cycore move beyond the same old questions, such as: How can we do what we do faster and better? How can we do what we do at a lower cost? I want you to go back to the essential question: "Why do we do what we do at all?"

Bob counters, "That makes it sound as if I haven't done anything right in the past."

"No, you've done a lot of things right in the past, but that doesn't mean they will be the right things for the future. That is what my coaching assignment with you is all about. Collectively, we need to ask ourselves whether we are doing the right things, but more important, we need to ask why we are doing what we are doing. Answering that question will put you in the right frame of mind to redesign your business processes. As your personal coach, I'll be there to help you every inch of the way."

Predictably, Bob signs up for your program. Over the next two months, you find yourself spending all of your time at Cycore either coaching Bob directly or gathering and assimilating data to corroborate pending decisions that Bob has to make. However, as time marches on, Bob becomes less reliant on you, which you secretly admit hurts your feelings. As you think through your own coaching process, you begin to realize that is the way it should be. If you are a good coach, the athlete you are coaching will soon learn all that you have to teach him. It is then time for you to move on to another coaching assignment.

It takes you the better part of two months to find another personal coaching assignment at Reynolds Corporation. And, unlike the assignment you had at Cycore, Inc., this one is a part-time assignment. You're spending a disproportionate amount of your time finding clients rather than coaching. Your net worth at the end of the year remains unchanged when you review your financial statement.

First Year Financial Summary

Beginning Year Net Worth	$210,000
Plus: First Year Revenues	$90,000
Less: Business and Living Expenses	$90,000
First Year Net Worth	$225,000

In the interest of attracting more clients, you consider establishing your own unique approach to coaching rather than relying on the traditional approaches you have been using. Or, you could join an established partnership that has already developed a client base. Both options have important benefits that you want to carefully consider before you make your final decision.

1. If you believe that establishing your own approach to personal coaching would be your best strategy, turn to Chapter 27.

2. If you believe that buying into an established partnership would be your best strategy, turn to Chapter 28.

CHAPTER 13

CHASING BIG CLIENTS

At precisely 8:00 A.M. on Monday, your taxicab stops in front of the Motorola building and as you step out of the car, the cold wind hits you in the face like an avalanche. After a lot of hard work and a long flight, you have finally landed your first appointment with a major company that is legitimately interested in retaining you as its consultant and trainer. You're set for a nice long lucrative contract if you can just figure out how to close this sale.

You walk through the front door and into the elevator with all the flair and confidence befitting an entrepreneur. The elevator stops at the eighteenth floor and as you step out, you're greeted with a "good morning" from Kori Rye, the executive secretary to Motorola's Senior Vice President Susan Raymond. Kori escorts you into Raymond's office and hands you a cup of coffee. "Mrs. Raymond will be here in a moment to hear what you have to say." Susan enters the office at the precise 8:15 A.M. meeting time. You introduce yourself and engage in some small talk with what you hope will be your new client. Susan is a tall, slender woman in her late forties with the bronze face of an avid golfer. You can tell she has a great deal of confidence in herself and probably works well with others as long as things are done her way. She asks you to start your presentation. "Let me show you on this first chart what my training and consulting goals are for Motorola". . . and the well-rehearsed words seem to just roll out of your mouth.

You've spent the better part of a year chasing big clients, fighting and sometimes scratching your way into the offices of key executives to present your case for their business. More than once, you were told that you had no more than five minutes to make your business case. Motorola is the exception; you have been allocated a full fifteen minutes of presentation time. It's also your first of a series of formal presentations that you will be making over the next several weeks. You have back-to-back presentations with AT&T, The Boeing Company, Microsoft, Loral Corporation, DEC, and a couple of other major companies that you can't remember right now. You've invested at least a month's time in each presentation, learning about the culture of each company, what their current problems are, and what are the hot buttons of the executive you'll be addressing. Motorola is your "test case" because you were told they are a hard sell on outside training services. Their internal training department is larger than most companies.

You can't believe you are making an important presentation and thinking about where you have been in the past at the same time. You focus your mind back on your closing remarks. "And in conclusion, I would very much like the opportunity to earn your business today. My motivational training program is quite unique and it works. As I pointed out in one of my earlier charts, the increase in employee productivity resulting from this program far exceeds the cost of the program. When can I start the program for Motorola?" You've done it now: you have applied Zig Zigler's assumed sales closing technique. After a long period of deadly silence, a broad smile crosses Susan's face. "Why don't you start tomorrow."

You do in fact start tomorrow and over the next few months, the Motorola reference base helps you establish your training and consulting credentials with other major corporations. You discover that if you provide excellent service to a major account, you suddenly become a part of its inter-network of preferred training subcontractors. No sooner are you done with one assignment than they are after you to start another. It's a great position to be in but you can't grow your business if you are the one who is always tied down with the training and consulting assignments.

In your first year operating as a small consulting and training business, you generate $90,000 in revenue and $55,000 in expenses, netting you $35,000. Your net worth drops from $210,000 to $170,000 since you had to cover living costs and some unexpected costs such as the hail damage to your roof that wasn't covered by your homeowner's policy. If you had a magnifying glass, you would have been able to spot the exclusion in your policy when you read it! You summarize your financial position on a Lotus spreadsheet:

First Year Financial Summary

Beginning Year Net Worth	$210,000
Plus: First Year Revenues	$90,000
Less: Business and Living Expenses	$75,000
Less: Supplemental Living Expenses	$35,000
First Year Net Worth	$190,000

However, because of your success with Motorola and several other big accounts, your income increases substantially in your second year. Chasing big accounts pays off for both your consulting and training business. Winning the Motorola account was a real coup. DEC, Boeing, and AT&T sign long-term training and consulting contracts with you because you are already supporting a reputable company. Your financial situation improves dramatically in the second year:

Second Year Financial Summary

Beginning Year Net Worth	$190,000
Plus: Second Year Revenues	$180,000
Less: Business and Living Expenses	$125,000
Second Year Net Worth	$245,000

Your consulting and training business is growing and you are faced with an ongoing dilemma: How can you keep it growing? You don't have any more billable hours that you can personally throw into the business. Your 80-hour work weeks are already beginning to take a toll on you physically and mentally. If you are not careful, you risk losing your marriage and family. As you consider the alternatives, you contemplate hiring trainers and consultants to leverage your billable income. The consulting industry standard billing ratio is 3 to 1. If you pay a consultant or trainer $25 per hour, his or her billable rate should be $75 per hour to cover overhead cost, and most importantly, your profit on the transaction. However, you remember from your corporate days that managing employees presents a whole new set of problems. There are hiring and firing issues to consider, sick and vacation leaves to schedule, personal conflicts, and a variety of other issues to address. Even if you could find a way to hire employees on a contract basis, you'll still be challenged with a number of typical employee-management problems.

The alternative is to continue working for yourself. If you could hire yourself out as a full-time contract trainer for a major corporation, you would definitely reduce your travel hours and 80-hour work weeks. But, if something happens to you—like a serious illness—that would be the end of the game since you're a one-person team!

1. If you believe that hiring associates to build project teams would be your next logical step to grow your business, turn to Chapter 29.

2. If you feel that you should concentrate your efforts on becoming a contract trainer to grow your business, turn to Chapter 30.

CHAPTER 14

BEGINNING WITH

SMALL COMPANIES

AS CLIENTS

American companies are spending over $15 billion annually on management training and consulting. Now that's a number that you can really get excited about and you are anxious to claim your share of the pie. You have decided to market small companies first, before you move on to bigger corporate clients. It makes sense to you because small businesses are growing at a much faster rate than their larger corporate rivals.

For the next several months, you throw yourself into the task of identifying exactly what types of training programs small companies want. You believe there is a definite need for good management development—or MD programs as they are more popularly called. You ask yourself: Why are companies interested in MD programs? What offerings do they want to see? To find the answers, you mail questionnaires to 500 randomly selected MD training specialists who are members of the American Society for Training and Development (ASTD). A 24-percent response rate is more than you had anticipated from the mailing and gives you the statistical significance you wanted out of the survey. After burning a few weeks of long midnight oil, you create a format for an MD program that precisely matches the needs identified in your survey. You call the program *The Six-Step Fast-track MD Program* and summarize the steps as follows:

1. Building new people skills for the year 2000.

2. Doubling everyone's productivity, including your own.

3. Implementing strategic planning with 100 percent of everyone's support.

4. Developing a succession plan so you are not left behind.

5. Improving morale every day and all the time.

6. Responding to and controlling changes with enthusiasm.

Anxious to test market the theme of your program, you meet Karen Long, the guest speaker at the ASTD regional meeting in Manhattan. During the course of the conversation, Karen tells you about her background. She graduated with a Ph.D. in psychology and started a career in family counseling with Louis A. Allen Associates, a well-known management-development firm where she inherited the Johnson & Higgins account. When she decided to make another career change, Johnson & Higgins beckoned, admitting that they weren't quite sure how they would utilize her but that she seemed to be the kind of person they wanted in their organization. She has since justified the wisdom of their decision and ascended into the position of Human Resources Vice President.

You show Karen your management-development course outline and ask her to give you a critical evaluation. She begins by telling you that MD is essentially an overview for people who have been in management for a while and suggests you don't spend too much time on any one subject. Emphasize delegation, performance counseling, and how to turn around nonperformers. Customize your presentations to include "hot buttons" that meet specific client needs. Show how you can help them resolve key internal issues and problems. If you can do all that, you'll have a dynamite program.

Convinced that your program is, in fact, a dynamite program, you hire 10 trainer associates during the slow summer season and subject them to a comprehensive MD train-the-trainers program to get them ready for the fall season. Everybody is excited about the program and their future with your company. As you move into the fall season, a traditionally good time to book training contracts, your marketing program starts to sputter; there's lots of verbal interest in MD but very few contracts. In a nutshell, you believe that the current downsizing trend is at the heart of the problem. Like giant yo-yos, the big companies have started their annual fall migration into their favorite programs: downsizing, rightsizing, and reengineering. Whatever sizing name is popular on Wall Street is what they call their respective programs.

As a result of the sizing exercises, concerned smaller companies stop hiring, hoard their good workers, and refuse to contract for any outside services including training. It's a completely opposite reaction from what their large company rivals do. The big companies are actively contracting for outside services, which do not show on their employee head count, to make up for employee services lost in their downsizing exercises. They use training programs to improve upon the productivity of employees who survive the head-count reduction. In hindsight, you now wish you had pursued larger clients.

To make matters worse, small companies believe they should pay lower fees for the same training and consulting services offered to their larger rivals. As one of your small clients so aptly put it, the small business mind-set has been to think small on the expense line and large on the retail price line for their product and service offerings. If they can't buy something for what they think it's worth, they'll do without it or find a cheaper substitute. That's the entrepreneurial way!

All of this creates a minefield of potentially explosive problems that you don't need right now. The erosion of your small company base of business for MD training programs is devastating the morale of your trainers. In two short months, your monthly MD revenue base of $40,000 is cut in half. Worst yet, trainer morale problems are coming across on the podium during training sessions. Your customer satisfaction index from questionnaires every client completes at the end of a session have dropped 20 percent in the last 60 days alone. Five of your best trainers have already quit and you suspect that the rest are actively looking for jobs.

To bolster sales, you mount an intensive marketing campaign to market big client accounts, but quickly realize that the cultivation process will take you at least six months to put something together, if you're lucky. You don't have six months of payroll money sitting idle in your bank account. You don't even have two months. Sadly, your start-up decision to focus on small clients brings your company to an end. Reluctantly, you calculate the financial damage that has occurred this past year:

Second Year Financial Summary

Beginning Year Net Worth	$210,000
Plus: Second Year Revenues	$90,000
Less: Business and Living Expenses	$110,000
Second Year Net Worth	$190,000

Looking back on where you have been, would you alter your decisions in order to create a different future for yourself?

1. If you would like to change your last strategic decision, return to Chapter 4.

2. If you would like to select another business venture to start-up, return to Chapter 2.

3. If you would like to conduct more analysis before you start-up another business, turn to Chapter 3.

If you're still feeling the sting of defeat and believe you could have made your last strategic choice work in real life, you may be right. After all, this is just a game. However, if you return to your last strategic decision and select the other alternative (Chapter 13), you will learn why the authors consider it a better choice.

CHAPTER 15

ACQUIRING LAND

Real estate is everywhere because the common denominator of all real estate is land. And land is everywhere. Well-selected real estate always increases in value. Why? Because, as Mark Twain put it, "They ain't making any more land. But they can make more and more people to populate the land." You have decided to invest in land, the subject of the book you're reading, appropriately titled *They're Not Making Any More Land.* You know land can be used in several different ways and some land increases in value faster than other land because of the way the land is used. It reminds you of the poker-game story.

Three wealthy poker buffs were playing a high stakes game of five card draw. After several hours of playing, there came a hand in which all three players had been dealt excellent cards. As the antes increased, each of them ran out of cash and began using their respective real-estate holdings to up the ante. The rancher from Montana began the last round of raises by pledging his entire 10,000 acre ranch, including all his cattle and equipment. The oil baron from Oklahoma met the challenge by pledging his 1,000 acres of oil-producing wells. The wealthy Texan ended the bidding by offering his seven acres of ground in Texas.

"Seven acres!" gasped the other two partners. "Here we have pledged thousands of acres and you expect us to accept your measly seven acres?" "Yup," replied the Texan. "My land is right in the middle of downtown Dallas." Obviously, some land is more valuable than other land. The shorter the supply, the higher the sales price and the higher the probability the property will increase in value.

The book you have been reading talks about four major categories of land use. Undeveloped land is located away from population centers and has no immediate development potential. It's the kind of ground that is only good for holding the earth together. Recreational land has little use except for limited recreational value. Agricultural land is used for either animal grazing or crop production. The fourth type of land utilization is urban land near population centers. Urban land typically has a higher value because of its various uses. It can be sold for home building lots, for apartments, factories, or warehouse building sites, or a wide variety of other commercial uses.

You decide to invest in urban land where the factors of supply and demand will be working in your favor. A typical acre (43,560 square feet) of raw undeveloped agricultural land in your area can be purchased for as little as $500. That converts to a penny per square foot. If the same land could be converted into subdivision lots, it would sell for at least $50,000 an acre, or about 87 cents per foot. If the subdivision could be used for apartments instead of private residences, its value would substantially increase. The highest-priced land is typically used to build shopping centers or office buildings, and can sell for $100,000 or more per acre. Your land-development strategy begins to take shape. Between any two categories of land, there are fantastic opportunities for profit. All you need to do is convert land from one use to another.

You call Cheri Dengel, your real-estate agent, and ask her to start looking for land-conversion investment opportunities. Over the next several weeks, you talk with Cheri about a number of different options, none of which meets your investment criteria. It's a beautiful Saturday morning and you are just about to take that first sip of hot coffee when your cellular phone rings. It's Cheri. "Let's look at a ten-acre parcel right outside of town that's currently being used to raise corn. The farmer is getting older and wants to retire before the sprawling city gobbles him up. Since his livelihood has been derived from the land, he's resisted offers from subdividers in the past. Now that he is older and has retirement in sight, he should be receptive to an offer."

As always, Cheri has done her homework. That's why she is the only real-estate agent you will work with. On average, agricultural land in the county has been selling for between $4,000 and $10,000 an acre. However, two parcels of land this close to the city limits recently sold for $20,000 and $30,000 an acre. Farmer John has kept close track of every land sale within a hundred-mile radius of his property. He wants at least $25,000 an acre. You thank Cheri for the front-end work she has done and tell her you will get back to her in a day or two after you have completed your own analysis.

You visit the city and county government offices, where you confer with local government officials to determine the level of difficulty you'll encounter in subdividing the land and obtaining building permits. Is there adequate water, sewer, and fire protection? Will there be any problems when the final plan is submitted to the planning department for approval? Has the land been properly surveyed? Is there a market for the property? What size lots can be sold and at what price? These are some of the questions you ask when you contact a land survey company.

After gathering all of the facts, you conclude that the signs point to GO for the purchase of the land. Building lots have sold for as high as $20,000 within the last three months. Your surveyor draws up a preliminary subdivision plan showing that once the streets and sidewalks are installed, there will be room for thirty lots on the property. Working with a local contractor, you put the financial plan together:

Cost vs. Profit Projections for Proposed Land Acquisition

Cost of the 10 acres	$250,000
Cost of streets, sidewalks, and utility hookup per lot	$150,000
Sales commission and advertising costs	$30,000
Total Cost	$430,000
Gross sale of 30 lots at $20,000 each	$600,000
Less: Total Cost	$430,000
Total Profit	$170,000

The profit picture looks outstanding for a relatively small piece of land. You estimate it will take about a year to complete the full transaction. You might even be able to sell lots to a local builder who may need the land for his next subdivision. The wholesale price of the 30-lot package could be $17,500 per lot, but you would avoid sales cost and still end up with a $125,000 profit. You purchase the land and proceed with your development plan.

Obtaining the building and zoning permits that you need before you can install the streets, sidewalks, and utilities turns into a nightmare. The Planning Commission insists on getting an environmental impact study first, before it will issue the necessary permits. Four months later and with your environmental impact study in hand, you get the permits you need. Because of the permit delay, the contractors you had contacted to do the paving and utility work took on other jobs and won't be available to start your project for another 90 days. The delay is costing you more money than you had ever anticipated. Not only are you paying for services and permits that you can't use, you've got your own personal living expenses to contend with. You receive a call from Dan Bridger, one of the home builders you had contacted earlier. Dan offers to buy your property for exactly what you have into the venture. After reviewing your projected financial statement, you accept Dan's offer, lick your wounds, and decide to start over.

Second Year Financial Summary

Beginning Year Net Worth	$225,000
Plus: Profit from Land	$0
Less: Business and Living Expenses	$74,000
Second Year Net Worth	$151,000

Looking back on where you have been, would you alter your decisions in order to create a different future for yourself?

1. If you would like to change your last strategic decision, return to Chapter 5.

2. If you would like to select another business venture to start-up, return to Chapter 2.

3. If you would like to conduct more analysis before you start-up another business, turn to Chapter 3.

If you're still feeling the sting of defeat and believe you could have made your last strategic choice work in real life, you may be right. After all, this is just a game. However, if you return to your last strategic decision and select the other alternative (Chapter 16), you will learn why the authors consider it a better choice.

CHAPTER 16

BUYING HOUSES

AND APARTMENT BUILDINGS

If it is so easy to become wealthy through real-estate investing, then why isn't everybody doing it? Most Americans recognize it as one of the surest and safest ways to obtain financial freedom. Like any sophisticated investment challenge, only a few are willing to work hard at finding investment opportunities and then take the risks to actually buy the property. The rest will simply stand on the sidelines and say, "I should have bought."

You have decided to invest in rental property and find yourself asking a basic question: How does a person with limited knowledge of real estate become an investor in property? You know from past experience that investors have different thresholds for risk and debt. You're still lamenting over why you didn't buy more real estate in the past. Had you been more "bullish" in the 1970s or 80s, your financial position would be a lot better today than it is. You've talked to several bankers and real-estate agents and based on their input, want to start investing in real estate now!

Most of what you have read about investing in real estate tells you that the safest investment is income property. This may include rental homes, apartment buildings, office buildings, shopping centers, warehouses, or industrial parks. Rental homes and apartment buildings seem to offer the least risk and least amount of expertise, which fits your current profile. Income-producing property, where the tenant pays you rent sufficient to cover your mortgage payments and operating expenses and produce a positive cash flow, is what you want. Should you concentrate on buying houses first before you invest in apartment buildings? The purchase of a rental home would offer you the opportunity to gain knowledge, experience, and confidence before moving up to apartments. Homes and apartments will always be in demand, regardless of what the economy does. People have to live somewhere and you decide to let the buying opportunity dictate what investment you start with, homes or apartments.

Several of your friends have made a great deal of money buying older or poorly maintained properties that just needed a coat of paint and some basic landscaping adjustments. After restoring the property, they sell the property for a significantly higher price than what they paid for it. They call their investments "fixer-uppers." The quickest money can be made in this kind of real estate, but it takes a dedicated individual who knows something about fixing buildings. You think you know which is the right end of a hammer and plan to do the basic "fixer-upper" work yourself rather than hire a contractor who can eat up your cash reserves in a hurry.

Common sense tells you to find well-constructed properties in growing areas regardless of the condition of the property. The long-run appreciation from such a property may be slow, but it will be steady and predictable. If the basic property is solid, then it should not require a lot of work to bring the property up to standards. In a recent real-estate investment class you attended at a junior college, you learned what you needed to do to become familiar with where to invest by studying the properties on the market. You were told to learn all you could about the city where you plan to invest, its growth patterns, its depressed areas, and where the growth is likely to extend. The more you learned about the market, the more confident you became at spotting good investment opportunities. Talking to real-estate agents and driving through neighborhoods noting all "For Sale" signs, stopping and asking questions whenever you could, helps you determine what constitutes a good buy in your area.

In your search for rental property, you find a five-unit apartment located in a growing part of town. The building is in good condition and the rental situation is excellent. Each unit has two bedrooms, one and three-quarter baths, and rents for $400 a month. Renters pay all utility bills. To determine if this is a good investment, you estimate the annual income and expenses for the property. The purchase price is $120,000 and there is an existing loan of $80,000 with monthly mortgage payments of $826. The seller is extremely motivated and wants a quick sale. He realizes that the value of the property is close to $135,000 but he will settle for $120,000. The listing real-estate agent tells you that is about 10 percent below market. The seller's equity is about $40,000 and he has agreed to sell the building to you with a down payment of only $10,000. You can secure a 25-year loan of $110,000 at 11 percent with monthly payments of $1,098.

1. Annual Rental Income: $400 per unit * 5 units * 12 months = $24,000. You have been able to determine that, on average over the last three years, the vacancy rate has been 5% and hence you adjust rental income down to $22,800 ($24,000 * .95).

2. Other Income: A candy-vending machine generates $20 a month in net profits or $360 per year.

3. Operating Expenses: Operating expenses should not exceed 30 percent, according to what you have read in *Apartments*, a trade magazine for apartment owners.

You proceed to complete the balance of Rental Property Operating Statement, making notes as you proceed. After all expenses and mortgage payments have been figured, you project a positive cash flow. The final area of analysis is to determine if the property is worth what you are about to pay for it. After all, who other than the seller says that the apartment is really worth $120,000! Why not $110,000? How do you make sure you are not being swindled out of $10,000? You hire an appraiser (Joan Woodward) who was referred to you by your real-estate agent to help determine the market value of the property. You were told she's an excellent appraiser and also very busy. When you call Joan, she tells you she won't be able to appraise your apartment for three weeks. In the interim, you decide to prepare your own estimate, based on a "how to appraise real estate" procedure in an appraisal book you got from the library. The book covers three appraisal approaches:

1. Cost Approach: where you determine what it would cost to replace the structure by obtaining estimates from local building contractors

2. Income Approach: where you determine the property value by analyzing the income generated by the property

3. Market Approach: where you determine what other similar properties have sold for recently.

In your own mind, you believe that the market approach is the most effective method for determining value. The prize for investing goes to the investor who knows, rather than guesses, current market prices. A ten-unit apartment similar to yours sold for $250,000 three months ago. Although it is located only four blocks from where your unit is located, you believe your location is preferable. The other unit is located right off an incredibly busy thoroughfare causing noise problems. According to the tenants you contacted, the congestion on the frontage road makes it difficult to enter and exit the apartment's parking lot. The apartment was built eight years ago and based on data from the County Clerk's office, costs $150,000 to build. The cost of the lot was $40,000.

Armed with all of the facts, you proceed to estimate the value of your property using the cost approach. You compare the cost of construction on a per-square-foot basis of the comparative apartment to the one you are considering. Both units are block-wall construction with Spanish tile roofs and asphalt parking areas. The interiors of both units are standard plaster walls and ceiling construction supplemented with medium-grade wall-to-wall carpet. Your cost approach calculations follow:

Cost per sq. ft. to build comparative apartment = Construction Cost / Total Sq. Ft.
= $250,000 / 8,000
= $31.25 per square foot

Cost Adjusted for Inflation = Cost per Sq. Ft. * Inflation Rate over 5 Years
= $31.25 * 1.21
= $37.81

Cost per sq. ft. to build proposed apartment = Purchase price – Value of land / Tot. Sq. Ft.
= $120,000 – $25,000 / 4,000
= $23.75 per square foot

Based upon your preliminary cost-per-square-foot analysis, the apartment you are considering compares favorably with the competitive unit. However, your property is three years older than the comparable unit, a factor that could affect the cost of replacing appliances, heating units, and air-conditioner units. You make a mental note of this issue.

You've been advised not to invest in real estate unless there is at least a 10 percent capitalization rate on the investment. You used the following formula to determine the capitalization rate of the apartment:

Capitalization rate = Net operating income / Price
                   = $13,000 / $120,000
                   = 11%

The property you are considering has a net operating income of $13,869 and based on an 11-percent minimum capitalization rate, its value would be calculated by multiplying estimated net income by 11 ($13,000 × 11 = $133,000). Based on your capitalization rate analysis and your estimate of net operating income, the apartment should be selling for $33,000 more than your offer of $120,000.

Having concluded your analysis, you buy the apartment for $120,000 and over the next four months, apply the same technique to buy two rental houses. As you approach the end of the second year, you sell the apartment for $135,000 and update your financial statement:

Second Year Financial Summary

Beginning Year Net Worth	$225,000
Plus: Net Revenue From Income Property	$18,400
Equity From Sale of Apartment	$15,000
Second Year Net Worth	$258,400

Satisfied with your early success in real-estate development, you consider two alternatives to further grow your business. You're intrigued with the idea of purchasing as much real estate as you can with zero down payments. However, based on the financial success you enjoyed with your first apartment, you are also contemplating building an apartment complex.

1. If you believe that playing the "zero down" game is the best way to grow your real-estate development company, turn to Chapter 31.

2. If you believe that building an apartment complex is the best way to grow your real-estate development company, turn to Chapter 32.

CHAPTER 17

ADDING NEW LOCATIONS

Finding the right location for a small business demands a combination of science, art, and luck. When you selected the location for your first Mail Boxes Etc. (MBE) store, your demographic research was thorough and complete. The chamber of commerce, city planning commission, economic development agency, and local office of the U.S. Census Bureau provided you with valuable demographic data such as average family income, length of residence, average age, mean income, and traffic patterns in all of the locations you considered. Most of the information was free or available at a nominal cost.

You learned all you could about your customers, who they are, what their buying patterns are, and where they live. You found out everything you could about their demographics and habits before you committed to your present store location. You had several locations in mind and visited the city planning office to see if zoning regulations would prevent you from selecting a specific location. You were particularly interested in regulations governing business signs and the types of businesses that were allowed at different locations. Were there any planned roads or developments that could affect your choice? You rule out locations that your competitors already control.

You narrow your search down to a couple of choices, which allows you to concentrate on specific locations. All of your efforts pay off when you select a location that is right for you and perfect for your customers. You locate your MBE franchise near your customers in a busy convenience mall anchored by an Albertson food store. Like clockwork, your customers do their shopping at Albertson and then stop by MBE for their mailing service needs.

However, your decision to hastily add additional Mail Boxes Etc. locations without getting the company's endorsement is about to pull you under if you can't break the lease agreements. When you leased space in the Albertson mall, you drew on everything from market research to consumer psychology to validate the site. Why didn't you go through the same check-and-balance steps for your other locations? Unfortunately, you already know the answer to the question. You thought you knew it all and price, price, price rather than location, location, location guided your decision.

You planned to use your Albertson mall store as your prime location and set up three feeder stores in industrial parks where you leased store space for a third of what the Albertson mall space cost. You were betting on the fact that the industrial park commercial clients would welcome a convenient mail outlet. You should have asked them first before you signed the leases, because, as you have belatedly discovered, they are not interested in your services. Most of your potential commercial clients already have their own mail rooms and in spite of your repeated solicitations to show them why it would be cost-effective to use your services, they are not interested in shutting down their internal mail operations. As a result, you're not making enough money to cover your monthly lease payments let alone direct and overhead costs. The entire operation is about to bury you financially.

Mr. Cohen is the property manager you dealt with to solidify the three industrial park long-term lease locations at a great price. What a great guy he was to deal with before you signed the lease agreements. There wasn't anything he wouldn't do for you. Now that he knows you're in trouble and want to negotiate an end to the leases, he won't even return your phone calls.

You decide to give it one more shot and call Cohen's office. "Good morning, Mr. Cohen's office. How may I help you?" You reply with an "Is he in?" By now, Cohen's snippy secretary knows your voice even though you have tried, without success, to disguise it on several occasions. "He's in a meeting. I'll leave him a message to call you back." You reply with a "don't bother" and hang up the phone.

Your next call gets results and solves your financial dilemma. Your attorney friend, Alan Gwant, answers the phone. "Alan, as we discussed in our lunch meeting yesterday, please file a Chapter 13 bankruptcy order on my behalf." Alan tells you it will be done by close of business today. You hang up the phone and a smile crosses your face. You've finally got even with that Cohen guy! Your smile fades as you assess the damage that has been done to your financial position:

Second Year Financial Summary

Beginning Year Net Worth	$225,000
Plus: Second Year Revenue	$190,000
Less: Business and Living Expenses	$225,000
Second Year Net Worth	$190,000

Looking back on where you have been, would you alter your decisions in order to create a different future for yourself?

1. If you would like to change your last strategic decision, return to Chapter 6.

2. If you would like to select another business venture to start-up, return to Chapter 2.

3. If you would like to conduct more analysis before you start-up another business, turn to Chapter 3.

If you're still feeling the sting of defeat and believe you could have made your last strategic choice work in real life, you may be right. After all, this is just a game. However, if you return to your last strategic decision and select the other alternative (Chapter 18), you will learn why the authors consider it a better choice.

CHAPTER 18

EXPANDING THE SCOPE

OF SERVICES

James Farling, your Mail Boxes Etc. store manager, walks into your office and shuts the door, obviously upset about something. "I'm concerned about your interest in expanding the scope of our services. I'm just beginning to learn this job and we both know the store is making money. I hear rumors that you want to expand the scope of our services. Why start changing things around when everything is going so well?" You like and respect James. He has been a great store manager, always on time, stays late when needed without complaining, and tracks your cash receipts with the honesty of an eagle scout. You don't want to lose him. "James, we'll just have to move beyond our current comfort zone and here is why."

"The seasonal cycles in the mailing business are becoming more and more difficult to manage. You know 40 percent of our business is done over the Thanksgiving and Christmas holidays. I'm not complaining about holiday business. What I am concerned about is that when things are slow in the off-season months, I still have to pay the rent, salaries, utility bills, and a bunch of other fixed costs. I'm looking for a way to financially smooth things out around here and I need your help to do it."

You hadn't realized how loud your voice had become until you glance out the open door of your office and catch several customers staring in at you. James catches your concern, shuts the door, and offers an apology. "I am sorry for thinking only about myself. Maybe we could collectively figure out how to get more sales out of your existing floor space. For example, do we really need two self-service copy machines in the front of the store? Why not go with one machine and use the space that is left over to display a rack of those Leanin Tree greeting cards that guy is always trying to sell us?" You tell James it's a start and by the end of the week, you're in the greeting-card retail business.

Over the next several months, you begin to expand the scope of your services to include on-site personal computer (PC) rentals by the hour, a brochure design service and an answering service. To your surprise, your greeting-card sales become an active part of your retail business, which causes you to add other retail product lines that complement your mailing business. A complete line of stationery products is added. You soon discover that people are willing to pay for PC coaching services when they rent your PCs. You offer coaching in desktop publishing, graphic design, word processing, and spreadsheet design. Nobody minds paying $25 for a half-hour consulting session.

During the start of the Christmas season, you're so busy that you don't even notice the start of the holiday business. When you review your financial statement and realize how good business has been to you this year, you're reminded of the help that James put forth to make it all come together. When you hand him an envelope, he asks you what it is. "That's your Christmas bonus." He starts to object by reminding you Thanksgiving was just last week. "James, if you don't open the envelope now, I'll take it back." The smile on his face when he peers into the envelope to see the amount printed on the check makes it all worthwhile.

Second Year Financial Summary

Beginning Year Net Worth	$225,000
Plus: Second Year Revenues	$260,000
Less: Business and Living Expenses	$224,000
Second Year Net Worth	$261,000

That evening as you head for home, you contemplate what you should do next to expand your MBE business. Adding delivery services would allow you to expand into markets that are currently outside of your territory. You're also thinking about adding direct-mail services to attract larger corporate clients. If you had the time and could afford it, you would do both but prudent judgment tells you to stick with only one alternative.

1. If you believe that adding delivery services would be the best way to expand the scope of your business, turn to Chapter 33.

2. If you believe that direct-mail services would be the best way to expand the scope of your business, turn to Chapter 34.

CHAPTER 19

You're having problems funding the development of software applications. You finally produce a multimedia CD-ROM version of your book, *The Corporate Game,* and thanks to your marketing, rather than your technical expertise, its sales are doing quite well. Unfortunately, you don't have the financial resources to produce another title and decide to search for a way to leverage your services to make more money. You manage to get a speaker's spot at the National Software Developer's conference in Boston next week. It wasn't easy! Your perseverance paid off when Bill Rhoades, the association's Executive Director, finally agreed to add you to the program agenda. You've got a half-hour slot to talk about the marketing needs of the industry. He doesn't know about your secret agenda; you're looking for software developers who need marketing help. You want to show them how, with your help, they can find new marketing channels for their services. You plan to use the fees from your marketing services to fund your own software-development activities. You'll use your presentation hopefully to pique their interest.

The NSD conference draws in excess of 2,000 software developers from all over the country. As you settle into your hotel room at the Boston Hyatt, you review your presentation material for tomorrow morning's opening session. The screech of your alarm startles you as you realize you had fallen asleep in the lounge chair last night while reviewing your presentation material. Your presentation starts in a half-hour, which barely gives you enough time to get ready. You make it to the podium with one minute to spare.

You begin your presentation by showing an exhibit that "pinpoints" target software development markets by industry. "As you can see, the target markets are broken down into four areas of opportunity. In anticipation of your question as to what you can expect to make by entering any one of the four target markets, let me show you my next chart. I have personally reviewed the sales projections and believe they are conservative." At the conclusion of your presentation, you ask, "Are there any questions?" Several of the people in the audience express an interest in meeting with you to discuss the marketing opportunities you identified in more detail.

It's nearly midnight and after a long evening of seminar networking, you finally make it up to your hotel room and switch on your laptop, which is becoming a nightly ritual to check your e-mail. There's a message marked urgent from Hal McBride, a highly regarded multimedia developer whom you met earlier, telling you about a group of software developers who want to meet with you tomorrow at 7 A.M. in the conference meeting room. Hal's message tells you they are interested in learning more about your marketing program. You settle in for a quick five hours of sleep, only to be awakened by the phone at 4:15 A.M. It's Hal checking to make sure you'll be at the morning meeting. Doesn't this man ever sleep? With controlled temper, you tell Hal: "I'll be there, now go back to bed!"

As you walk into the conference room that morning, you're surprised by the number of people waiting for you; there are about thirty. Hal McBride walks up and rapidly begins shaking your hand. "Let me tell you what this is all about. As the group spokesman, we would like to learn more about your marketing program. We all need marketing support. How you can help us? How much will it cost us? We want lots of specifics, if you don't mind. Remember, we would not be here if we weren't interested."

You've got about an hour to cover the details of your program before the seminar starts. You would have preferred to meet with interested players on a one-to-one basis rather than on a group basis for obvious reasons. If you say the wrong thing, you could lose the entire group. However, if you say the right thing, you could win over the entire group.

You thank Hal for his comments, introduce yourself to the group, and begin explaining the program. "Most of my consulting work with companies these days is collaborative work where cross-functional teams are used to resolve challenging problems in a give-and-take atmosphere. The team concept works well with one significant exception. The information systems (IS) teams don't have the technical depth to cover all critical technical disciplines. Internal turf issues tend to bias the objectivity of the teams. For example, the local area network (LAN) expert will almost always defend a LAN solution to a problem that may clearly call for a wide area network (WAN) solution." Hal raises his hand and before you can acknowledge him asks, "What does all this cross-functional team stuff have to do with us and our desire for marketing support?"

"I'm glad you asked that question, Hal, because I was just about to give you the answer. Companies that rely on cross-functional teams to resolve IS-related problems need outside software developers to participate as collaborative team members. They believe consultants can be more objective (i.e., no turf barriers) and you offer them a source of expertise that they may not have covered internally. In addition, you may be able to offer them a solution that requires the development of software, which you can cover. As I see it, your participation on cross-functional teams is a win-win situation for you. As a team member, you have the opportunity to earn prime consulting fees that may also lead to software-development contracts. I can provide you with all the collaborative consulting work you want, if you are interested."

You conclude your presentation by asking if anybody is interested in the program. Hal recommends a follow-up session at 8 P.M. "The seminar will be over today and most of us don't have to leave until tomorrow morning." Everybody agrees to the meeting time.

That evening, you tell the group what you want out of the deal. "My fee will be 25 percent commission on your gross earnings for all work that is contracted through me. All participants in the program must agree to provide software-development support to my company at a 25-percent discount off your published price. "Nobody challenges your numbers as you go into the details of the agreement and identify the specific types of technical support you will need. Over the next six months, your cross-functional team-support program proves to be an outstanding success with both the companies and the software developers you represent. Your net earnings in the second year of the program catapult your salary into six-digit figures.

Second Year Financial Summary

Beginning Year Net Worth	$215,000
Software Development Revenue	$85,000
Plus: Commission Revenue	$75,000
Less: Business and Living Expenses	$70,000
Second Year Net Worth	$305,000

As you look forward to a successful third year, you consider what you should do next to further the growth of your business. On the one hand, you are intrigued with the idea of keeping your business small. You believe that, with the support of a small team of five software developers, you could develop two or three top software products that could make you millions. On the other hand, if you choose to expand your software-development horizons to include multimedia applications, you'll need additional capital to buy multimedia hardware and camera equipment.

1. If you believe that raising additional funds to develop multimedia applications is your best choice to grow your start-up, turn to Chapter 35.

2. If you believe that developing a few software products with a high market potential is your best choice to grow your start-up, turn to Chapter 36.

CHAPTER 20

DEVELOPING YOUR OWN

SOFTWARE PRODUCT

Over the past 12 months, the most pervasive subjects in every trade journal you read are about the Internet and multimedia software products. And they all say the same thing: the market is untapped! You are looking for a "ground-floor opportunity" and have subsequently decided to focus your efforts on developing your own software product, a universal database that can interpret both legacy data and multimedia data. The database you have in mind will integrate sound, images, text, and other complex data forms into one relational database pool of information on or off the Internet.

If you can pull this thing off, the demand for a universal database system will be huge. The database would allow users to simultaneously manage text, images, sound files, and other multimedia file components inside the database. You discuss the idea with John Foley, Vice President of Internet Shopping Network in Palo Alto, California, a company that sells over 35,000 products on the Internet each year. It represents national clients like Teleflora, JC Penney's and Black & Decker. John is legitimately fascinated with your universal database idea and tells you, "Our company's cyberstore is limited to relational data where only small product pictures can appear as attachments to our front-page web advertisement. We are well aware of the fact that future transactions will require much richer data combinations. We need a database that can handle unlimited sound, advanced automation, video excerpts, and seek-and-find text information. Whoever comes up with a universal database that can interpret both digital data and multimedia analog data will become an instant millionaire."

Your excitement for this project mounts as you thank John for his input, hang up the phone, and head out to the airport for your flight to Dallas and the National Software Association conference. Michael Stonebaker of Infomix Software is the keynote speaker and you need to talk to him. Michael was responsible for developing the first object-oriented database called Postgres when he was a professor at the University of California. He and a team of students developed and completed the program under a Federal-government grant last year.

Your flight arrives on time in Dallas and the 300-yard walk from the terminal to the Dallas Regency Hotel where the conference is being held greatly simplifies the logistics of avoiding rush-hour traffic. You check into your room and as you review the program agenda, abruptly realize that Mike will be addressing all new arrivals in the Alamo room in less than an hour. You hope to talk to him at the reception that immediately follows his address.

The Alamo Room is packed with people who have come to hear what Mike has to say about universal databases. He talks about Postgres, an object-oriented database written in a software query language (SQL). "We used SQL rather than a third-generation language such as C+++ to minimize development costs. In the early stages of the project, we realized the challenge we face to develop a relationship between digital and analog data, a marriage that nobody knew how to perform. The fundamental problem is that relational architecture has been stretched to its limits and therefore, can't cut it for new applications."

At the cocktail party that follows, you get a chance to talk to Mike. After telling him how much you enjoyed his presentation about Postgres, you ask him how you can get a copy of the program. He tells you, "All of the source code for Postgres is available free since it was developed with Federal grants. You can download the software from the Internet at address http://techweb.cmp.com. You'll need about 20 diskettes to complete the copy."

Your trip to the conference turns up a potential gold mine. All during your flight home, a single thought continues to race through your mind: If you can figure out how to commercialize Postres, a universal database that has already been blessed with $4 million dollars of Federal grant money and thousands of hours of student research and development time, then you're on your way to making millions.

No sooner are your feet on the ground than you find yourself planted in front of your PC, connecting into the Internet and downloading the Postgres programs. Mike was right; it took exactly 20 diskettes to complete the task.

Stabilizing Postgres proves to be a technical challenge that is beyond your capability. Every time you run the program, it blows up at random intervals. The problems you encounter are not unexpected since Postgres was developed in an academic lab with limited funds to fix all program bugs and little time to create adequate documentation. In desperation, you hire a couple of "topnotch" SQL programmers who, to your delight, succeed at stabilizing Postgres so that it can be demonstrated without blowing up!

Anxious to demonstrate Postgres's capabilities, you rent a booth at the northeast regional Comdex show. If all goes well, you're headed for the national Comdex show in Las Vegas where attendance has been known to exceed 750,000 people. On the first day of the conference, your friend from IBM, Kurt Carpenter, stops by your booth. You ask Kurt, "What do you think about the marketing prospects for a universal database?" The answer he gives you stings. "You're trying to sell a Swiss Army knife to the database market. Most database professionals are still trying to get their existing relational databases working. A fully integrated database system that's capable of accessing digital and analog data files is not one of our top priorities. Two years from now, it might be!"

You thank Kurt for his opinion, which you believe is demonstrating the short-sightedness of a typical IBM executive. However, the enthusiasm that you expected for Postgres at the show doesn't materialize. You get a lot of comments like "Nice concept, might need it someday" to "How would you use it?" During the course of the show, you collect over 1,000 business cards and zero sales orders.

When you arrive home, the current issue of *InformationWeek* is ominously waiting for you in your mailbox. The entire issue is dedicated to databases and what the major corporate players like DEC, Microsoft, and Oracle are doing in the universal-database development market. Oracle announces its Universal Server, which integrates Oracle's relational database with six different data types. As you read on, none of the "big three" can agree on the technical format that universal databases of the future should adapt to accommodate all data formats.

You suddenly realize you are not even a pawn in this giant chess game. You try to leverage what you know about universal-database architecture by calling the major database companies for a job or consulting position but you get the same answer. "What do you know that we don't already know?" Reluctantly, you decide to review where you are financially, before you plot your next move.

Second Year Financial Summary

Beginning Year Net Worth	$210,000
Plus: Second Year Revenues	$22,000
Less: Business and Living Expenses	$94,000
Second Year Net Worth	$138,000

At your current rate of financial deterioration, you will be bankrupt in two years. While you still have some financial resources left, you mount a major campaign to find another job. Looking back on where you have been, would you alter your decisions in order to create a different future for yourself?

1. If you would like to change your last strategic decision, return to Chapter 4.

2. If you would like to select another business venture to start-up, return to Chapter 2.

3. If you would like to conduct more analysis before you start-up another business, turn to Chapter 3.

If you're still feeling the sting of defeat and believe you could have made your last strategic choice work in real life, you may be right. After all, this is just a game. However, if you return to your last strategic decision and select the other alternative (Chapter 19), you will learn why the authors consider it a better choice.

CHAPTER 21

BUYING AN EXISTING MOTEL

Prior to moving to Montana, you subscribed to the *Billings Gazette* and learned about a motel that was for sale in Flathead, Montana. It is definitely not what you have been looking for, but as Chris told you, there are no lodges available for sale anywhere in Montana. Your "fallback" position is to acquire a motel, learn all that you can about the hospitality industry, and buy a lodge when one comes on the market. After your meeting with Chris, you called Flathead Realty and talked to Jim Carleton about the motel ad you had seen in the paper. Jim tells you it's still on the market and you agree to meet with him early that afternoon.

After gulping down an Egg McMuffin, you point your Hertz car north on Interstate 17 toward Kalispell, the gateway into Montana's Flathead Lakes region. Two hours out of Billings and you arrive at Kalispell only to find that you have another hour's drive up a winding mountain road to get to the town of Flathead, population 2,000 during the summer season. The population drops to 50 in the winter.

There is only one main street in Flathead and it doesn't take you long to find Jim's office. As soon as you step out of your car, Jim appears from nowhere and shakes your hand. He's a tall, slender man dressed in a wool shirt and Levis that are somehow held up with the longest set of suspenders you have ever seen. Once inside the office, Jim proceeds to tell you about the motel. "Joel Sorenson died three months ago and left the Sorenson Motel to his son and daughter. Joel had been running that motel for over fifty years but his kids never wanted any part of it before his death and they don't want it now. The son lives in Denver and I believe the daughter lines in Cheyenne. Both have good corporate jobs and even though they were raised in this country, they're not anxious to come back on a permanent basis. They have asked me to sell the motel for $300,000 or the best offer I can get. Before I go any further, why don't we jump in my truck and I'll show you the property."

Your first sighting of the Sorenson Motel was a memorable event. It did not fit the picturesque mental image you had created in your mind. Built shortly after World War II, this had to be one of the first motels in the state. Jim tells you it was definitely the first motel in Flathead and with the exception of a couple of guest houses down the street, it is still the only motel in Flathead. There are 30 units on the property with a separate main unit that serves as the reservation office and home for the motel manager. When Joel Sorenson died, his brother agreed to run the property until it was sold. By even Montana standards, the property is rustic and in dire need of repairs. Everything could use a coat of paint and when you walk into one of the units, the carpet and drapes look like they are original equipment. Could they possibly be 50 years old?

You return to Jim's office and as he hands you a cup of coffee, he asks, "Well, what do you think?" When you tell him not much, he looks like you had just insulted his wife. "What do you mean, not much? Joel Sorenson spent his life building and maintaining that place. The Sorenson Motel is a town landmark." You carefully choose you next set of words. "Jim, I am looking for property that represents a solid investment, one that I can run and make a living at while I'm doing it. I also want to have some reasonable assurance that if I should decide to sell, I'll be able to get my money back out of the place. Quite frankly, I don't believe the Sorenson Motel meets any of my investment criteria."

As you get up from your chair to make a polite exit out of the office, Jim steps in front of the door and asks for five more minutes of your time. You reluctantly agree and Jim starts in on what you guessed would be his "last ditch" sales pitch. "Suppose I told you the Sorenson netted $75,000 a year out of that motel over the last five years and I can prove it because I did his tax returns before he died." You stop dead in your tracks thinking how anybody could net $75,000 a year out of a $300,000 investment. You tell Jim, "I'm tired and I want to get home. What's the catch?"

Jim asks you to spend one night at a room he's reserved for you at the motel. "In the morning, I will show you everything you need to see to confirm that this is the investment of a lifetime." You agree under one condition. "Point me toward the best steakhouse in Flathead." Jim tells you how easy that is because there is only one steakhouse in the town. When you ask him if it is also the only *restaurant*, he doesn't answer. That evening, as you enjoy one of the best T-bone steaks you have ever had, you tell yourself to keep an open mind when you meet with Jim tomorrow morning.

Your morning meeting begins at 8 A.M. as Jim proceeds to roll-out the five-year occupancy records for the Sorenson Motel. "As you can readily see, this motel has enjoyed a 75 percent year-round average occupancy rate. Winters are harsh up here and the place still gets its fair share of skiers and hunters. To confirm what I am saying, let me show you Sorenson's tax returns over the past five years. As you begin to pore through the numbers with Jim, you suddenly realize that this motel could be a money-maker. It has generated a positive cash flow over the past five years and returned an income to its owner that is 25 percent of the estimated value of the property.

Instinctively, you decide to make an offer on the motel. "Jim, tell the Sorenson kids I am prepared to offer them $225,000 for their dad's motel." Jim almost catapults out of his chair. "That is an insulting offer that they would never accept. I won't even submit it." You calmly look Jim squarely in the eye and ask him how many offers he has had on this property since it came on the market. His glowering silence tells you what you already know—none! By the end of the meeting, Jim calms down and steadfastly insists he can rise to the challenge and will submit your "low-ball" offer to the Sorensons in the morning. You tell Jim, "The renovation work you identified might convince them that this is a fair offer." As you leave Jim's office, you thank him for his support and return to your room at the Sorenson Motel.

Jim calls you early the next morning and tells you your offer has been accepted. You meet him in his office, sign the final papers, and head back down the mountain to Billings to refine the strategic plan you've held in your hip pocket. You believe you have just purchased a motel for well under its market value. Your first thought is to put it back on the market, sell it, and take your short-term profits all the way to the bank. On the other hand, if you can indulge in a little patience and renovate the motel, you could stand to gain a far greater profit in the future. Either way, your financial situation looks good.

Second Year Financial Summary

Beginning Year Net Worth	$190,000
Plus: Second Year Revenues	$275,800
Less: Business and Living Expenses	$190,000
Second Year Net Worth	$275,800

1. If you believe it would be in your best financial interest to renovate the Sorenson motel, turn to Chapter 37.

2. If you believe it would be in your best financial interest to sell the Sorenson motel, turn to Chapter 38.

CHAPTER 22

BUILDING A NEW LODGE

Chilling January winds whip off Penobscot Lake as you duck into the Rainbow restaurant for lunch. Like most local businesses, the place is nearly empty since Montana isn't terribly popular in the winter. Even the local business owners close up shop and flee to kinder climates. Among those who remain is George Stevens, a well-respected residential and commercial builder in the area who has agreed to meet you for lunch. You find George sitting in one of the fifties-style booths discussing the toboggan race with a waitress as he takes some good-natured ribbing about what he had to do to win the race last week.

The personal part of the conversation abruptly stops when you walk up to the booth and shake George's hand. The waitress politely asks if you want a cup of coffee; you nod and she returns with your coffee. You met George last week when Cheri Dengel, the local real-estate agent, introduced you to him at a sparsely attended chamber-of-commerce meeting. "He's the best builder in the area," Cheri told you. You later learned that George is also the only builder in the Penobscot Lakes area.

After exchanging a couple of introduction niceties with George and placing your order for lunch, you open up the conversation to business. "George, as we discussed last week, I have decided to build a lodge on Penobscot Lake. I'd like you to be the prime contractor on the project. Are you interested?" After an incredibly long pause and a lot of head scratching, George appears to be about ready to give you an answer to your question. You wonder why it's taking so long to answer what you thought was a simple question. The man can't be overloaded with work right now. But, as Cheri told you, "Montanans are casual and calculating folks who have to like and trust you before they will even consider doing business with you. The fact that you're an outsider automatically puts you at a disadvantage." George finally answers your question. "That depends. . . ."

Carefully controlling your irritation, you politely respond with, "That depends on what?" You hope your contorted smile doesn't give away the internal irritation you are feeling for the way this conversation is digressing.

"It depends on whether or not the lodge you have in mind can survive as a business in this area. I do not want to build a lodge unless I am convinced that it will survive. I've seen many pioneers just like you come into Montana with a similar vision and fail financially in their first year." You are suddenly taken back by what you believe are legitimate concerns of this "good old Montana boy." You ask George to be more specific.

The ensuing discussion gets into depths that go beyond your expectations. George continues, "An existing lodge can be appraised by several formulas that depend on its actual or potential operating income and capitalization rate. As you know, capitalization is the process of converting income into a capital value. The rate at which this occurs is called the capitalization rate. Do you want me to continue?" You quickly nod your head.

"As I understand it, the lodge you're planning to build will be comprised of two investment components, a mortgage loan and your equity in the property. I bring this point up because not only will the lodge have a capitalization rate, but each investment component will have its own capitalization rate. Consequently, the capitalization rate for your lodge is the sum of the interest rate or rate of return on invested capital and the recapture rate or rate of return on invested capital."

"If the invested capital is a mortgage loan, then the lender's investment is the loan amount. Each payment on the loan consists of an amount for interest and an amount for principle. The interest and principle is the return on the lender's investment or the mortgage capitalization rate. Your down payment in the lodge represents your equity position. It follows then that your return on the investment comes from the cash flow of the property. The capitalization rate is the sum of the mortgage interest rate and the property recapture rate. Are you still with me?" As George catches his breath, you ask him where all of this is going.

"Let me show you. You want to build a $500,000 lodge on land that you are about to buy for $150,000 for a total cost of $650,000. You have projected an annual net income of $51,000 from the venture. The current interest rates are running at 8 percent and the capitalization rate is 11 percent. What is the estimated market value of the lodge? Is it still worth $650,000 when I get done building it? Here is the formula I use:"

PV = Present Value, INT = Interest Rate; CAP = Capitalization Rate; INC = Income

PV = $650,000

INT = 8%

CAP = 11%

INC = $51,000

$$\text{Property Value} = PV + ((INC - (CAP \times PV)) / INT$$
$$= \$650{,}000 + ((\$51{,}000 - \$71{,}500) / .08))$$
$$= \$650{,}000 + (-\$20{,}500 / .08)$$
$$= \$650{,}000 + (-\$256{,}250)$$
$$= \$393{,}000$$

With calculator in hand, George scratches out the numbers to his formula on a napkin, which he hands to you when he finishes. "You can see from my calculations that the lodge you are about to build for $650,000 including the land would be worth an estimated $393,000 based upon your projected net income figure of $51,000. As you can see from the formula, your lodge would have to earn a minimum of $71,500 of net income per year before it would be worth what you would have in it:"

$$\text{Property Value} = PV + ((INC - (CAP \times PV) / INT))$$
$$= \$650{,}000 + ((\$71{,}500 - \$71{,}500) / .08))$$
$$= \$650{,}000 + (\$0 / .08)$$
$$= \$650{,}000 + (0)$$
$$= \$650{,}000$$

"Like I told you at the start of our meeting, as much as I would like to build your lodge, I can't in all good conscience do it if I don't think it will represent a good investment for you." A numb feeling begins to take over your mind. You thank George for his expert advice and as you politely excuse yourself from the table, ask him what he did before he became a contractor. "I was a professor at Montana State University. I have a Ph.D. in economics!" The meeting ended on a note that you had not anticipated as you step outside to let the cold Montana air bring you back to your senses.

In the interest of deciding what you should do, you spend the next several weeks talking to several lodge owners throughout Montana. They all shared one common business acclamation: Making money in the lodge business is tough! From your observation, the lodges that were successful were able to demand a premium for their rooms based on their location and reputation. Although you believe you have selected a great location for the lodge you want to build, you realize that it takes years to establish a reputation. You decide to project what would happen to your net worth if you were to build a lodge:

Second Year Financial Summary

Beginning Year Net Worth	$190,000
Plus: Second Year Revenues	$0
Less: Business and Living Expenses	$75,000
Second Year Net Worth	$115,000

You can't afford to cut your net worth almost in half, which would happen if you built a lodge. Thanks to George, it was better that you found out now rather than finding out after you built it. Maybe there is some other endeavor that you can get into without risking your personal finances. Looking back on where you have been, would you alter your decisions in order to create a different future for yourself? You'll think about it tomorrow!

1. If you would like to change your last strategic decision, return to Chapter 9.

2. If you would like to select another business venture to start-up, return to Chapter 2.

3. If you would like to conduct more analysis before you start-up another business, turn to Chapter 3.

If you're still feeling the sting of defeat and believe you could have made your last strategic choice work in real life, you may be right. After all, this is just a game. However, if you return to your last strategic decision (Chapter 9) and select the other alternative, you will learn why the authors consider it a better choice.

CHAPTER 23

JOINING A BIG-6

ACCOUNTING FIRM IN THE

CONSULTING AREA

Susan Harrison is the Senior Executive Recruiter retained by Peat Marwick to find the company a replacement for George Capana, one of the company's senior consultants who retired last month. Once the world's largest accounting firm, Peat Marwick fell into second place behind Andersen in the early 1990s. The company blamed the drop on currency fluctuations, which lowered the value of its overseas revenue, which accounts for 70 percent of its business. Peat Marwick's recent alliance with Toshiba to provide hardware and software for sales-force automation applications could bolster the company's international position. George Capana was a key figure in the project. His sudden stroke left him with no other option but to retire.

As Susan studies the stack of resumes for the hundredth time, she can find nothing she dislikes about *you*. You have the brains, ambition, energy, impatience, and good looks to be anybody's consultant. You certainly look good on paper and you talked a good story during the countless interview sessions. You're Peat Marwick's top prospect for the job.

Weary of the long hours and months that have been spent on the recruiting process, Harrison calls her associate recruiters into her office for a hastily held meeting. "Let's get this Peat Marwick show on the road and extend an offer to our top candidate. Peat Marwick's partners have authorized the offer. Do you all agree on our first choice?" They all agreed that you are the best person for the job.

Harrison picks up the phone and calls you at your home. You answer, listen to Susan's offer, and accept the position.

Your decision to join one of the Big-6 accounting firms was a compromise between what you really wanted to do (start-up a business from scratch) and what made more sense from the practical side. Your new consulting position offers you an opportunity to remain somewhat independent and to apply your entrepreneurial talents as you consult with a variety of different clients. Technological consulting, once a mere appendage to the tax and audit practices of the Big-6 firms, is now the tail that wags the dog. Your newly found colleagues at Peat Marwick told you that nobody wants to be known as just a tax-and-audit firm anymore. By adding the information technology (IT) consulting line, it secures a way to lock up a client base and keep them billable. To do that, all of the Big-6 firms, including Arthur Andersen, Coopers & Lybrand, Deloitte & Touche, Ernst & Young, Peat Marwick, and Price Waterhouse are redefining and restructuring themselves. You discover that Peat Marwick is unifying its practices on a worldwide basis, focusing its tax and consulting practices on vertical industries, beefing up technological capabilities through acquisitions and alliances and adding people like yourself with high-demand IT skills.

You initially thought all of these changes were occurring so that Peat Marwick could remain competitive with the other Big-5. However, its bigger challenge is coming from computer equipment and service companies. Amdahl Corporation recently acquired Trecom Business Systems, a computer-service company rich in systems integrator talent to augment Amdahl's mainframe computer client base. Amdahl is hardly alone. AT&T launched AT&T Solutions, its consulting, systems integration, and outsourcing unit. IBM is already well entrenched with its ISSC consulting division, and the list goes on to include MCI, Hewlett Packard, Microsoft, Unisys, and a host of other companies.

In spite of the heightened pace of competitive activities, it's all working to your advantage. Consulting is fast becoming the biggest piece of the revenue pie. In fact, the Big-6's collective revenue from consulting is growing at 20 percent a year as compared to a 3 percent growth rate for their tax and audit practices. Most expect consulting to represent half their business within the next few years. Information technology consulting kicked in 40 percent of Peat Marwick's U.S. consulting revenue last year.

All of the Big-6 are expanding to take on global clients. Peat Marwick has already taken on significant global responsibilities, including the construction of national banks in emerging nations. The marketplace is such that some software vendors refer to the Big-6 as their value-added resellers. Ted Harrington, one of the Peat Marwick partners you have gotten to know reasonably well, tells you, "We're not resellers, but I'm not sure you can define what a Big-6 firm is today. Application packages have been one of the Trojan horses that have been driving a lot of our services. Whether the Trojan horse is a software vendor bearing a consultant or a consulting firm bearing software appears to matter little to our customers. They simply want one organization to handle their reengineering efforts. What matters is whether the company they choose has the right mix of global resources to do the job.

No wonder you have been so busy since you accepted this job six months ago. You've been on the "flight road" 60 percent of the time traversing from client to client, but you have done well. Your first assignment was with Lam Research Corporation, a $1.2 billion semi-conductor company that has historically relied on service bureaus and manual bookkeeping to hold its worldwide operations together. Its patched IS measures could scarcely keep up as Lam's overseas revenue quadrupled over the past four years. Last year's overseas sales rose to 40 percent of total revenue.

Lam, an audit client of Peat Marwick, needed a consultant to quickly activate financial reporting and software to manage its sudden growth. You were the only one available at the time and got the assignment. You chose SunSystem accounting software from Systems Union Inc. and Esspace decision support software from Arbor Software Corporation to "jump-start" Lam into the 20th century. Six months later, Lam's financial reporting system has been installed on an in-house computer capable of generating a wide variety of financial reports to a battery of financial analysts. Speed of implementation and global adaptability were critical to your success on this assignment. There were times when you were sure you were not going to make it, but you did.

As companies rely increasingly on Peat Marwick to manage their audits, build and run their IT operations, and reengineer and staff their business processes, you allow yourself to once again to be taken in by a corporate monolith. Your clients like you, Peat Marawick likes you, and you know you could walk across the street at any time and get another consulting job. It's nice to know you're wanted and have job security. As you review how well you have done financially over the last four years, you realize you didn't get rich working for a Big-6 Accounting firm, but you are enjoying a very comfortable standard of living:

FINANCIAL SUMMARY OVER 5 YEARS

	Year 2	Year 3	Year 4	Year 5
Beginning Year Net Worth	$190,000	$190,000	$245,000	$312,000
Estimated Annual Income	$55,000	$105,000	$122,000	$135,000
Estimated Living Expenses	$55,000	$50,000	$55,000	$80,000
Ending Net Worth	$190,000	$245,000	$312,000	$367,500

Your net worth over the past four years has accumulated to almost $400 thousand. If you stay on your financial plan, you'll pass the half-million mark in two years. This ends this track of play.

1. If you would like to see how well you did as compared to other start-up strategies, turn to Chapter 77.

2. If you would like to see what would have happened if you had linked-up with a group of independent consultants, turn to Chapter 24.

3. If you want to select another start-up strategy, turn to Chapter 2.

4. If you want to conduct more analysis before you choose an alternative strategy, return to Chapter 3.

CHAPTER 24

LINKING-UP WITH A
GROUP OF INDEPENDENT
CONSULTANTS

Wall Street calls it "downsizing" but IBM, true to its culture of creating its own terms, calls it "rightsizing." The bottom-line effect is the same regardless of the term used. Big corporations quickly surplus hundreds of thousands of highly qualified people that they can no longer support. Although you are affiliated with a consulting firm, you have a driving ambition to link up with a group of independent consultants, a group of wild mustangs bent on doing their own thing. Your good friend, Dale Mosier, was recently an IBM rightsized victim. Dale invites you over to his ranch home for a barbecue to view his new mustang mare, which he just adopted from Wyoming. There is a business agenda attached to the barbecue. He's invited forty "rightsized" individuals to hear what he has to say about forming an independent consulting group.

Barbecues are traditionally fun events with everyone laughing and having a good time. Dale's barbecue is different. With the exception of Dale, nobody knows each other and everyone there is looking for a job. Conversations are guarded, particularly when you ask, "How are you doing?" During the initial stages of the barbecue, you discover that there is an incredible depth of talent just standing around eating hotdogs and hamburgers. On average, each person has 20 years of "hard-core" technical experience in all of the engineering disciplines and most have been in high-end management positions. They are all used to working long hard hours and they understand what the word productivity means.

Sensing the urgency in the atmosphere that is restricting casual conversation, Dale decides to jump into the subject of forming an independent consulting firm earlier than he anticipated. Ringing an old chuck wagon bell that hangs over his barbecue, he quickly captures everybody's attention with his opening remark. "Friends, I have a vision that I want to share with you. I want to create an independent consulting company called Niwot Technology, Inc. You see, the Niwot Indians were a tribe that was downsized the hard way by the Crow Indians. But, due to their tenacious spirit, they survived and we will survive under the name of Niwot Technology. I have landed a contract with AT&T that will provide a six-month consulting contract for 20 people. Although the technical and management requirements mix of the contract varies, I believe that any one of you could qualify for a position on this assignment. Obviously, I cannot guarantee that there will be a follow-up contract on this assignment, but if we turn in an outstanding performance, we should be in good shape for additional AT&T work. I need 20 good men and women to sign up for this contract by close of business tomorrow. Who is with me and are there any questions?"

Marty Albaugh raises the first question, which sounds more like a heated objection. "Why are you pressuring us to make a decision now? We all need more time to think about it and to consider our options. Even if I agree to sign up, I reserve the right to change my mind later and back out of the deal."

In a controlled voice, Dale answers Marty's questions and further clarifies his position. "I'm not dictating the sign-up schedule. The client, AT&T, wants 20 highly qualified people that they can count on to assist them in implementing a major IT project, which is confidential. You will be told what you need to know about the project once you commit to it. I forgot to mention one important detail pertaining to your commitment. Your respective commitments must be backed with a $5,000 personal check that is not refundable if you back out of your commitment prior to the end of the six-month assignment. Did I answer your question, Marty, and are there any other questions?"

You've known Dale for a number of years and have the highest degree of respect for his judgment. Your car is the last one to leave his driveway late that evening. A number of guests left with Marty right after Dale made his presentation. As Dale later put it, "I wanted to flush out the quail first so that I could get at the meat-eating animals." You are the first to officially sign up for the Niwot Technology independent consultant program and with some reservation, hand Dale a check for $5,000. By close of business the next day, 15 of the 40 invited guests had joined Niwot Technology. When you ask Dale what he is going to do to fill the other five positions he needed, he tells you he really only needed fifteen people to fill the contract order. He inflated the number to impress the audience.

The group comes together and incorporates under the name of Computech since no one with the exception of Dale liked the Niwot Technology name. Like all good corporations, Computech needs a president, which everybody assumes will be Dale. He declines the offer and recommends that you take the position. After much discussion, you accept the position as long as everybody recognizes that Computech is really a partnership organization. Your contract assignment with AT&T proves to be both technically and financially rewarding as you review your year-end financial statement:

Second Year Financial Summary

Beginning Year Net Worth	$190,000
Plus: Second Year Revenues	$260,000
Less: Business and Living Expenses	$225,000
Second Year Net Worth	$225,000

AT&T offers Computech an opportunity to pursue a follow-up contract, which puts pressure on you to establish the consulting direction for the company. The tough national and international economic situation leads you to believe that the firm would be well advised to specialize in marketing. However, the safer route might be to simply concentrate on following the latest consulting fads.

1. If you believe that Computech should specialize in marketing, turn to Chapter 39.

2. If you believe that Computech should follow the latest consulting fads, turn to Chapter 40.

CHAPTER 25

OBTAINING TEMPORARY JOBS

Anybody with a car and a credit card can relocate anywhere they want with relative ease in the continental United States. The challenge is to figure out what you are going to do and how you're going to live once you get to where you want to be. Fortunately, you have assessed both these issues as part of your plan to relocate to Montana. Your decision to relocate to Billings involved more than just a coin-flip. You considered two other locations, the capital Helena and Great Falls. After researching the advantages and disadvantages of the three cities, you selected Billings for several reasons.

The total population of Montana is still less than a million people living in the fourth largest state in the country. Billings is by far the largest city in the state and its residents enjoy a healthy economy. Although Billings's economy is still tied to the state's agricultural economy, mining, tourism, and a variety of service industries are important parts of Billings's job market, which was your strongest draw to Billings. You decided to obtain a temporary job or, if necessary, temporary jobs in Billings to cover your living expenses while you search for a lodge or find some other line of work that would fit with your entrepreneurial drive. If you can obtain a good temporary job, you won't have to touch your savings, which you have "earmarked" for the down payment on a lodge. Billings is perfectly located in the center of the state just to the east of the Rocky Mountain range that dominates the western half of the state. The eastern half of

Montana is dominated by prairie land that is great for raising cattle, but it is not where you want to be. The Rockies are what attract the tourist and that is where you are going to find a lodge.

It's Sunday afternoon as your car passes the "5 miles to Billings" sign that every city seems to have. Your exit onto Montana Avenue brings you to the Best Western Motel, your temporary home. Your reservations are confirmed and in a few minutes, you find yourself lying on the bed in your motel room, gazing at some television show, sipping a cup of tea, and thinking to yourself, "I'm officially relocated to Montana and it feels good." You vow to get a good night's sleep in preparation for tomorrow's interviews. As you scan through your agenda, you take note of your appointments with four temporary employment agencies:

1. Accountants on Call, who specialize in providing permanent and temporary accounting positions.

2. Royal Personnel Services, who specialize in providing permanent and temporary management positions.

3. Kelly Technical Services, who specialize in providing permanent and temporary computer-related positions and technical writing assignments.

4. Olsen Staffing, who specialize in providing permanent and temporary production and manufacturing-related positions.

You admit to yourself that you have quite a spread of positions to cover tomorrow but that fits with your temporary job-search strategy. When you retired from the corporate world of management, you had to wrestle with the fact that there are a lot of retired management professionals just like yourself out there in the market looking for another management job. While that may be where the bucks are, in your opinion, it's not where the jobs are in this downsized economy. Companies are looking for worker bees and not management drones.

The reality of the situation forced you to assess your trade credentials. At one time in your career, you were a darn good accountant, could design computer applications with the best of them, write COBOL programs, handle technical-writing assignments with ease, and run just about every aspect of a manufacturing facility. Most of your trade background was learned the same way you learned to ride a bike when you were a kid; it was tough learning how to get that bike to stay up, but once you learned how to do it, you never forgot how to ride a bike again. You haven't forgotten your trade background either.

Your 8:30 A.M. interview starts with Accountants on Call. In quiet frustration, you fill in the blanks on the employment application that duplicates what you already have recorded on your resume. It's their prerequisite before you will be allowed to talk to their employment counselor, Florence Snyder. Your completed application is dispatched into Florence's office while you patiently wait for her to summon you into her office. A half-hour later, Florence comes out of her office, introduces herself, and invites you into her office. She tells you that based upon your qualifications, she may have a three-month cost-accounting position with Mobil Oil that might be a good fit with your background. When she asks if you would be interested in the assignment, you give her an emphatic "yes" answer. Your objective today is to obtain as many job offers as you can so that you can select the one that offers you an opportunity to learn something and pays a decent wage at the same time. Florence tells you she will contact Mobil, and if they are interested, she'll schedule an interview. You thank Florence for her time and with your Billings street map in hand, arrive just in time for your 10:30 appointment with Royal Personnel Services.

Your morning interview session with Royal and afternoon sessions with Kelly Technical Services and Olsen Staffing follow a path almost identical to the one you encountered with Accountants on Call with two notable exceptions. Jane Watson of Kelly Technical Services identifies an opportunity to develop a PC-based reservation system for the Timber Wolf Lodge, a major resort complex located on Canyon Ferry Lake near the town of Helena. As the old expression goes, that would allow you to "kill two birds with one stone." You could learn more about what it takes to run a lodge and make some money at the same time.

Ken Olsen of Olsen Staffing tells you about a technical-writing assignment with Cole & Weber, a major advertising agency in Billings that is actively involved in tourist trade advertising techniques. You have some background in advertising and know intuitively that an effective advertising program is critical to the success of any lodge. Working for Cole & Weber would afford you an opportunity to learn all you could about how to exploit different advertising media to attract customers into your future lodge. After a long and tiring day, you close out your last interview session and head back to the motel satisfied with what you were able to accomplish in just one day.

Like an alarm clock, the ring of the telephone jolts you out of bed the next morning as you quickly glance at your watch and realize it's already 9 A.M. Jane Watson of Kelly Services asks you if you would be available for an afternoon interview session with the Timber Wolf Lodge. You give her an enthusiastic "yes" answer and she proceeds to provide you with specific details on exactly what they are looking for, who you will be talking to, and how to get to Canyon Ferry Lake.

Anxious to get to the lake at least two hours before your interview, you jump into the shower. As you are getting out of the shower, the phone rings again. This time it's Ken Olsen who wants to set up an interview with Cole & Weber. He asks, "Can you meet with the management team this afternoon?" You tell Ken that you have a personal commitment that would be difficult to break and ask if the interview could be scheduled for tomorrow. He assures you that would probably work and in fifteen minutes calls you back to confirm a morning meeting with Cole & Weber.

Over the next two weeks, all of your time is spent bouncing back and forth between interviews at the Timber Wolf Lodge and Cole & Weber. Both ventures offer you amazingly similar opportunities, six-month full-time positions at $25 an hour for your time (separate fees are paid to the employment agencies) and an opportunity to move into a full-time position if the temporary assignment works out to your mutual satisfaction. You calculate what effect either position would have on your year-end financial position:

Second Year Financial Summary

Beginning Year Net Worth	$190,000
Plus: Second Year Contract Income	$44,300
Less: Business and Living Expenses	$35,000
Second Year Net Worth	$199,300

You have only been in Montana for three weeks and you have two job offers on the table, which will more than cover your anticipated living expenses if you move into an apartment and afford you an opportunity to learn more about the lodging industry. Unfortunately, since both offers are for full-time temporary positions, you cannot elect to work for Cole & Weber and the Timber Wolf Lodge. It's Friday and you are committed to make a decision today. You pick up the phone and dial. . . .

1. If you decide to work the Timber Wolf Lodge, turn to Chapter 41.

2. If you decide to work for Cole & Weber, turn to Chapter 42.

CHAPTER 26

INTENSIFYING YOUR SEARCH

FOR AN APPROPRIATE LODGE

You have decided to intensify your search for a lodge in Montana, which will require your full-time effort to meet your financial goal. As you think through what you want to accomplish, you come up with a couple of answers. "I'd like to buy a lodge someday and make enough money to retire in ten years." As you step back and listen to yourself, you can't believe you are thinking like this and realize you'll never reach either goal because they are too vague.

When you go to the hardware store to buy a tool, you know what you want to accomplish with the tool. You have an established goal and have identified the tools that will help you obtain that goal. If you need a quarter-inch hole drilled through a metal plate, then you need a quarter-inch drill designed to cut through metal. You might also need a high-speed electric drill to meet your goal. How ridiculous it would be to buy tools without knowing what goal you wanted to accomplish with the tools. None of the tools in the entire store would mean anything if you didn't have defined tasks to complete.

To test the feasibility of your financial goal, you decide to first determine where you are financially. If you don't know where you are financially, how do you expect to get to where you want to be? Your recent move to Montana was not cheap. It cost more than you anticipated and depleted some of the funds you had earmarked for the lodge. You've leased an apartment in Billings for six months, which is the time you have allocated to find a lodge. After living expenses, you hope you'll have enough money to make the down payment on a lodge. Just to make sure your financial projections are right, you estimate what your cash reserves will be over the next six months while you're looking for a lodge:

SIX-MONTH CASH-FLOW PROJECTION

	Month 1	Month 2	Month 3	Month 4	Month 5	Month 6
Beginning Cash Balance	97,500	94,500	91,500	88,500	85,500	82,500
Less: Living Expenses	3,000	3,000	3,000	3,000	3,000	3,000
Total Available Cash	94,500	91,500	88,500	85,500	82,500	79,500

After reviewing your cash position, you realize you're cutting it close. You have no room for any miscalculations and it causes you to reconsider your overall financial goals. There's nothing wrong with a desire to become wealthy, but you need to identify the steps in detail that will get you there. The lodge you want is only a picture in your mind with nothing filled in like its location, size, construction, or cash requirements. You begin to shape your financial goal by compiling a list showing the investment objectives you want to accomplish:

1. Buy a well-maintained lodge located on a lake somewhere in Montana within the next six months.

2. Any improvements to the lodge must be minimal (e.g., painting, landscape, clean-up, minor carpentry, etc.) and you must be capable of performing the work rather than relying on subcontractors.

3. The lodge must be located in an area that attracts winter as well as summer visitors with an emphasis on winter guests to assure a cash flow in the off-season. It must be near a ski area, snowmobile trails, and public hunting areas.

4. The lodge must be capable of generating a positive cash flow in excess of $50,000 a year after taxes to meet your minimum personal living expenses.

You expand your financial plan by preparing a spreadsheet that quantifies your minimum financial requirements for a lodge:

TWELVE-MONTH CASH-FLOW PROJECTION

	Jan–March	April–June	July–Sept	Oct–Dec	Totals
Beginning Cash Balance	97,500	82,000	67,800	54,900	38,100
Plus: Net Lodge Sales	97,500	104,000	110,500	91,000	97,500
Less: Operating Expenses	78,000	83,200	88,400	72,800	78,000
Less: Mortgage Payment	35,000	35,000	35,000	35,000	35,000
Total Available Cash	82,000	67,800	54,900	38,100	22,600

ANNUAL MINIMUM FINANCIAL REQUIREMENTS FOR LODGE

	Jan–March	April–June	July–Sept	Oct–Dec	Totals
Projected Gross Sales	247,300	272,030	299,233	269,310	1,087,872
Operating Expenses	209,970	232,227	256,710	229,779	928,685
Mortgage Payment*	12,600	12,600	12,600	12,600	50,400
Net Profit (Loss)	24,730	27,203	29,923	26,930	108,787

* Assumes 80% loan on $750,000 lodge.

You call your real-estate agent, Cheri Dengel, and tell her about your financial requirements for a lodge. She agrees to meet with you later that afternoon to review your numbers and to see if she can find a property that meets your investment objectives. As your meeting with Cheri begins, you ask her to review and comment on your financial requirements worksheet. She tells you, "None of the lodges that you can purchase for less than a million dollars are making a 10 percent net profit, which is what you need to realize your profit objectives. The economies of scale are just not there in the smaller lodges to get to that profit level."

You ask Cheri how much you would have to spend on a lodge to realize the economies of scale you need to make a 10-percent-plus profit. "You are talking about a lodge that sells for a minimum of $1.5 million and most of those are owned by corporations. Even if they were for sale, most corporations won't deal with small investors. No offense, but they will quickly tell you it is not worth their time."

You thank Cheri for her time and walk across the street for an unscheduled meeting with Harold Smith, the loan officer at the First National Bank of Montana. You learn that it would be very difficult to buy a lodge with just 20 percent down when Harold tells you First National and most other commercial banks will require at least 25 to 30 percent down. You review your personal financial statement to determine if you can meet a 30-percent down-payment obligation, which would be $225,000 on a $750,000 lodge, which exceeds your projects second-year net worth:

Second Year Financial Summary

Beginning Year Net Worth	$190,000
Plus: Second Year Income	$0
Less: Temporary Living Expenses	$36,000
Second Year Net Worth	$154,000

You quickly determine that the additional down payment would take more than you have to meet the obligation. You are not opposed to taking risks but you also know you need some reserve cash for unplanned emergencies. You decide to stop your search for a lodge since it is not economically feasible for you at this time. At least you have managed to relocate to Montana. Tomorrow, you plan to start looking for a job. Looking back on where you have been, would you alter your decisions in order to create a different future for yourself?

1. If you would like to change your last strategic decision, return to Chapter 11.

2. If you would like to select another business venture to start-up, return to Chapter 2.

3. If you would like to conduct more analysis before you start-up another business, turn to Chapter 3.

If you're still feeling the sting of defeat and believe you could have made your last strategic choice work in real life, you may be right. After all, this is just a game. However, if you return to your last strategic decision and select the other alternative (Chapter 25), you will learn why the authors consider it a better choice.

CHAPTER 27

ESTABLISHING YOUR OWN
APPROACH TO COACHING

You don't want to get bogged down in your personal background, but it bears directly on your plan to establish your own approach to personal coaching. When you were in the corporate world and were assigned your first management position, you reported to Neil Larson. Neil was by far the best boss you ever had. He was the ultimate coach and made you feel like you could do the impossible. He built phenomenal management teams by using his personal warmth and charisma. You honestly enjoyed going to work every day. As a Junior Sales Manager, you wanted to lead your reps to the top of the mountain just to please Neil. Over time, he taught you how to use his techniques to accomplish the same thing with the people who worked for you. Using Neil's approach, you want to establish your own approach to coaching. By applying his techniques combined with a tight, well-executed coaching process tailored to all levels of salespeople, you will have a dynamite coaching program.

That's exactly what you set out to do and you select Cleveland as your target market. Your objective is to offer personal coaching sessions to managers in a "mentor format" where you would show them how to apply personal motivational techniques to themselves and to their employees. After several months of prospecting for clients in the Cleveland metropolitan area, you have managed to convince 50 men and women in sales management positions that they may need your help. They have agreed to meet with you at the Hilton in the Hospitality Room to hear what you have to say.

You've scheduled the meeting at 7:30 A.M., which came as a shock to your guests. Morning meetings usually start at a more civilized hour. What you are saying is this: You're in trouble. You're going to need an extra hour or so to dig out while the other "corporate ladder climbers" are still in bed. As 7:30 arrives, your attendees begin to stagger into the room. It's not until 8:15 that all of the attendees are seated. Only 25 people show up, which is half of what you expected. You find yourself reaching deep into your own motivational tool kit to make sure you're up for this presentation.

Since all of the managers in attendance are in sales or fields closely related to sales, you decide to start your personal coaching presentation off with the magic word: competition! You use it repeatedly that morning to show them how, with proper coaching, they can learn how to thrive on competition just like an athlete does. In your opening remarks, you tell them, "When a competitor makes a sale, the race is over. You have one less unit to sell. When that happens, it suggests that someone else out there was smarter, faster, and harderworking than you. There is no sense agonizing over what went wrong or your personal failure when the competition beats you fair and square. Yesterday, they may have been smarter, faster, and harderworking than your team. What can you do to significantly improve your odds of winning more sales?"

You stop for a moment to assess the audience's reaction to what you have said. Your perception is that you are getting a lot of blank stares, but you continue anyway. "What went wrong? We can blame the lost sale on the market, bad luck, lousy products or services. We can blame it on the so-called "shrinking pie" or the agglomeration of resources that's always being divided into smaller pieces of the pie by an increasing number of competitors. Or, we can simply blame it on a competitor, analyze why we lost, go back out into the field, and fight for the next account. It means learning from what they have done right, going back out and doing it better. That is what personal coaching is all about. If you and your sales team will incorporate those procedures into everything you do, you will become the best there is."

The thrust of your presentation is based on what you believe is Cleveland's business attitude. Like business people across the United States, they have literally forgotten how to compete. In the process, they have forgotten how great it is to win. You proceed with your concluding remarks by telling your less-than-enthusiastic audience that in the beginning, humankind's survival depended upon the instinct of winning. You tell them, "The thrill of winning ensures that we keep moving, keep hunting, keep foraging, fighting, and selling. It feels good to win and I would like to help you improve your win rate. I don't buy the notion that the desire to compete and to win is a primitive instinct that needs to be suppressed in men and women. I believe the opposite is true. Nonetheless, I'm bucking decades of conditioning that starts at an early age. Many parents, teachers, and employers find it easier to smother the competitive instinct in the interest of decorum and orderly behavior. A thick fuzzy blanket is thrown on top of conflict, emotion, and turmoil. It's not "nice" to exult in being the smartest kid in the class, the fastest runner or the best sales person. As a sales manager, you should give your people permission to win, to exult when they're the best and to despair when they are not. Learn how to become their personal coach and watch your sales climb off the chart. If you would like to sign up for one of my personal coaching training sessions, see me after the presentation. Thank you for your time."

You watch in amazement at the speed with which everyone is able to exit the meeting room at the same time. In less than a minute, with the exception of a woman who remains seated in the far corner of the room, you are left standing by yourself. As you rock back on your heels and begin to lick your wounds from what you conclude must have been a bad presentation, your single remaining prospect approaches you. "Allow me to introduce myself. My name is Rita Gant and I want to tell you that in my opinion, the presentation you just gave was one of the best I have ever heard. I'm the President of the National Speaker's Association so I believe there is some credibility in my observation."

You thank Rita for salvaging a portion of your ego and ask her the question that has been nagging at your mind. "Why didn't I solicit any interest in my personal coaching offer?" Rita gives you a delightfully simple and yet, complex answer: "Salespeople are unique animals in that they are only capable of hearing positive statements and are incapable of hearing anything that's negative. Have you ever attended a sales seminar by Anthony Robins or Brian Tracy, for example, and heard them utter one negative word? They don't because they know their audience doesn't want to hear it and they subsequently make millions spreading nothing but positive verbiage. We both know that the sales world is far from purely positive. Your message and coaching service was all about improvement, which implies fixing problems. Your message fell on deaf ears. They cannot and will not hear you."

After spending over a year working to develop you own approach to personal coaching, you decide to cut your losses and try something else. Although you believe that there is money to be made in the relatively new venture of personal coaching, you wish now that you had affiliated yourself with an established partnership before you ventured out on your own.

Second Year Financial Summary

Beginning Year Net Worth	$190,000
Plus: Second Year Revenues	$40,000
Less: Business and Living Expenses	$75,000
Second Year Net Worth	$155,000

Looking back on where you have been, would you alter your decisions in order to create a different future for yourself?

1. If you would like to change your last strategic decision, return to Chapter 11.

2. If you would like to select another business venture to start-up, return to Chapter 2.

3. If you would like to conduct more analysis before you start-up another business, turn to Chapter 3.

If you're still feeling the sting of defeat and believe you could have made your last strategic choice work in real life, you may be right. After all, this is just a game. However, if you return to your last strategic decision and select the other alternative (Chapter 28), you will learn why the authors consider it a better choice.

CHAPTER 28

BUYING INTO AN

ESTABLISHED PARTNERSHIP

Hesitant about your ability to quickly build a personal coaching client base, you decide to join an established partnership. Although you would prefer to be on your own, you can't risk making the wrong financial decision. After surveying a field of possibilities, from large, multidisciplined consultant firms to smaller niche specialists, you decide to accept a position with Personal Dynamics, an established partnership specializing in personal coaching. Personal Dynamics is also engaged in an impressive seminar circuit.

Your entrance into Personal Dynamics is not free. Its senior partner, Ron Stein, explained the membership rules to you. "You have one year to become a partner at Personal Dynamics. In the first year, your progress will be carefully evaluated by every partner in the firm. We will of course coach and help you along the way because it is in both of our interests that you meet Personal Dynamics' high partnership standards. It goes without saying that the general partnership will invest a significant amount of their time, unbillable time I might add, to you as you progress through the year. We ask that you contribute $50,000 as a membership fee to help offset our costs. If you stay with the program for the full twelve months and become a partner, we'll refund $25,000 of your membership fee. If for whatever reason we decide to terminate our relationship with you, we'll refund your full membership fee. If you elect to terminate the program for whatever reason, you forfeit your membership fee. Fair enough?"

You agree to pay Personal Dynamics' membership fee, which is risk-free as far as you are concerned. You don't plan to quit and you are good enough to know they won't fire you. Five months into Personal Dynamics' program and you run into problems with the general partnership. You've developed excellent relationships with every client you work with to the point where they are requesting you for coaching support over the tenured partners. You sense there may be a tinge of jealousy brewing in the pot. Anxious to avoid a major confrontation, you ask Ron Stein to join you for lunch. Your lunch with Stein begins pleasantly enough but soon erupts into a battle of egos as Stein enumerates a list of reasons why you are not partnership material.

When you threaten to terminate your position with Personal Dynamics, he quickly reminds you about the $50,000 membership fee. You know you'll lose it but why should Ron care? This infuriates you, but you manage to keep calm until you can figure out where Ron is coming from. After forcing yourself to compliment Ron on how vital he is to the ongoing success of Personal Dynamics, the conversation settles down to normal tones. You let Ron talk and learn that the general partners are concerned over the fact that you have developed a strong professional relationship with their clients. They are concerned that if you leave the firm, you'll take several of their clients with you. The sudden increase in interest in personal coaching promises to increase revenues 25 percent by year end, and as a result, none of the partners wants to see any disruptions to the firm's growth pattern.

You assure Ron that you are not interested in leaving Personal Dynamics and you are anxious to contribute to the growth of the firm when you become a partner. On your one-year anniversary day, you become a partner, and are refunded your $50,000 membership fee rather than the required $25,000. Ron tells you to treat the full refund as a bonus, which you do. As you review your year-end financial statement, you applaud the increase in your net worth.

Second Year Financial Summary

Beginning Year Net Worth	$190,000
Plus: Second Year Revenues	$130,000
Less: Business and Living Expenses	$60,000
Second Year Net Worth	$260,000

The options that you have been unable to consider until now come to the front of your mind. The impressive rate of growth that Personal Dynamics enjoyed over the past year gives you cause to want to stay with this company and help it grow. However, the entrepreneurial spirit is calling you to break out on your own. You've established a reputation in the personal coaching business that will eliminate the past problems of finding clients.

1. If you believe you would be better off breaking out on your own to leverage yourself, turn to Chapter 43.

2. If you believe you would be better off working with Personal Dynamics to grow the partnership, turn to Chapter 44.

CHAPTER 29

FINDING ASSOCIATES TO
BUILD PROJECT TEAMS

Chasing big accounts has paid off for both your consulting and training business. As it turned out, winning the Motorola account was a real coup. Two weeks after you landed Motorola, Intel and AT&T signed long-term training and consulting contracts with you. Their decisions were in part based on the fact that you were already supporting a reputable Motorola client.

Despite all the positive advancements you've made in your consulting and training programs, your marketing and sales efforts have been less than exciting. You're concerned that you may not know the consulting market as well as you thought, which makes you hesitant about proceeding with your decision to hire new associates. You used to be in marketing several years ago and wonder if the market has perhaps changed over the past five years. Maybe you have become obsolete, a chilling thought that you decide to keep to yourself.

Kathy Simon enters your office for her scheduled four-hour marketing and sales recovery presentation. You met Kathy at a chamber-of-commerce mixer three weeks ago and asked for her help. She's in her mid-thirties and has an impressive background with Arthur Andersen, her current employer.

Kathy proceeds to lay out a market segmentation program that is one of the best you've ever seen. "Let me first show you where the consulting and training industry has been over the past five years." Her charts show market share by region and service line. Customer and competitor demographics are clearly depicted. Her segmentation analysis also identifies several underserved information-technology marketing opportunities. After more than two hours of presentations and discussion on market segmentation analysis, Kathy turns her attention to the future. "The rapid growth and popularity of the Internet has fueled the training and consulting markets into what promises to be a $50 billion market within the next five years." She summarizes the hot-technology topics to consider:

1. Client server hardware and software applications every company needs to survive.
2. Website development approaches and marketing techniques that can dramatically increase sales.
3. Using object-oriented database architecture on the Internet to accelerate research and development efforts.
4. Internet security options and techniques to protect a company's information assets.

She shows you a new sales-and-marketing approach that could instantly move your company into a position of significance by capturing new markets that show great promise. In order to take full advantage of the marketing opportunities Kathy has identified, you'll have to significantly increase the size of your consulting staff. For the next two hours you discuss the options that could be quickly employed to get the people you need. In the end, the idea of developing a pool of consultants with varying degrees of talent who could be called upon to participate in project teams is an attractive alternative. Resumes could be easily solicited, stored on a relational database, and extracted to form custom-designed project teams on demand.

Kathy joins you for lunch and agrees to work with you on a retainer-fee basis to help implement the program. Two months after Kathy's presentation, your project-team work force is in place. By the end of the third month, seven project teams have been dispatched to client locations throughout the country and by the end of your third year, project-team sales reach $1.2 million. Your year-end financial position looks great:

Third Year Financial Summary

Beginning Year Net Worth	$245,000
Plus: Third Year Revenues	$1,200,000
Less: Business and Living Expenses	$1,160,000
Third Year Net Worth	$285,000

However, in your fourth year, the crisis you had temporarily fore-stalled mounts. Your project teams are overloaded and overworked. It finally dawns on you that you have been mercilessly increasing the pressure on your project teams by asking them to do more and more. One of your team members summed it up for you: "We have already lost 10 of our best team members and that's just the start. You can't work people 16 to 18 hours a day for extended periods of time and not suffer some human breakage." Project team sales fall to $800,000 in your fourth year, which limits the growth of your net worth:

Fourth Year Financial Summary

Beginning Year Net Worth	$285,000
Plus: Fourth Year Revenues	$800,000
Less: Business and Living Expenses	$755,000
Fourth Year Net Worth	$330,000

As you wrestle with the problem, you wonder whether it is time for you to get out of the consulting business before you also burn yourself out. Let someone else grapple with the challenge of manag-ing project teams. But then again, the money is good and perhaps a compromise is in order. You move quickly to eliminate all weekend work at client locations. You offer your team members the option of flying home on weekends or let them pocket the flight money instead for their own personal use. The weekend-off flight program cuts 25 percent out of your profit margin but what the heck, it's only money and the program proves to be immensely popular with your associ-ates. Although your financial position at the end of the fourth year only showed a 10-percent increase over last year, it jumped to 30 per-cent in the fifth year:

Fifth Year Financial Summary

Beginning Year Net Worth	$330,000
Plus: Fifth Year Revenues	$1,149,300
Less: Business and Living Expenses	$1,095,000
Fifth Year Net Worth	$384,300

Your contract employee base stabilizes as you close out your fifth year of operation. The weekends-off program has helped turn the morale of your staff around. Reduced working hours, coupled with a generous 401K plan that you offer in the fifth year boost morale and help catapult your net worth to an all-time record high. It feels good to finally be on a winning team, particularly when you own the team. You've come a long way from the corporate quagmire and are making over $250,000 a year. One of your old friends whom you had to ask for advice back in the beginning and from whom you got none calls you to ask how you are doing. You tell him you're managing to get by!

This is the end of this path of play. If you would like to see how well you did in comparison to the alternative start-up paths you could have taken, turn to Chapter 77.

1. If you would like to find out what would have happened if you had become a contract trainer, turn to Chapter 30.

2. If you would like to try another start-up path where you take action now, turn to Chapter 2.

3. If you would like to try another start-up path where you can conduct analysis before you take action, turn to Chapter 3.

CHAPTER 30

BECOMING A CONTRACT TRAINER

Although you have been pleased with your success at marketing training programs for big companies, the nerve-wrenching exercises you have to go through to keep your training calendar booked is dragging you down. Most of your training assignments are for one- to two-day engagements with an occasional five-day program thrown in. You are beginning to realize that downtime is an Achilles' heel of the consulting industry. Last week, you scheduled a training session at CompUSA for Monday and Tuesday, but were unable to book another client for the balance of the week. As a result, you lost half the week to downtime and had to return home to call everyone you could think of to book next week's training schedule. It is a never-ending cycle that you have been constantly challenged to resolve in the two years you have been in this business. Next week, First Interstate Bank wants you to conduct a five-day training session. At least a week will be full of billable work.

It's Friday morning and you are wrapping up a week-long training program at First Interstate Bank's Phoenix office. Anxious to get in a round of golf before you fly home Saturday, you gladly accept Hal Redding's offer to play a twosome at the Scottsdale Country Club. Hal is Intestate's Senior Vice President who endorsed, and more importantly signed, the purchase order for your training session.

Somewhere between the seventeenth and eighteenth hole, the typical casual conversation associated with golf turns to the inevitable business conversation, but not in a way you had anticipated. Hal begins to talk about internal recruiting problems he's having finding a qualified candidate to conduct and direct the bank's training program. He goes on to say, "I've had to do it all, and quite honestly, it's not my job. I'm not qualified and it's more than I can handle along with my current level of responsibilities. We have not been able to find anybody inside the bank with the training qualifications we need and when we look to the outside, we can find trainers, but they don't know the banking industry. The problem is further compounded by the fact that we have got a hiring freeze on all exempt positions. It takes the signature of the President and the Board of Directors to override the mandate. Even if a suitable candidate could be located and hired, he or she would lack job and organization-specific knowledge about this bank's unique procedures and culture. A new hire, no matter how experienced, would lack the social and technical support network to ease the transition from the outside. And, to be perfectly honest with you, First Interstate does not have a good track record of retaining people hired from the outside to fill training positions. They stay with us for six months, then leave as soon as something better comes along."

As your golf cart pulls up to the eighteenth green, Hal stops talking and prepares to make a four-foot birdie putt, which he proceeds to miss by a foot. You diplomatically decide not to disturb the iced silence that ensues as you point the cart back to the clubhouse for lunch with Hal in tow. The silence persists as you and Hal sit down to what appears will be a very dull lunch. You knew the man was upset, but you had no idea he was that upset.

A small light begins to flicker in the center of your mind. "Hal, I have a solution to your dilemma. Have you considered hiring a contract trainer, like me for instance?" Hal's mouth drops wide open and the only thing you can determine from his stare is that you definitely have his attention. "Hal, before you say anything, let me explain what I would like to offer you." His mouth closes, which you assume is his statement inviting you to proceed.

"Effective immediately, I am prepared to accept the position of contract trainer for the bank. Here is what I can bring to the bank's table. I have been providing the bank with training support for the past two years and during that time, I have learned your internal procedures, understand your unique culture, and I know your people. They respect me or you would have fired me a long time ago. As a contract employee, I will not be on the Bank's official head count, which bypasses the presidential approval process. And, I have the external social and technical support networks that you referred to earlier to develop and continue to develop a viable training program that would meet the specific needs of the bank. What do you think?"

The ensuing silence is almost more than your impetuous nature can tolerate. But, as Brian Tracy says, "Once the sales pitch is made, shut up and wait for as long as it takes to get a reply." You have just made one of the fastest sales pitches of your life. If you can pull this contract trainer program off, it will solve your immediate training down-time dilemma. You'll think about what you will do with your other training commitments tomorrow. First things first! Hal's mouth opens again but this time you think he will say something as the sparkle returns to his eyes. "I'll see you in my office the first thing Monday morning and we can draw up a contract. I like the idea. But, if you say anything to anybody about that birdie putt of mine, the deal's off."

By the end of the third year, you have built a solid, professional relationship with everyone you touch at First Interstate. The bank has you running hard on the training circuit four days a week but pretty much leaves you alone on Friday to catch up on your paper work and to leave early if you want. It's a far cry from the 80-hour workweeks you used to put in and financially, you are in great shape:

Third Year Financial Summary

Beginning Year Net Worth	$245,000
Plus: Third Year Revenues	$150,000
Less: Business and Living Expenses	$125,000
Third Year Net Worth	$270,000

However, you begin to wonder if, over time, you won't get bored at First Interstate dealing with the same people day in and day out. The numbers are exciting when you consider what would happen if you brokered other trainers into training positions and received a straight commission for your work. You would inherit some of the employee-management problems you've been trying to avoid, but they should be superficial with contract employees. If you decide to broker trainers, you realize you will have to leave your secure position at First Interstate. But then again, if you remain the sole employee of your company, you won't have to deal with all of the employee-related management headaches.

You decide to think about it in the morning and make your final decision after a good night's sleep, which doesn't happen. You lie awake all night thinking about what you should do.

1. If you think you would be better off remaining solo, then turn to Chapter 45.

2. If you would like to change the course of your business and start brokering trainers, turn to Chapter 46.

CHAPTER 31

PLAYING THE

"ZERO DOWN" GAME

Your goal is to buy real estate with nothing down. You realize "nothing down" does not mean that the seller receives no down payment. It means that the down payment comes from somewhere else instead of out of your pocket. You've learned to incorporate creativity in your life and now is the time to apply what you have learned.

You receive a call from Joe Kipplinger, whom you met at a recent "zero down" investment seminar that you were both attending. He tells you about a seven-unit apartment located in your town that has been advertised for several months in the local paper. Joe tells you he checked it out with his real estate agent when it first listed and he was not impressed. The seller wanted too much of a down payment and the rents were below market rates for comparable units.

You and Joe had discussed your interest in purchasing real estate for as close to "zero down" as you could get at the seminar. Joe tells you that the listing agent for the apartment told him the seller is now anxious to sell and is willing to be creative on the terms of the sale. Based on Joe's tip, you call Cheri Dengel, the listing agent, to get the facts pertaining to the property:

- The asking price of the apartment is $170,000.

- The seller has an assumable $155,000 mortgage with payments of $1,250 at 9 percent.

- The seller wants $25,000 to cash out his equity position.

- The twelve-month average unit rent has been $250 for 6 units. One unit rents for $375. Total rent is therefore $1,875 (6 units × $150 + $375).

- Tenant security and cleaning deposits are $200 per unit or $1,400.

- The real-estate agent's commission on the sale is 6 percent or $10,200 assuming a sell price of $170,000.

Cheri agrees to show you the property later that afternoon. You are impressed with the location and sound structure of the apartment, based upon your preliminary review. The apartment looks like the investment opportunity you have been searching for, if you can figure out a way to eliminate the $20,000 down payment. Over the next two weeks, you carefully analyze the market value, capitalization rate, and the replacement cost to make sure the selling price is reasonable. From what you learn, this appears to be an excellent investment opportunity. You call Cheri to tell her of your intent to submit an offer on the property, based upon the fact that the property appears to offer a favorable cash flow, and based upon the operating statement you have prepared:

ANNUAL INCOME AND EXPENSES

Gross rental income	$22,500	5 × 400 × 12
Other income	$600	Vending machine
Total gross income	$23,100	
Less: vacancy credit	$1,125	Assumed 5% gross rent
Net income	$21,975	
Operating expenses:		
Accounting and legal fees	$600	
Advertising and licenses	$375	
Property insurance	$1,025	
Property management		Not required
Payroll - resident manager		Not required
Payroll taxes		Not applicable
Property taxes	$960	
Maintenance services	$1,230	
Supplies	$400	
Utilities	$600	
Miscellaneous	$200	
Total operating expenses	$5,390	
Net operating income	$16,585	
Annual mortgage payments	$15,000	
Cash flow before taxes	$1,585	

You organize your thoughts as to how you are going to eliminate the $20,000 down payment issue. The seller agrees to carry a $12,000 second trust deed, which gets you to well within the range of where you want to be. Cheri tells you the rents are due on the first of each month. Because of this and barring any major vacancies before closing day, $1,875 in rents and $1,400 in security deposits would be transferred to you if you close on the first day of the month, which you stipulate in the purchase agreement.

The closing date coincides perfectly with the first mortgage payment, which is due on the last day of the month or thirty days after the closing date. You're already pre-qualified to assume the loan on the property. When the mortgage payment comes due in thirty days, you collect next month's rent to pay the mortgage payment. You can apply all of the security deposits to the down payment but that raises a couple of questions in your mind. Some state laws require security deposits to be held in an escrow account, which cannot be touched. A call to an apartment owner you know confirms that's not a problem in your state. What about the fact that you have to return deposits to tenants when they move out? As you think about the problem, you find the solution is simple. When a tenant moves out, another moves in; the deposit from the new tenant can be given to the old tenant.

The seller has the obligation at the completion of the sale to pay real estate commissions. That $10,800 amounts to a large share of the required down payment. You ask Cheri to lend you $5,000 of her commission secured with your personal note guaranteeing to pay the money back in two $2,500 annual installments over two years. You convince Cheri to take the note when you tell her if she doesn't help you out, you can't buy the property. Then, there would be no sale and no commission. To sweeten the pie, you agree to list the property with her when you sell it in the future. Cheri quickly agrees to your terms.

You take mental note of the fact that it would have been much more difficult to have arranged this kind of loan if the agent was not a broker or operating out of a 100-percent commission pay house where the agent receives all of the commission in return for paying a monthly service fee to the broker. If the agent had been working for another broker on a commission-share basis, up to 50 percent of the commission goes to the broker. This would have significantly reduced the amount of commission Cheri could have lent you.

It has been a long and productive week. You sign the closing papers at the escrow office and as you point your car toward home, you mentally review what you did to buy the apartment with zero down:

Real estate agent's fees borrowed	$5,000
Security deposits	$1,400
Prepaid rents	$1,875
Deferred second mortgage	$12,000
Total money derived for down payment	$20,275
Money needed for down payment	$0

Your financial situation looks solid and you should realize a substantial increase in your net worth as your properties appreciate.

Third Year Financial Summary

Beginning Year Net Worth	$258,400
Plus: Third Year Revenues	$150,000
Less: Business and Living Expenses	$115,000
Third Year Net Worth	$293,400

As you round the corner and turn into your driveway, you can hardly wait to dive into your new swimming pool. Your car phone goes off with an irritating blast. Reluctantly, you answer and listen to Cheri's excited voice on the other end of the line. "I have just found two perfect investments for you if you can make a decision within the next hour. One is a residential property that would make a perfect rental. The other is a large project similar to the apartment you just bought that's hot! I'll meet you in my office in 30 minutes, okay?" After a long pause, you give her your answer, and as Paul Harvey would say, "You know the rest of the story."

1. If you believe you would be better off sticking with houses for investments, turn to Chapter 47.

2. If you believe you would be better off moving to larger projects for investments, turn to Chapter 48.

CHAPTER 32

BUILDING AN APARTMENT

COMPLEX

As you drive into the construction site where your apartment complex is being built, your mind shifts to the many problems you have encountered, which is the subject of this morning's meeting with Steve Regan, your prime contractor. You spot Steve talking to one of his supervisors. They stop talking when they see you and his supervisor takes off before you can get a chance to meet him. As you approach Steve, he gives you a disgusted look. "Steve, I know my decision to cut costs by insisting that you use fiber board instead of plywood for side panels did not sit well with you but I have got to do something. With all of the construction delays, I'm running out of money."

The confrontation you expected starts with Steve speaking first. "Quite frankly, I am concerned about your ability to pull this project off. The whole program runs counter to good construction and business practices. You're late on getting payments to me, which means that I'm late on meeting my payrolls. My crews don't like it and if it continues, they will walk off the job. Then you'll really find out what a delay is all about." A moment of tense silence ensues.

You counter Steve's concerns with one of your favorite analogies: "Does anybody want a heart transplant? The obvious answer is no, but if the surgeon tells you the change is necessary if you want to live, you'll probably change your answer to yes. Given the alternatives, you'll do everything you can to make the change work." A frown crosses Steve's face. "I hear what you are saying, but we are also talking about some other changes besides the fiber-board issue that are outside of either of our control."

You know exactly what Steve is referring to. You've encountered delays in getting the building permit, some bad whether, a carpenters' strike, and bank-funding delays that have stretched your financial resources to the limits. Your initial plan was to start and complete the construction in four to five months. You believed you had sufficient cash reserves to cover your living expenses during that time so that you could devote your attention to the project and lining up renters. You're eight months into the project and according to Steve, the apartment might be completed in two months. By the end of this month, you'll be out of money.

In retrospect, you realize you didn't have sufficient cash reserves to build an apartment complex. Most of the delays you have encountered were completely outside of your control, which makes you feel better but it doesn't help. You've contacted several large construction companies that specialize in building apartments and negotiate a buy-out offer from Handly Construction. They are willing to pay you 75 percent of what you have invested in the project and will take over your bank loan. All told, you stand to lose about $70,000 dollars on the project as you assess the impact on your financial statement:

Third Year Financial Summary

Beginning Year Net Worth	$210,000
Plus: Third Year Revenues	$0
Less: Loss on Sale of Apartment	$70,000
Third Year Net Worth	$135,000

Looking back at where you have been, would you alter your decisions in order to create a different future for yourself?

1. If you would like to change your last strategic decision, return to Chapter 16.

2. If you would like to select another business venture to start-up, return to Chapter 2.

3. If you would like to conduct more analysis before you start-up another business, turn to Chapter 3.

If you're still feeling the sting of defeat and believe you could have made your last strategic choice work in real life, you may be right. After all, this is just a game. However, if you return to your last strategic decision and select the other alternative (Chapter 31), you will learn why the authors consider it a better choice.

CHAPTER 33

ADDING DELIVERY SERVICES

Over the past year, you learn that running a successful franchise is much like running any other business, with one major exception—the limited financial support you get from the franchiser. While the franchiser alternately helps you with advertising, promotional ideas, and management assistance, it falls short of offering you viable suggestions on how to increase your personal income. It consistently insists that if you strictly follow its operations manual and its system, you will succeed. But it's not that easy. For starters, the personal income projections in its brochure are 25 percent higher than what you are now making, which you readily admit you should have caught before you bought a Mail Boxes Etc. franchise. When all is said and done, you believe you made the right decision to buy into the franchise. You consider yourself an astute entrepreneur and, having identified a problem, you will find a way to manage it!

You religiously track the profile of your customer base over the past year. When a customer enters your store, you offer him or her an opportunity to receive a copy of your free monthly newsletter. The newsletter offers helpful hints on how to save money on mailing services, direct-mail advertising techniques and always includes money-saving coupons. In return for the newsletter service, customers agree to complete a simple questionnaire that asks questions about their business and why they choose to use Mail Boxes Etc. You have collected over a thousand questionnaires and up to now, have been too busy to tabulate the results. You admit that is not a very good excuse but it's the truth. Since procrastination is not the entrepreneurial way, you ask your daughter who is home for spring break to enter the responses into CrossTab, a questionnaire tabulation program that runs on your PC. You offer to compensate her, which she enthusiastically accepts. The results of the tabulation provide you with some interesting information:

CROSSTAB RESULTS

	Response Percentage	Average Monthly $ Per Customer
Private-use customers	78%	$52
Business-use customers	22%	$235
Business Size		
Less than 5 employees	68%	$198
5–10 employees	15%	$225
11–25 employees	11%	$250
26–50 employees	5%	$305
Over 50 employees	2%	$365

It's no surprise that the bulk of your clients are made up of two groups: private individuals who like the convenience of using a local mailing and packing service rather than facing the inconvenience of waiting in post office lines, and small business owners with less than five employees, many of which are home-based businesses. What catches your eye are the larger small businesses that use your mailing services. Five percent of your customer base is made up of businesses with between 25 and 50 employees. Although the percent is relatively small, they are on average spending $305 a month as compared to $52 a month for private-use customers. A quick review of their invoices tells you why. They're shipping larger packages, consistently require overseas shipments, always buy shipping insurance, are heavy users of overnight mail, and often require the use of complex packaging materials.

If you could somehow increase your larger small-business customer base from 5 to just 10 percent, you would quickly realize your goal of increasing your personal income by 25 percent. The question that first needs to be answered that was not addressed on your questionnaire is why they are using your services as opposed to the post office or their internal mailing department.

You add this question to your questionnaire and call 45 of your larger clients to find the answer to your question. George Hemming, one of your regulars summed it up best for you: "I'm the President of a small wholesale distribution company and, like every small business owner, I have to pay close attention to my bottom line. I have looked into what it would cost to add a mail-room operation to my business and, quite frankly, your services are cost competitive. I live in your neighborhood so it is relatively easy for me to dump our daily output of mailing on your doorstep on my way home. If your location wasn't convenient to me, I wouldn't use it!" You ask George a carefully worded, pre-rehearsed question. "George, if I could offer you free pick-up and delivery service during the week, would that be of any benefit to you?" George gives you an emphatic "yes" answer but questions what you would be delivering. You cut in with the second part of your prepared statement. "George, if you will agree to meet me for lunch on Friday, I will tell you what I can deliver to your company that will save you additional time and money." George agrees to the meeting.

Your strategy of providing pick-up and delivery services is beginning to take shape. Although you realize that accounts like George's will probably remain with you because of your convenient neighborhood location, the opportunity to expand your mailing services into small business marketing areas (i.e., business and industrial parks) presents you with an exciting opportunity to grow your business base. However, as George pointed out, you are picking up business (e.g., mail) but you're not delivering anything. If you could figure out a way to make a single client delivery trip earn revenue by both picking up business and delivering some product the client needs, then you will have created a profitable situation.

Friday arrives and as is always typical with Fridays, everybody is in a good TGIF mood. George is no exception as he sits down to join you for lunch and proceeds to tell you about the fantastic bass fishing trip he's going on this weekend with his son. Halfway through lunch, he stops talking, and apologizes for having dominated the conversation talking about fishing. You assure him that no apology is necessary since you love to fish, which you really don't. He invites you to tell him more about your delivery program. You ask George if his company uses a lot of forms and how they get reproduced. To your surprise, George takes off on an impassioned 15-minute explanation. "We have so many forms that I defy anybody to keep track of them. Everybody has a form for something and because we have so many of them, I can't tell which ones we need and don't need. We must use five different printers plus our own copy machines just to keep us supplied with the darn things. I admit we need some forms but I am obviously frustrated over the sheer number we use. Did I answer your question?"

You thank George for his answer and suggest to him that you have a solution to his problem. He invites you to continue. "Suppose I were to offer you the following service. One of my employees, at no charge to you, would spend a day at your company and collect a copy of every form you're currently using. We would assign a unique number to each form and insert them in a large spiral binder organized by form type and function. You would have a complete binder of all your forms and we would have a complete binder at MBE. Here is what this program would do for you:"

1. Anytime anyone in your company needs additional forms, they call MBE, give us the form number, and we print the necessary copies.

2. Printed forms are delivered to your company through our daily delivery service.

3. If you or whoever you authorize chooses to discontinue the use of a form, call us and we would delete the appropriate one from our binder. This prevents your employees from ordering discontinued forms.

4. Both your forms binder and ours are simultaneously updated whenever you add or modify a form.

5. Once each quarter, at your option, I'll meet with you to review and make recommendations on your forms usage, printing costs, and forms-design criteria. We'll also discuss your overall level of satisfaction with MBE's service.

With baited breath, you ask George; "Would this be a service that would interest you?" His response is immediate. "When can you start? If you can do all those things to solve my forms problem plus provide me with mail pick-up service, you've got my account forever. You can use me as a reference whenever you want." George's company becomes your first pick-up and delivery account. Satisfied with the service, George refers five business clients to you in the first month. Initially, you use your Cherokee wagon as your pick-up and delivery vehicle but over the ensuing months, your delivery client base grows substantially beyond the cargo capacity of the Cherokee. You decide to review your financial position before you consider purchasing a vehicle for the store.

Third Year Financial Summary

Beginning Year Net Worth	$261,000
Plus: Third Year Revenues	$295,000
Less: Business and Living Expenses	$250,700
Third Year Net Worth	$305,300

Excited about the initial financial success of the program, you feel your pulse racing with a desire to add more delivery business, and your stomach clenching as you carefully consider your next step. The increase in your printing business has cut deeply into the production areas of your store. Boxes of completed forms are piled everywhere waiting for delivery. You're concerned about the safety hazard if one of them should fall on an employee or client. The last thing you need is an OSHA audit. Moving to a larger facility would solve your storage problem. On the other hand, if you added delivery trucks with drivers to accommodate a twice- or even three-times-a-day delivery schedule as opposed to the current daily schedule, you could keep ahead of the printing backlog and not have to move. Either way, you've got to do something soon or stop offering the service to any new clients.

1. If you believe that moving to a new building with more space would be the best strategy for you to take, turn to Chapter 49.

2. If you believe that remaining in your existing office space and adding delivery trucks would be your best strategy, turn to Chapter 50.

CHAPTER 34

PROVIDING DIRECT-MAIL SERVICES

Ever since you were a kid, you've been fascinated about the direct-mail industry. You certainly receive enough of it and while most people call it "junk mail," somebody out there is making a lot of money out of this junk. You might as well jump on the bandwagon with the rest of them. Besides, it would be a perfect extension of your Mail Boxes Etc. (MBE) business offerings.

You subscribe to *Direct Marketing* magazine, a leading publication in the direct mail field. Although you realize that direct marketing involves the use of telephone sales, mail order, promotional postcards, television home shopping, billing inserts, party plans, radio ads, and door-to-door selling to get your advertising message across, the best direct-marketing approach for certain types of businesses is still direct mail. One primary benefit is that you can track the results of direct mail to verify if it's working. For example, you can count the number of returned coupons customers present from a direct-mail ad campaign, the number of calls received from a mailing, and ultimately, the sales dollars that are generated as a direct result of the mailing. You list the advantages and disadvantages of direct-mail advertising:

Advantages

- Advertising message is targeted to those most likely to buy your product or service.

147

- Direct-mail message can be as long as necessary to tell your story.

- Can measure the response of direct-mail campaign to determine if it is working.

Disadvantages

- Long lead times are required for creative printing and mailing.

- Direct mail requires coordinating the services of many people (e.g., artist, photographer, printers, etc.).

- Mailing list must be constantly updated to remain current.

Having reviewed the advantages and disadvantages of direct mail, you outline in your mind what direct mail will do for your business. For starters, you believe that customers who come to your store for direct-mail services will be inclined to use the other services MBE offers such as your bulk-package mailing service. Most direct-mail customers are commercial accounts, which you desperately need to help defray your overhead expense. Commercial accounts spend on average five times more per visit than does a private account. Direct mail will allow you to expand into geographic markets that you are not currently serving. Your private accounts come predominately from the local neighborhood because it is convenient. If your rates are competitive, commercial accounts will travel across town to use your service.

If you add direct-mailing services to your business, you'll need a computer-controlled database system to record and retrieve the names of customers and prospects. A mechanism must be in place to measure the actual purchases that occurred as a result of the direct-marketing program. Ongoing direct communication with prospects or customers would be an important part of the program. You'll also need equipment to handle the direct-mail preparation process, which you summarize in the price list that follows:

Direct Mail Equipment, Software, and Materials Needed	*Purchase Price*
Computer Hardware	$6,000
Computer Software	$2,000
Envelope Stuffer/Sealer	$45,000
Paper Folder	$16,200

Cheshire Label Applicator	$22,000
High-Speed Computer Printer	$6,000
Forms Buster	$3,240
Annual Supplies (paper, forms, glue, etc.)	$4,900
Computer and Equipment Maintenance Contract	$12,300
Total Costs	$117,640

Your accountant, Chandler Phillips, tells you that with the exception of the supplies, which can be expensed, you can depreciate computer hardware, software, and processing equipment. Chandler explains, "Depreciation is considered an expense to the business just like any other expense. Depreciation expense gets charged against certain fixed assets that depreciate in value over time, such as equipment, computers, furniture, and other similar items. The loss of value could be attributable to obsolescence and the general use of the asset. There are two basic accounting methods that are used to calculate depreciation; straight line and declining balance. Straight-line depreciation is based on the expected life of the asset. Here's how the straight-line method is used to determine depreciation expense:

"Let's assume you purchased a $5,000 personal computer that has an expected 'asset life' of 5 years. This means that at the end of the fifth year, the computer will be obsolete or worn out based upon your best judgment. In other words, at the end of the fifth year, the asset will be worth nothing. The annual depreciation expense of the personal computer can be easily calculated."

Annual depreciation expense = Total asset cost / asset life
= $5,000 / 5 Years
= $1,000 / Year

Chandler continues: "The declining balance depreciation method can be used if it is to your advantage to obtain a quicker write-off of an asset. Under this method, assets are depreciated by a percent of their remaining balance each year. The depreciation expense of the personal computer that was used in the previous example can easily be calculated for each year of the asset's useful life of 5 years. The declining balance percentage is based upon twice the equivalent straight-line percentage."

You thank Chandler for his in-depth explanation of depreciation. According to a direct-mail magazine, the average processing fee charged in your geographical area for one unit of direct mail is eight cents. You calculate how many units of direct mail you would have to process to break even on just your annual equipment and material costs:

Total Annual Equipment Depreciation Costs = Total Equipment Costs / 5 Years
= $100,400 / 5 Years
= $20,088

Direct Costs = Material Costs + Equipment Maintenance Costs
= $4,900 + $12,300
= $17,200

Direct-Mail Volume to Break Even = Total Equipment and Direct Costs / .08
= ($20,088 + $17,200) / .08
= $37,288 / .08
= 466,122 units

You wonder if it is even feasible to process 466,122 pieces of direct mail per year just to cover your equipment and material costs. You haven't even included your labor costs into the formula. How convenient it would be if you could just call your competitors and find out what kind of direct-mail volume they are processing annually. Being the tenacious person that you are, you call several direct-mail companies only to be told the information you seek is confidential. You are planning to visit your parents in Los Angeles next week, which is completely outside of your marketing area. On a whim, you call Joe Snyder of LA Mailers who agrees to meet with you to share his production numbers with you. Your meeting with Joe proves to be a real eye-opener. Joe tells you that the direct-mail processing business has become so big and competitive that it now takes a minimum of 100,000 pieces per month just to break even. When you show him the list of equipment that you plan to purchase to get into the business, he laughs. "My envelope-stuffer machine cost twice what you think you are going to spend for your entire set-up. Sure you can buy a Pitney-Bowes Stuffer for $45,000 but it can't run at anywhere near the capacity you will need to stay competitive in this industry. I've got over $2 million invested in equipment and I'm just making it! The big direct-mail houses have five times that much invested in their high-speed equipment."

You thank Joe for his input and wisely decide not to venture into the direct-mail business. You are thankful that you waited, before you financially committed to the equipment you thought you needed. Had you gone forward with your direct-mail service plan, your MBE franchise would have lost money.

Third Year Financial Summary

Beginning Year Net Worth	$261,000
Plus: Third Year Revenues	$350,000
Less: Business and Living Expenses	$370,000
Third Year Net Worth	$241,000

This ends this track of play. Looking back on where you have been, would you alter your decisions in order to create a different future for yourself?

1. If you would like to change your last strategic decision, return to Chapter 18.

2. If you would like to select another business venture to start-up, return to Chapter 2.

3. If you would like to conduct more analysis before you start-up another business, turn to Chapter 3.

If you're still feeling the sting of defeat and believe you could have made your last strategic choice work in real life, you may be right. After all, this is just a game. However, if you return to your last strategic decision and select the other alternative (Chapter 33), you will learn why the authors consider it a better choice.

CHAPTER 35

One thing you have discovered in the two years you have been in the software-development business is that the most difficult part of developing software is figuring out how the application will work with the people who use it. On the consulting side of your business, the problem is financially minimized because your clients pay you to develop what they think they want. If they change their minds, they'll pay you anyway. On the software-development side, you earn nothing until your developed application hits the market. If you were correct at interpreting what consumers want, and your application sells you will ultimately be reimbursed for your development efforts. If they don't like it, you lose!

You have been contemplating developing multimedia applications. Multimedia offers an opportunity to create applications that are closer to human reality. You can create software that sings, speaks, displays graphics and animation, plays video excerpts, and displays text for those users who still want to read. The really exemplary aspects about multimedia are that it's fun to use, is very productive, and is where the market is going. Every new PC is equipped with CD-ROMs that can read multimedia disks. The computer and office supply stores now feature "blister pack" racks of a growing number of multimedia applications and even the paper-based bookstores are converting their hard stock over to multimedia disk. In just a few years, the number of multimedia disks-in-print will exceed the number of books-in-print. Clearly, if you want your software-development business to grow and remain competitive, you have to start developing multimedia applications.

Your decision to develop multimedia applications presents you with a financial challenge. The development of traditional software applications required a relatively inexpensive PC and a printer and that was about it. However, the development of multimedia applications requires a whole new level of developmental equipment. To get started, you'll have to upgrade your PC's processor, memory, and fixed-disk storage. You'll need to add additional peripheral equipment such as a high-resolution flat-bed scanner, VCR camera, CD-ROM reproduction equipment, a number of interface boards, and the list goes on. When you total the cost of the equipment you'll need, you jump at the $100,000 figure. How are you going to get your hands on that kind of money?

"When in doubt, access the Internet to find whatever it is you're looking for." Who said that? You can't remember but it's a thought as you sit down in front of your trusty "old" PC and dial the Internet. Using the search word "venture" you access a website called *The Center for Venture Research* at address http://www.venture.com/eid and moments later, you're listening to a multimedia VCR clip entitled *Venture Capital Angels:*

"The availability of start-up capital is fading as the traditional financial sources (i.e., commercial banks and finance companies) are reluctant to provide early-stage risk capital. Start-ups just don't fit into their long-range plans. The major venture-capital companies are also leaving the small start-up field. Most of them won't touch a venture that's worth less than a million dollars. However, don't despair—there is an enormous explosion of private equity investors who are specifically interested in emerging companies. Many of these investors are self-made millionaires and entrepreneurs from past generations. The capital and know-how of this largely untapped economic resource is well worth your consideration. These venture capital "angels" are capable of bringing both money and know-how to the table where their knowledge can be more valuable than their capital."

There is a directory attached to *The Center for Venture Research* website, which lists over 100 private equity investors complete with addresses, telephones, and e-mail addresses. The e-mail address fuels an idea that just might trigger the interest and financial support from one of these investors. Why not create a multimedia proposal that precisely depicts what you want to do and distribute your proposal through e-mail? Not only would you eliminate the cost of printing and mailing multicolor proposals but you could more accurately demonstrate precisely what multimedia applications you want to develop with their money. By using Astound's author development tool, you're able to create your multimedia proposal, which you distribute to the e-mail locations of 125 potential investors.

Within a week, you receive requests for more information from 15 prospective investors. Larry Harrington, the CEO of Venture Investments, calls you and tells you if you're willing to meet him in his San Francisco office, he will devote a half-day to listen to your proposal. You gladly accept Larry's invitation for an afternoon appointment tomorrow. You head out to the library to find out more about Larry Harrington. He's listed in *Who's Who in the West,* and as it turns out, he is one of the largest and most successful venture capitalists in the business. You decide to keep your appointment for tomorrow and confirm your flight to San Francisco.

The Transamerica building towers above as you look up and wonder what it must be like to have an office on the 50th floor, where Larry Harrington's office resides. You walk into the reception area of Larry's office and are transfixed by the beautiful black walnut paneling that lines the entire office suite. Larry emerges from his office, shakes your hand, and ushers you into a chair in front of his desk. "Let's get started" he announces with an abrupt tone. "How much money do you want and what will it be used for?"

You are about to tell him you need the money for working capital when you admit to yourself the stupidity of that kind of response. This man will demand specific answers to his questions and if he doesn't get them, you're out. There are only three things to do with a loan. You can buy new assets, pay off old debts, or pay for operating expenses to accomplish a specific objective. "I need capital to develop multimedia courseware for colleges and universities. Here is an example of the types of multimedia products I will be developing."

Satisfied with your response, Larry asks; "Why don't you have enough of your own money to do this?" You respond by showing him a projected cash-flow statement that identifies the money you will invest into the program and the specific equipment you anticipate obtaining for the program. You tell Larry that if you do not get the investment capital you need, you will simply reduce the scope of your development effort and fund it with your own money.

Larry smiles and tells you he's impressed with your "well-thought-out" answers to his questions. "Be careful when you answer my next question because it is the most important of all the questions I have asked so far. When and how will you pay the loan back?" This isn't the time to be vague. You show Larry your sales projections and marketing plan to convince him of the long-term profitability of your business and your ability to repay the loan.

After over three hours of intense conversation with Larry, he asks you to join him for dinner to celebrate. "Celebrate what?" you ask. "I'll loan you the money you need."

You are reminded that one of the most important parts of the loan process is what happens after you get the money. Maintaining a good relationship with Larry is essential to making sure things go smoothly. Over dinner that night, you negotiate an agreement you can live with and sign the loan documents.

The injection of Larry's capital into your software-development company allows you to release two new multimedia products into the educational market. Several major universities include your material in their fall semester schedules, which accelerates your sales beyond your original projections. Your financial statement is in great shape as you contemplate your next strategic business move:

Third Year Financial Summary

Beginning Year Net Worth	$305,000
Plus: Third Year Revenues	$150,000
Less: Business and Living Expenses	$116,100
Third Year Net Worth	$338,900

Raising the additional capital you needed proved to be a wise decision on your part. It allowed you to realize sales revenue from two new products this year, which would not have happened if you had been forced to use your own capital. However, venture-capital money is expensive and since you will need more capital to fuel the growth of your business, you mount a search for a less expensive source of funds. The Small Business Administration might be a good place to start your search for capital. You also have an opportunity to merge your company into a larger and more established software-development company.

1. If you believe your personal and financial objectives would be better served by merging with an established software company, then turn to Chapter 51.

2. If you believe your personal and financial objectives would be better served by getting a Small Business Administration loan, then turn to Chapter 52.

CHAPTER 36

PICKING THE TOP TWO

PRODUCTS WITH THE MOST

POTENTIAL

The headlines in the *Wall Street Journal* invite your attention: Rockwell International Under Siege. The target: the aerospace giant's research and development resources. The weapon: the Internet. Hackers are trying to break into Rockwell's computer systems via the net. "Someone may already be inside," says Ray Richards, Rockwell's information systems (IS) manager. "There's no way to tell because these hackers know how to cover their tracks. What is especially alarming is that the attempted break-ins are happening even though Rockwell uses the latest firewall encryption technology available. If they can crack our code, they can break into any company they want."

The article continues by stating that Rockwell's break-in problems are causing some businesses to cancel plans to use the net. According to an *InformationWeek* survey, one out of four IS managers said that "fear of Internet break-ins is keeping them from using the net. Many companies refuse to use the net for any important corporate information." An Ernst & Young survey of 2,000 IS managers corroborated *InformationWeek*'s findings. One in five suffered a break-in or attempted break-in.

All of this bleak news is great news for you because it reinforces the viability of your software-development strategy. Two of the software developers that you connected with last month (Jim and Arlene Davis) are a husband and wife team who recently retired from the IRS.

Collectively, the two of them have over 35 years of experience developing security-access systems for the IRS's huge network of computers.

They have developed two program applications that, when implemented, will prevent any hacker from accessing a company's data files. Jim arbitrarily named the programs Firewall 1 and Firewall 2. Arlene explains how the programs work: "Firewall 1 is designed to set off an alarm the moment it detects anyone who is attempting to access secure data files. It automatically goes into a "search-and-find" mode to determine the exact terminal address of the person attempting to obtain unauthorized access. Firewall 2 is a default program that activates in the event that an intruder is successful in breaking into an unauthorized file. It has been designed to shut the file down and if one of its high-level security options is invoked, it will physically shut the computer down before any data can be extracted from secured files. Based upon what Jim and Arlene have told you, if these two tandem programs perform to their specifications, every Internet user in the world is a potential client.

You've devoted countless hours to work out a strategic plan for marketing the Firewall programs and have persuaded the heads of Rockwell International to test the software. Its Chief Information Officer, Jerry Madden, agrees to beta test the programs on one of Rockwell's highly secured computer systems. You've stuck your neck out for the future of your new start-up by betting you can deliver a security program that the "heavyweights" at Rockwell have not been able to accomplish. Its IS security team is out to sink your ship before it even gets launched.

Despite enormous odds, you have pushed your company's software applications out into the wave of the future—Internet security. If you can prove to the Internet world that you have a security system that's endorsed by Rockwell, all of the selling will have been done. A properly staffed software-order department is all that you will need to catapult your start-up into stardom.

The "beta test" rules of the game are relatively simple. At an assigned time, you will install Firewall 1 and 2 on one of ten Rockwell computers. The decision as to which computer to use will be determined five minutes before the installation by drawing a number (1 through 10) out of an empty coffee can. A team of five of Rockwell's best hackers, who have been code-named Fire Breakers, will be housed in a secured and guarded U.S. Air Force building, which is equipped with Internet terminals. The Air Force was quick to volunteer its facilities and support for the program for obvious reasons: a significant portion of Rockwell's proprietary data is owned by the government. Rockwell's Fire Breaker team has exactly 40 hours to break through your Firewall programs and extract data from a published list of 25 secured files. Everything starts tomorrow morning at 0800 hours and instead of feeling excited, you start to sweat. You've heard about "bulletproof" products that have been torn apart, or about massively sophisticated decryption products that are available to anyone as "freeware" on the Internet.

Tomorrow morning arrives as you, Jim, and Arlene pull up to Rockwell's security gate in your Jeep Cherokee. Ray Richards is at the gate to meet you and minimize the security-access requirements. At the prescribed 0800 hour, Firewalls 1 and 2 are installed on Rockwell's computer number one. At this point in the game, you and your team have completed the first round of play. The second round will be played by Rockwell's Fire Breaker team.

Although the three of you sit together on the flight home, the conversation is ominously silent. None of you elects to break the ice. As you walk into your home office, the red light on your answering machine is flashing. The recorded message is from Ray Richards, who says "call me in the morning." The next morning you return Ray's call and hear the dismal news. "Our team cracked your Firewall code in a little over 9 hours and retrieved data from all 25 assigned files, which has been certified by the Air Force." You feel like a tornado just slammed you into a brick wall as you blurt out the words, "How could that happen?"

"Several reasons. I had security experts working against you armed with sophisticated automated tools that have been explicitly designed to find and exploit holes in any security program like your Firewall programs. What's scary is that these same tools are readily available to even novice intruders. The program we used to break through Firewall is called CRACK. It's an encryption-breaking program that's widely available on the Internet. When we activated CRACK and it "touched" Firewall 1, CRACK immediately recognized that a 12-digit security code was required to pass through your program. The rest of the break-in routine was really quite simple. CRACK started replicating all of the possible combinations for the first digit in the security code until it found the one Firewall would accept. The process was repeated for the remaining 11 digits. Now, armed with the correct security code, we were able to pass through your Firewall programs. Access to the secured files in Computer 1's database was routine. And you know the rest of the story."

You thank Ray and his staff for giving you and your team the opportunity to test your programs. Ray interjects, "What are you going to do now?" You take a deep sigh to collect your thoughts. "I've devoted over a year of my time to help develop the Firewall programs. Clearly, it was a waste of my time. To be honest with you, I'll lick my wounds and find something else to do."

After what seems like an extremely long silence at the other end of the line, Ray cuts back in. "I'm impressed with the work you have done. Rockwell could use someone like you. If you would be interested in a position in my IS department, why don't you join me for lunch tomorrow and spend a couple of days to look over our operation? I'll pay for everything and there is a 6 P.M. flight you can take tonight." You think to yourself, it's an option, and right now, it's your only option when you review your financial statement. "Ray, I would be glad to join you for lunch tomorrow."

Third Year Financial Summary

Beginning Year Net Worth	$305,000
Plus: Third Year Revenues	$150,000
Less: Business and Living Expenses	$170,000
Third Year Net Worth	$285,000

Looking back on where you have been, would you alter your decisions in order to create a different future for yourself?

1. If you would like to change your last strategic decision, return to Chapter 4.

2. If you would like to select another business venture to start-up, return to Chapter 2.

3. If you would like to conduct more analysis before you start-up another business, turn to Chapter 3.

If you're still feeling the sting of defeat and believe you could have made your last strategic choice work in real life, you may be right. After all, this is just a game. However, if you return to your last strategic decision and select the other alternative (Chapter 35), you will learn why the authors consider it a better choice.

CHAPTER 37

RENOVATING THE MOTEL

You bought an existing motel at a fixer-upper price because the seller was willing to accept the fact that its motel fell into this category. Your rationale was simple; over the next 12 months, you will refurbish on average two to three units per month so that by the end of the year, you'll have all thirty units restored. You can do all of the cosmetic work yourself. You'll contract out the plumbing and electrical work, which are beyond your construction expertise.

When you went on a "walk-through" with Jim Carleton, your real-estate agent, he pointed out the major fixer-upper issues you need to address. He told you, "I want to see you get the best, the absolute best price for your motel should you ever decide to sell. That will depend on two things that do not exist now. The overall curb appeal of this motel is at best a 3 on a scale of 1 to 10. Not only is that going to hurt you on the resale value, but your potential clients will take a second look before they drive in to rent a unit. Let's face it, people want to stay in a clean overnight accommodation." You interrupt Jim by calling his attention to the fact that every unit is immaculately clean, which he has seen during the walk-through.

Jim agrees but is quick to remind you that there are only three people who know the units are clean, "your janitorial service, you, and me and I am sorry, but we don't count! We are not the ones who will be renting these units. Again, judging from the overall lack of curb appeal, there is an implication that the units are dirty. Every exterior wall needs paint and the rust that extends down from the drains in the roof certainty doesn't help." Over the next two months, you discover that unfortunately, Jim is right. For every three customers who stop to rent a unit, only one stays. They're usually the ones who stop late at night when it is too dark to see anything or they are too tired to search for a better alternative.

The insides of the units need some fixer-upper help as well. Every dishwasher in the kitchenettes is tired. When you opened one, the hinges gave way and the door almost fell off. All of the oven doors were solid but as near as you could tell, none of them had ever been cleaned.

You wonder if you are not selling yourself short by stretching the maintenance work out for a year. You are approaching the peak of the tourist season, and with a couple of nights' exception, the average occupancy of your motel has only been 60 percent. On several occasions, you drive through town in the evening to check on how the other motels are doing. Almost without exception, the "no vacancy" signs are flashing while you are still at half-occupancy.

It's another one of those 60-percent-occupancy nights and as you sit at the registration desk near midnight hoping for a late arrival, you pull up your Lotus spreadsheet on your PC to estimate what your lost occupancy rate is costing you. The numbers that appear on the spreadsheet are cause for concern:

Occupancy and Rent Analysis

Number of units rented over past 3 months	1,728 units
Average occupancy percent per month	60%
Average unit rate per night	$45
Total revenue in past 3 months at 60% occupancy	$77,760
Estimated total revenue in past 3 months if at 90% occupancy*	$116,640
Estimated lost occupancy revenue	$38,880 ($116,640 – $77,760)

* 90% summer season occupancy rate based on average occupancy rate in your area. Source: National Motel Owners Association

After a sleepless night worrying about the income you are losing as a result of operating a Class C as opposed to a Class A motel, you decide to accelerate your refurbishment plan by hiring a subcontractor to complete the task for you. Several phone calls later, you finally find a subcontractor who has the time to stop by and give you a cost estimate. You take his cost estimates and add them to your original Lotus spreadsheet to see if the anticipated increase in clients will off-set the cost of refurbishing all of the units:

Refurbishing Cost vs. Expense Analysis

Estimated cost to refurbish one unit	$995
Cost to refurbish all 24 units	$31,840
Estimated increase in rental revenue assuming 90% increase in occupancy rate	$38,880
Difference between refurbishing cost and increased revenue	$12,400

To your delight, you can offset all of the refurbishing costs with the projected increase in your occupancy rate. Sharon Morgan, Bank of America's loan officer, agrees with the premise of your estimates if the work can be accomplished within the next thirty days. She quick-ly points out that if the construction goes beyond thirty days, you'll miss the best part of the tourist season and if that happens, you might as well wait to do the work in the off-season winter months. You call your contractor from Sharon's office and learn the dismal news. All of his work crews are booked on summer construction projects and would not be able to start on your motel until November, at the ear-liest. He tells you, "Even if I could do it now, we would have to shut your entire motel down to accomplish what needs to be done in a month. Could you afford the downtime?" To save face in front of Sharon, you tell him "yes" even though you know that would wipe out your last remaining cash reserves. You tell Jim you'll get back to him and hang up the phone. Sharon tells you the bank would be will-ing to loan you half of the money you need to refurbish the motel. You thank Sharon for her time and head back to the motel.

You are in a "Catch 22" situation. Without getting the motel refurbished, you can't get the occupancy you need to meet all of your expenses. If you have the work done this winter, you won't have enough cash reserves to keep everything going until the start of the tourist season next spring. In the quiet of your office, you switch the "no vacancy" sign on even though you still have 10 vacant units. Reluctantly, you exercise the only viable option you can think of and call Jim. You ask him to list the property for a price that will hopeful-ly cover your equity position. Your personal net worth drops in the third year:

Third Year Financial Summary

Beginning Year Net Worth	$275,800
Plus: Third Year Revenues	$330,000
Less: Business and Living Expenses	$380,200
Third Year Net Worth	$225,600

Looking back on where you have been, would you alter your decisions in order to create a different future for yourself?

1. If you would like to change your last strategic decision, return to Chapter 4.

2. If you would like to select another business venture to start-up, return to Chapter 2.

3. If you would like to conduct more analysis before you start-up another business, turn to Chapter 3.

If you're still feeling the sting of defeat and believe you could have made your last strategic choice work in real life, you may be right. After all, this is just a game. However, if you return to your last strategic decision and select the other alternative (Chapter 38), you will learn why the authors consider it a better choice.

CHAPTER 38

SELLING THE MOTEL

Over the next several months, you throw yourself into the task of finding a buyer for your motel. You have concentrated your attention on everything you should know about selling property for maximum gain. To maximize your gain, you have to know how to pick the times when it is advantageous to sell. You made a profit during the two years you've owned the motel and you realize that when you sell, you will need to invest precious time locating another investment property. Finding the right property takes time, sometimes a great deal of time. Selling the motel will dilute your investment program unless you are able to immediately reinvest your profits into another comparable property. Your wealth accumulation goal is based upon holding property. As soon as you sell a piece of property, you alter your accumulation plan. It's difficult to reinvest quickly enough to maintain the cash accumulation you were enjoying when you owned property.

You have discovered that you can't invest in another property without money. You've run across several investment opportunities that would have significantly advanced your financial goal; properties that were at the right place, at the right terms, but you didn't have the money to make the down payment. You need to sell your motel so that you will have the down payments for new investment opportunities. You're considering investing in a larger motel or lodge somewhere in Montana and you recently located a seventy-five unit motel/lodge combination that is selling for $750,000. The seller wants

$100,000 down payment. You can't come up with the $100,000 unless you sell the motel. Although the motel you are considering is twice the size of the one you've got, your management problems won't double and you will substantially increase your cash flow. That's the key to your investment strategy. If the sale of a property improves your investment position, you sell. If your investment position is not improved, you don't sell.

Although you will pay capital-gains tax on the property when you sell, the tax would have been a lot higher if you owned the property for less than six months. You are considering a property exchange to minimize your tax exposure if you can find an investor who would be interested. Some sellers are glad to accept smaller equity properties in exchange for their properties, which might be just the solution they are looking for. If you can exchange the property, you will not be taxed as long as:

1. The property you exchange to is of greater value than the property you are currently exchanging.

2. There is no mortgage relief. The mortgage you assume on the new property is greater than the mortgage on the previous property.

3. You don't receive any cash or other non-real estate property in the exchange.

You're in a market where commercial properties are in high demand and you're tempted to try to sell the property on your own to save on real-estate fees. *The Five-Step Property Sales Plan* seminar that you attended at the University of Montana outlined what you need to do:

1. Consult with an appraiser who can do a realistic appraisal on the property. Appraisers who perform the same function for lending institutions will typically under-appraise properties to cover their "backside." You want an appraiser who can give you a realistic appraisal on your motel. If the appraisal is more than you expected, you can use this to support your market price. If the appraisal is less than what you expected, you can either adjust your market price or get a second opinion from another appraiser.

2. Decide in advance what you want from the sale of the property. Depending upon your personal circumstances, do you just want to

get rid of the property as soon as possible or do you want to test the market for the best price? In either case, you need to be realistic about what you expect to get from the sale of your motel. You've been told to not let pride-of-ownership enter into the equation. The more flexible you can be, the easier it will be to sell. The question that should always be in your mind should be, "How can I structure the sale so that the buyer gets what he or she wants and I get what I want?" Can you accept an increase in monthly payments instead of cash down? Are you willing to accept paper for a future payment on your cash down requirement? Does the paper need to be secured by property so that you can sell it if you so desire?

3. Write an ad that attracts buyers and reflects your flexibility on sales terms. The more buyers that are attracted to your ad, the more likely you are to find a buyer. The best way to attract buyers is to let them know they are going to get a good deal. That is where your appraisal comes in. Your ad should indicate that the buyer is getting a good deal on the price and terms if appropriate.

4. Prepare a flyer on your motel complete with pertinent details and pictures. Show all of the benefits that the buyer will acquire when buying the property. Pass the flyer out at all investment clubs and free display stations (i.e., grocery stores, banks, savings and loans, etc.).

5. Talk to everyone you know who might be in the market for your motel, including other motel owners, apartment owners, office-building owners, and any major income figures in the area. Present the project at one of the local Chamber of Commerce meetings to see if you can attract local interest.

Since time is a precious commodity to you, you decide to list the motel with a real estate agency. You spend the next two weeks searching for a real estate agency that has an aggressive advertising program in place backed by a large senior sales staff. The more exposure you can get in the same office, the better. After countless interviews and phone calls, you land on ReMax and a sharp agent, Cheri Dengel. She pushed you for a six-month listing but you settled for a 90-day listing with appropriate wording in the contract that will allow you to rescind the listing agreement for lack of performance. Just to make sure you were on the safe side of the tax laws, you asked your accountant Joe Leonard to help you structure the terms of the sale to maximize your tax benefits. You sign a sales contract with Cheri and ReMax as follows:

Acquisition $$		Proposed Price		Profit %	
Purchase Price	$225,000	Listed Price	$300,000	33%	
Mortgage	$168,750				
Equity	$56,250	Estimated Equity	$131,250	Change in Equity	233%

Working closely with Cheri, you determine your sales price by first determining the capitalization rate on the motel. The capitalization rate is a percent derived by dividing the motel's net operating income (Total Income – Total Expenses) by the selling price of the property. Your calculations follow:

Capitalization Rate = Net Operating Income / Property Sales Price
        = $43,000 / $300,000
        = 14%

Cheri explains to you why the capitalization rate, or "cap rate" as realtors call it, is important: "As a general rule, the higher the cap rate the higher the price of the property. Most investors look for cap rates of 10 percent or higher to prequalify solid investment opportunities." Low cap rates are an indication that one of three things are wrong:

1. Rents are too low.

2. Operating and overhead expenses are too high.

3. The price of the property is out of line with reality.

Cheri shows you how to determine the value of your motel based upon its cap rate:

Value = Net Operating Income / Capitalization Rate
      = $43,000 / .14
      = $307,000

After having completed the capitalization analysis and compared your estimated sales price with the estimate that you received from the appraiser, you believe that $300,000 is a fair price for your motel. To leave yourself some room for negotiating, you list the property for 10 percent above your acceptance price. Three weeks later, Cheri informs you that a cash buyer wants to purchase the motel for $290,000, or 5 percent above your acceptance price. You accept the offer over the phone to save time as you prepare for your next profitable investment adventure and review your financial statement.

Third Year Financial Summary

Beginning Year Net Worth $275,800

Plus: Third Year Revenues	$330,000
Less: Business and Living Expenses	$280,200
Third Year Net Worth	$325,600

With the money from the sale of your motel resting safely in your pocket, you contemplate your next investment move. Your success with the motel invites you to consider buying a larger and potentially more profitable unit. You'd also like to pursue your desire to buy a lodge, but realize you don't yet have enough money to make that transition. However, you could form a limited partnership to raise the money you need.

1. If you believe you can improve your financial position by buying a larger motel, turn to Chapter 53.

2. If you believe that it would be in your best financial interest to form a limited partnership to buy a lodge, turn to Chapter 54.

CHAPTER 39

SPECIALIZING IN MARKETING

In a world of accelerating change, the leverage of time represents one of the surest ways to achieve competitive advantages. You commit to specializing in marketing programs that, when implemented, will allow your clients to introduce new products and services in the least amount of time possible. You have always considered yourself an action-oriented entrepreneur, able to run circles around your competition, and since your sense of expediency has always helped you seize the opportunity of the moment, you feel especially well-qualified to specialize in marketing programs that are based on speed and timing.

As you probe more deeply into time-based marketing, you contact an old friend at the Fielding Institute who tells you why the old assumptions about market price and customer behavior no longer hold true. He sends you a recent article from the *American Marketing Journal* that features a case study where time-based marketing is being used.

When you announce your decision to focus on marketing at Computech's partnership meeting, Henry Riley storms out of the room in an emotional display of disapproval of your decision. The rest of the partners react with much less emotion, although a rousing discussion ensues for the next three hours. To your delight, the persuasive arguments of Kristi Rene and Tony Berger finally settle emotions and convince the other partners that the marketing emphasis can provide a key to success over the next 5 years. Kristi and Tony cite several examples of the power of specializing in marketing because it is needed by several of Computech's major clients. One example, Home Depot, comes up again and again as proof that even a company with a terrible operations track record, but stellar marketing and sales abilities, can outperform its competition. Kristi Rene hands out copies of *Fortune* magazine's article on the home-products retail industry in which Home Depot garnered high praise for its marketing and sales prowess, resulting in a 46 percent return on equity, second only to Home Base. Tony Berger chimes in with all the financial analysis he can muster to demonstrate that a marketing focus would solve Computech's growth and development problems. "Once our marketing consulting services are top-notch, we can then worry about bolstering our other consulting efforts." By the end of the day, the Computech partners, with the notable exception of Henry Riley, unite behind a five-year marketing emphasis.

Two days later, after a long and stormy confrontation with Riley, you accept his resignation. Then, at 3 P.M., just as you are getting ready to leave the office early after a string of 12-hour days, Tony Berger walks into your office and closes the door behind him. By the look on his face, you know he's upset.

"I've been in meetings the past two days with Kristi Rene. "We're trying to come up with a broad sketch of the marketing plan you requested, but we're having real difficulty ironing out our philosophical differences. To be honest, I think we're stuck." As Tony finishes his last sentence, your secretary buzzes to tell you that Kristi wants to meet with you as soon as possible.

You sigh. "Tell her to come up as soon as she can." So much for calling it an early day. While you're waiting for Kristi, you ask Tony to describe the philosophical differences as he sees them.

After a moment's thought, he says, "Kristi believes our marketing strategy should be based on a detailed market-segmentation process that allows for what she calls "micromarketing" or "database marketing." She wants to reconfigure our consulting line and customize services based on the needs of multiple market segments, and she's not thinking in terms of just four or five segments, she's thinking thirty or more. In my view, our consultants already do a good job of identifying and meeting different customer needs, so we don't need to analyze a bunch of different segments to death. We really should be worrying about specializing in a select set of market segments. We could increase our consulting sales by 25 percent just by adding the marketing and sales-training services our customers want."

Kristi comes in just as Tony is summing up his position. "Our philosophical differences really boil down to traditional versus results-based market consulting. Kristi doesn't see the need to offer traditional marketing consulting. She just wants to figure out the peculiar needs of a hundred different customer segments to achieve results-based marketing."

Kristi immediately launches into her own impassioned speech. "That's right! We don't need more traditional marketing, we need to provide our customers with exactly what they want, and that requires modifying our consulting offerings to meet the very different marketing needs of our customers. And, in all honesty, if we don't do a good job meeting all these different needs, we can kiss our customer base goodbye. Tony wants to play the game the same old way by specializing in traditional marketing services. It just won't work anymore."

As Tony and Kristi argue back and forth for the next several minutes, you begin to wonder if a compromise would be in order. When you ask about that, Tony and Kristi both concur. After another hour of discussion, you say goodnight to Kristi and Tony. During your half-hour commute home you think about the possibility of doing what they both suggest. Unfortunately, Computech does not at the moment possess the financial resources to do both well. Besides, even if you tried to do some of both, one of the two approaches should take precedence, or you'd invite the same sort of squabbling you just listened to for two hours. Surely, such contention could do nothing but cause confusion and inefficiency. Results-based marketing determines how, when, and where to modify products or increase services, whereas traditional marketing gets you back to the basics of market research and analysis. You've got to do something to stir some financial growth back into Computech's and your own financial statement as you project where you think you will be by year-end:

Third Year Financial Summary

Beginning Year Net Worth	$225,000
Plus: Third Year Revenues	$150,000
Less: Business and Living Expenses	$60,000
Third Year Net Worth	$315,000

As you pull into your driveway, you feel once again that your job as President of Computech boils down to playing "tie-breaker." You're tired, but confident that you can make the right decision tomorrow.

1. If you think Computech would be better off offering tradition-al market-consulting services, turn to Chapter 55.

2. If you think Computech would be better off offering results-based services, turn to Chapter 56.

CHAPTER 40

FOLLOWING THE LATEST FAD

In a shiny-floored, brightly lit corridor seven floors down from Teledyne's boardroom, you walk slowly out of Ralph Brady's office. Your head hurts and your shoulders slump as you struggle back to your temporary office in total frustration. This has been your third session with Ralph, Teledyne's Human Resources Vice President and nothing has been decided. By your estimate, finalizing the action plan to respond to the latest employee opinion survey should have been wrapped up in three meetings, but for some reason, Ralph has been dragging his feet. He's always pecking for more details than are necessary and reciting anecdotes about the company's good old days, which are a drain on valuable time. So far, the discussions about the dismal employee opinion survey have led nowhere. It reminds you of the story about the stranger asking an old man about directions to Muddy Gap, Wyoming. "Well, son," the old man said after sucking his pipe for a while, "don't rightly think you can get there from here." You don't rightly think you can get anywhere with Ralph.

This has been your fifth consulting assignment at Teledyne and based on your excellent rapport with Kelly James, Teledyne's Executive Vice President, you will be here forever, if you want. But that is becoming a problem with this latest Brady assignment. Two more weeks of this mundane "we'll think about it tomorrow" attitude and you're out of there! In desperation, you decide to take the issue up with Kelly. You walk into her office and, after the usual "how

174

are you doing" acknowledgments, you ask Kelly if you can speak off-line. You have used this approach with her before and trust her impeccable credibility. She quickly invites you to continue. In some detail, you explain your frustration in shaping an action plan out of the employee-opinion survey. "You don't need a consultant whom you are paying over $100 an hour to baby-sit one of your department heads. You can hire baby sitters for a lot less!" Now you have said it and probably cut your own throat.

A strange sort of smile crosses Kelly's face that has you perplexed. You think to yourself, "She is about to fire me and is simply expressing her delight before she pronounces her sentence." Kelly's smile disappears as she speaks. "As you know, I have the greatest degree of respect for you and Computech. Every assignment that I have given you has been delivered on time, within budget, and to my exacting expectations. With the exception of the current Brady baby-sitting assignment, your past assignments at Teledyne have been, for the most part, technical in nature. I'm here to tell you that although technical consulting is important, it's not where the true action is; human-interaction reengineering is where the action is at! Some executives are calling it the latest fad, while I simply call it getting back to the basics. Do you know what I mean?"

You're not sure you understand anything about what Kelly is talking about but in the interest of smart politics, you tell her you know exactly what she is talking about and ask her to continue. "Your employee survey assignment with Brady is, and I apologize for this, a set-up. I wanted you to witness firsthand—the real problem we have in this company—inaction due to lack of interaction. I would suggest to you that we are not the only company who is suffering from the inaction syndrome. Now, since I have already acknowledged the fact that I have given you a trick assignment, let me explain the good intent of my action. I believe that if you can shift out of your technical consultancy gear and help Teledyne solve its inaction problems by using interaction reengineering, we will both benefit. I'll gain productivity out of my management team and you'll develop a new expertise in interaction reengineering, the latest consulting fad. Now, are you up to the assignment and challenge?"

Again, in the interest of politics and keeping a good client, you muster all the enthusiasm you can to assure Kelly you are the one for the job and you have no intentions of letting her down. As you dismiss yourself from her office, she tells you to see her in exactly one week for a formal Brady progress report. Now your head really hurts as you shift your car into auto-pilot and head home. What do you know about interaction reengineering, the latest consulting fad?

Your trip to the local library turns up nothing. Although your subject search located a book on the subject, all five copies were checked out. Noting the author and title, you stop at five book stores and finally find one who has a copy of the book, *The Color Code* by Taylor Hartman. Maybe Kelly was right when she said interaction reengineering is the latest fad.

The book talks about new ways to see yourself and your relationship with others. It talks about personalities, that core of thoughts and feelings inside you that tells you how to conduct yourself. It's a checklist of responses, based on innate values and strongly held beliefs that direct your emotional as well as rational reaction to every life experience. It even determines which type of emotional reaction you're likely to have in any given situation. It certainly has dictated the reaction you have had when dealing with Ralph.

As you read on, you learn how important it is to understand how to recognize the strengths and weaknesses of your own personality type and the personality types of others like Ralph. The book elaborates on the four basic types of personalities and how to work with each type. It doesn't take you long to figure out what type of personality fits Ralph. He has what the book refers to as a "yellow" personality type.

Yellows are fun lovers. They are spirited, exciting, and have an innate ability to always be happy. They have a mental attitude that allows them to appreciate what they have rather than be miserable about what they lack. Yellows struggle to understand why anyone wants to look for problems rather than look for the easy road through life. Maybe that is why Ralph has chosen to ignore all of the negative aspects of the employee opinion survey.

You learn how to motivate yellows to accomplish tasks that are in your best interest, like implementing a "get-well" action plan for the employee survey. Despite their struggle with self-discipline and commitment, yellows are eager to experience all facets of life. They naively call for the spotlight to be placed on them as they play out their life as though it were on center stage. Yellows always promote the good in others and are willing to ignore their limitations.

Armed with new insight on how to work with and motivate "yellow" personality types like Ralph, you call him and arrange for a morning meeting to discuss an action plan to resolve the issues identified in the employee opinion survey. During the course of your conversation with Ralph, you suggest that the overall morale of the employees at Teledyne is excellent, which he tells you is a valid observation. You know better, but in keeping with your agenda to work with the man's personality, you continue. You tell Ralph, "You have an opportunity to demonstrate real leadership in human resources by suggesting ways to further improve on what is admittedly a high level of employee morale." When he asks you what areas need to be improved upon, you diplomatically suggest that he review the recent survey to gleen some helpful hints. By the end of the week, Ralph proudly presents a set of employee morale improvement recommendations to Kelly and her executive staff. On the surface, Ralph takes all of the credit. In the back room, Kelly congratulates you on your ability to implement interaction engineering to move one of her departments off dead center, as she hands you a $20,000 check for your consulting services. Following the latest fad in consulting has proven to be a reasonably profitable venture for you as you review your personal financial statement.

Third Year Financial Summary

Beginning Year Net Worth	$210,000
Plus: Third Year Revenues	$150,000
Less: Business and Living Expenses	$55,000
Third Year Net Worth	$305,000

Unfortunately, everyone else is following the latest consulting fad too. As you search for ways to differentiate your business from the other consulting firms, you contemplate focusing on personal productivity. In your mind, everybody can improve their productivity. You also consider developing an entirely new approach to training people that would differentiate you from all of your competitors.

1. If you think focusing on personal productivity issues would be the best path to take, turn to Chapter 57.

2. If you think developing a new approach to training would be the best path to take, turn to Chapter 58.

CHAPTER 41

WORKING FOR A

WELL-KNOWN RESORT LODGE

The ad in the *Sunday Billings Times* appears to be just the kind of interim job you've been looking for. It reads:

SYSTEMS ANALYST WANTED

The Canyon Lake Lodge is now accepting applications for the above position. A qualified candidate would be highly motivated, mature, willing to learn, and knowledgeable in PC database architecture. Person must possess outstanding people skills as well. If you would like to join our winning team, please fax your resume to: 406-555-7764.

With the help of Kelly Technical Services and after several interviews with Timber Wolf's General Manager, Steve Harding, you convince him you are the right person for the job. The Timber Wolf Lodge is located on the north end of Canyon Ferry Lake surrounded by the beautiful Helena National Forest. All 172 suites in the lodge look out over the lake and offer majestic views of the bordering Rocky Mountains. The lodge offers every conceivable recreational activity, including superb rainbow and native trout fishing, horseback riding, overnight rides, four-wheeling jeep rentals, mountain biking, and rental boats of every size and shape. Fall and winter activities include exotic snowmobile excursions into prime elk country, guided big and small game hunting, and some of the best skiing in the state.

With all of the sophisticated recreational services the lodge has to offer, you are perplexed over the fact that it relies on a manual reservation system to control over 300 daily room and recreation event bookings. The process is choking its staff and errors are causing serious customer-satisfaction problems. Steve Harding, the lodge's general manager, spends the first two weeks with you patiently going through every facet of the lodge's operation.

He bluntly explained the situation in a way that clearly defines the problem you were hired to resolve. "Our manual reservation system is the Achilles' heel of our operation. We are averaging a 10-percent error factor throughout our reservation system. A guest who wants to go on a breakfast horseback ride ends up being booked on a jet ski. Room reservation foul-ups are so prevalent that we have been forced to hold 15 percent of our rooms in reserve to cover missed room assignments. I'm talking about guests who show up with confirmed reservation cards that have not been recorded in our reservation book. It costs a lot of money for people to travel from all over the country to get to the Timber Wolf Lodge. When they finally get here, they expect to have their recreational desires met without a hitch. When we foul up, we have got one irate customer to contend with and chances are, he or she will never return. Our inadequate reservation system is costing us in excess of a half-million dollars a year in lost business. I've got six months to fix the problem or I'm out of a job. What can you do to solve our problems?"

Fortunately for you, the basic computer architecture for hotel and motel reservation systems has been around for several decades and over that time, has been refined to near perfection. You tell Steve that you need four weeks to analyze the situation before you can make any concrete recommendations. He reluctantly agrees to your timeline, which irritates you. He reminds you of another typical manager who wants instant computer solutions to long-standing problems. By the end of your first month, you've struck on a solution you believe will solve Timber Wolf's reservation problem. Lotus Notes is IBM's highly respected database package that can be easily connected into a local area network (LAN) of personal computers.

Your decision to go with Lotus Notes was reinforced when you learned that it already had a reservation module that's available to anyone who purchases the application software. When you present the proposed solution to Steve, he gives you his "rubber stamp" of approval. The PC hardware that you need is available "off the shelf" in Helena, just 20 miles east of the lodge. It takes you just sixty days to install both the hardware and software to initially automate room reservations. After thirty days of careful monitoring, Steve is ecstatic over the reliability of the system and pushes you to expand the system to accommodate reservations for recreational activities. By the end of your six-month assignment, the Timber Wolf Lodge has a fully automated reservations system that is working beyond even your wildest expectations.

Steve insists that you join him for a celebration dinner at the finest steakhouse in Helena, Montana (and in the world, according to Steve). During the course of the evening, Steve offers you a permanent position with the lodge. He tells you, "I need you to help move the Timber Wolf into the twentieth century. The reservation system proves beyond a doubt that we have got to automate all of our processes if we are to remain competitive. Will you accept my offer?"

He's shaken when you politely decline his offer and he aggressively asks you why. Over the past six months, you have gotten to know Steve reasonably well but because of the serious nature of your assignment, both of you have restricted conversations to business matters. With the success of the reservation system behind you, you decide to confide in Steve. "Steve, to be honest with you, I want to open my own lodge somewhere in Montana. I want to own the whole thing and run it myself."

Steve interjects with, "Let me tell you what you are up against. Starting one of these puppies is not cheap. How much money do you have to invest?" When you tell him you have about $200,000, he laughs! "I don't mean to make fun of you but you're going to need at least twice that much to start a successful lodge. I'll show you our books, which will tell you exactly what it cost to get Timber Wolf off the ground and into a profitable state. If you are intent on starting a lodge on your own, you'll need to raise more money perhaps from limited partners. As an alternative, I can put you in touch with some investors who might be interested in joint-venturing a lodge with you. That would give you some but not all of the control you are looking for in a new lodge. Will you stay with me until the end of the year before you strike out on your own? I'll help you out all that I can."

You agree to accommodate Steve's request and remain with the lodge until the end of the year. Unfortunately, Steve's hidden agenda for other automation assignments takes up most of your time. You haven't been able to resolve which direction you want to take on a new lodge, for either a joint venture to raise the money you need or borrowing the money you need. As the new year approaches, you review your current financial position, and prepare yourself for a tough decision.

Third Year Financial Summary

Beginning Year Net Worth	$199,300
Plus: Third Year Revenues	$90,000
Less: Business and Living Expenses	$35,000
Third Year Net Worth	$254,300

1. If you believe that you would be better off joint-venturing a new lodge, then turn to Chapter 59.

2. If you believe that you would be better off raising the money you need for a new lodge, then turn to Chapter 60.

CHAPTER 42

WORKING FOR AN
ADVERTISING AGENCY

Advertising is like weight lifting. If you don't do enough of it, you're wasting your time. When you create an advertisement, you don't want your customers to tell you they find it creative. You want them to find it so interesting that they buy whatever product or service you're advertising. You have an opportunity to work for Cole & Weber, a prestigious advertising agency in Billings. To help minimize the time you spend in determining if this would be the right job for you, you develop selection criteria to guide your choice. A good advertising agency offers personal attention to specific client advertising needs. In order to determine if Cole & Weber is as good as the agency says it is, you formulate several questions to ask during the interview process:

- How long has Cole & Weber been in business?

- Does Cole & Weber specialize in serving any one industry?

- Does Cole & Weber have experience in serving businesses with modest budgets?

- Can you give me some examples of successful advertising programs Cole & Weber has implemented?

- If there are account problems or disagreements, how are they resolved?

The chemistry you feel between you and the people you would be working with will be a big factor in choosing Cole & Weber. Will there be any personality conflicts? Will you be able to get along with the agency's creative people and its account executives? You like everyone you meet at Cole & Weber and accept a temporary Account Executive position with the firm.

You attend Cole & Weber's comprehensive week-long training session where you learn that every business makes advertising mistakes. The instructor, Jan Engin, tells you, "We are not immune from them, but you should know how to avoid the common mistakes. Don't try to do too much with too few advertising dollars. You cannot afford to be something to everyone. Too often businesses try to say too much by using many different media or expensive one-time flashy ads. A clear focus with just one powerful message may be all you need to create a successful advertising program. Choosing a medium based on its low cost rather than on its cost-per-thousand readers, listeners, or viewers can be a costly mistake. You should compare audience size, image, and the selling results for businesses that have advertised in various media. Don't just look at the ad rates of a medium."

Toward the end of the week, you learn that not advertising frequently enough is another common mistake. You may need to run several ads to increase the awareness and recall of your message. Don't make an advertisement bigger than it needs to be. Make sure your advertisement concentrates on the reader, listener, or the viewer. Don't expect too much from creativity in copy and art. A flashy and innovative ad will not overcome a defective product.

Failing to fully utilize the unique advantages of the medium, television especially, is another common mistake. For example, if you use TV, then demonstrate the virtues of your product. Avoid just talking through a TV script without demonstrating your product. If you use billboards, avoid using excess words. People will not have time to read them. Always capitalize on the inherent features of your product, service, or company. Match your market's preferences with the strengths of your offerings.

You learn that according to the Federal Office of Consumer Affairs, 95 percent of all dissatisfied customers never bother to complain to the seller. They make their dissatisfaction known in other ways by taking their business elsewhere and by criticizing your business whenever they get the opportunity. Replacing lost customers is an expensive proposition. Unfortunately, more attention is spent on acquiring customers than on retaining existing customers. It makes good dollars and sense to keep your current customers. The advertising costs of attracting new customers are five times greater than selling to existing customers. You list several ideas you can use to help your clients keep their customers:

- Solicit customer criticism and suggestions by installing a customer suggestion box.

- Teach all employees the importance of respecting your customers.

- Constantly remind employees of the value of good customer relations.

- Conduct telemarketing programs with new customers to gauge their level of satisfaction.

- Use direct-mail surveys to measure overall customer satisfaction.

- Conduct personal customer interviews to determine their level of satisfaction.

- Use hired shoppers (shoppers hired by an employer) to determine how well employees are treating customers.

- Use conveniently located customer comment cards to encourage customer comments.

- Use toll-free numbers to solicit comments from out-of-town customers.

- Establish a special complaint department to review and objectively evaluate every customer complaint.

- Publish a newsletter featuring product and service use bulletins, helpful news briefs, and calendars of local events.

- Conduct educational seminars where you can demonstrate different features of your business and offer product demonstrations.

- Offer goodwill gifts or special discounts to key customers to show your appreciation.

On the last day of the training session, Jan's closing remarks say it all. "Measure the success or failure of every ad you place. Otherwise, you will never know which ads are working or not working. Watch and evaluate your ads to see if they're drawing customers into your business. Discover what it takes for advertising to succeed. Advertising cannot overcome a structural business weakness, nor is it an automatic solution to all of your problems. If your prices are too high or you are in an inconvenient location, you've got problems that go beyond your advertising campaign."

Cole & Weber's training program was excellent. Over the ensuing months, you have an opportunity to apply what you learned by working with several different accounts, including The Montana Cattlemen's Association, Target Stores, and the Department of Natural Resources. You know that if you open a lodge, you must know how to achieve top results out of your advertising dollars. Advetising is a necessary investment and you must squeeze every penny out of your client's program if you are to be successful. As the executive director of the Montana Cattleman's Association told you, "I know that half my advertising dollar is wasted but I don't know which half." In order to leverage the advertising dollars of your clients, you find yourself constantly evaluating several media alternatives before you make your final recomendation:

1. Classified ads placed in newspapers, magazines, or weekly shoppers where the ads are arranged by product or service categories.

2. Display ads in selected pages of newspapers and magazines. They differ from classified ads in that each ad is custom-designed by the advertiser. They may include artwork, color, illustrations, and photographs to supplement the text copy.

3. Brochures that talk directly to the customer and are loaded with tantalizing graphics and interesting copy.

4. Flyers that quickly tell readers how they can benefit from a special offer. Unlike brochures, they are typically one-page handouts and are less expensive to produce. Flyers are often used to announce special opportunities to consumers such as limited offers, sales, or coupons.

5. Direct marketing that uses one or more advertising media to create a measurable response, such as telephone sales, mail order, promotional postcards, television home shopping, billing inserts, party plans, radio ads, or door-to-door selling to get the advertising message across.

Impressed by your quick grasp of advertising and public relations techniques, Mr. Weber asks you to join him in his office for a little "chit chat." He tells you what you already know. "Your clients like and trust you." He goes on to tell you; "I would like to make you an offer you cannot refuse. How would you like to become a partner at Cole & Weber? Now I know you have some crazy idea about opening a lodge in Montana so let me offer you an added incentive. We're about to mount a major marketing campaign to solicit accounts from lodges throughout Montana initially, and the United States on a broader scale. How would you like to head that effort?" You are speechless! You thank Mr. Weber for his generous offer and ask if you can give him your answer in the morning, which he agrees to. That evening, you review your financial situation as you contemplate your next strategic move.

Third Year Financial Summary

Beginning Year Net Worth	$199,300
Plus: Third Year Revenues	$95,000
Less: Business and Living Expenses	$35,000
Third Year Net Worth	$259,300

The opportunity of obtaining major lodges as accounts would certainly bring you one step closer to where you ultimately want to be but it also creates a dilemma. It would be awkward to establish a client relationship with a lodge and tell the owners you want to buy their lodge when and if it comes on the market. If you can diplomatically avoid taking the lodge advertising program responsibility, you would be free to look for a lodge in the evenings.

1. If you believe it would be in your best interest to look for lodges in the evening, turn to Chapter 61.

2. If you believe it would be in your best interest to obtain major Montana lodges as clients, turn to Chapter 62.

CHAPTER 43

BREAKING OUT ON YOUR OWN

TO BETTER LEVERAGE

YOURSELF

Deciding when to quit and move on to a better opportunity is one of the most important decisions any entrepreneur ever makes. You've done all you can do to contribute to the success of Personal Dynamics and now it is time to break out on your own. During your brief and emotional meeting with the senior partners, you announce your decision to leave the firm.

Over the course of your year with Personal Dynamics, you have learned a great deal about personal coaching. Although there is a tremendous need for the service, it carries with it the same stigma of admitting that you have to see a psychologist. Most people won't openly tell others they are seeing a psychologist and will do everything they can to avoid seeking psychological help, even when they need it. The implication is that if managers admit they are seeing a personal coach, their peers might ask, "What's wrong with you?"

To help eliminate this stigma, you write and publish several articles in magazines such as *Forbes* and *Careers* that are well received. *USA Today* asks you to syndicate a weekly column on personal coaching. You accept the assignment and have subsequently been inundated with calls from all over the country by people who want to use your service. Most of the callers are executives who recognize the value of having access to a coach to help them make tough business decisions.

You wanted to leverage yourself and this was one of the key reasons why you decided to leave Personal Dynamics. Several executives want to pay you a retainer, which would allow them to contact you by phone whenever the need arises. What a perfect way to leverage your time. No travel is required and if documentation is needed to augment the conversation, you just fax it before the call. Welcome to the electronic age. In your spare time, you pursue acquiring the equipment needed to add videoconferencing to your telephone system.

Over the next twelve months, your coaching business grows exponentially as you rapidly shift into offering retainer packages to the executive market. *Business Week* features a profile of your business complete with your picture on the magazine's front cover that swamps you with phone calls and thousands of letters asking for more information about your coaching services. You find yourself clearly in a position where you have more business than you can personally handle.

To further leverage yourself, you decide to begin selectively adding partners to your company. You choose a full partnership organizational structure to grow your one-person operation, which will necessitate some wrenching changes on your part. Up until now, you have been making all the decisions. As you discovered in your brief tour at Personal Dynamics, most of the critical decisions were subject to vote by the general partners. Admittedly, the senior partner of the firm could influence the outcome of the vote, but in the end, "yes" and "no" votes were counted. You understand the necessity of allowing democracy to prevail in a partnership setting. Each partner must believe he or she is a vital part of the partnership as a whole, or they will leave.

When you sense some hesitation from the future-minded Karen Wallington, one of the first partnership candidates that you like, you decide to explain the logic behind your organization more fully than you had planned: "Remember, the innovative organization approach, as we've discussed, represents a highly organic structure. There's little formalization here. It will allow us to strengthen our emphasis on project teams, particularly cross-functional teams to help broaden all of our knowledge in personal coaching. Remember, personal experience is the primary textbook since not much has been written about the subject. In particular, I want to make sure we avoid any sharp divisions that would undermine our efforts to constantly innovate."

Karen shakes her head. "I must admit you really surprised me. I expected you to land somewhere in the middle or more toward the position where the senior partner dominates. Instead, you have chosen the path of least resistance. Why?"

Though you hesitate momentarily, wondering whether you should expose your deepest thoughts and feelings about your new organizational structure, you decide to put all your cards on the table. "First of all, I don't believe that we should throw away everything we've learned over the past hundred years about centralized organizations. I am the central and only figure in my current organization, so this will be a tough personal transition for me to make. I believe the organization should be modified to incorporate principles of the classic innovative organization because those principles will enable us to best meet the needs of our clients and the rapidly changing business environments. We could waste months trying to reengineer or invent some new kind of organization, each day losing our position in the market, neglecting our customers and ultimately, probably going out of business. Frankly, I'm not willing to risk the future of this company on some radical new organizational perspective. Let's take advantage of what we have already learned about personal coaching, making sure we allow for sufficient innovation to move us forward and more fully satisfy our clients' needs now and in the future."

When you ask Karen if she can support the type of organization you want to build, she responds with an enthusiastic "Yes, it's exactly the kind of organizational structure I have been looking for." You extend an offer to Karen, which she accepts. After weeks of continuous interviewing, you fill the remaining open partnership positions. By the end of your third year, your partnership-team organization is working better than you expected. The referral coaching business that you had to turn down in the past is now being absorbed by your general partners. Thanks to their participation, your personal income increases substantially in the fourth quarter as you review the favorable impact it has on your net worth:

Third Year Financial Summary

Beginning Year Net Worth	$268,000
Plus: Third Year Revenues	$100,000
Less: Business and Living Expenses	$45,000
Third Year Net Worth	$323,000

Toward the end of the year, you continue mulling over the possibilities further growing your coaching business. The entire issue of

PC Magazine is devoted to creating websites on the Internet. After reading the magazine, you think you understand what a website is and since everybody seems to be getting into the web, maybe you should create one for your coaching business. As an alternative, you're also considering staying with the basics and launching a personal-coaching cable TV program. You don't have the resources to pursue both alternatives so you need to choose the program that you believe makes the most sense.

1. If you believe that creating a website focused on personal coaching makes the most sense for your business, then turn to Chapter 63.

2. If you believe that launching a personal coaching cable TV show makes the most sense for your business, then turn to Chapter 64.

CHAPTER 44

GROWING THE PARTNERSHIP

Stan Lee, the Senior Partner at Personal Dynamics, has for some reason taken an interest in you. During the course of your breakfast meeting with Stan, he candidly tells you about his concerns for the future of the partnership. "While I recognize that we are all busy and making a darn good buck at personal coaching, the supermarkets of the consulting industry are moving into our territory. Just last week, Arthur Andersen announced the formation of a new personal-consulting division with expectations that the division will go international in twelve months."

You interject your own thoughts. "Why is Arthur Andersen suddenly interested in personal coaching when it already has a corner on every other aspect of the consulting market?" Stan says, "The answer is obvious: Who are the predominant personal coaching clients?" You respond, "The executives of middle to large corporations" and you have the answer to Stan's question. If you're successful at personally coaching the executive, then he or she who controls the corporate purse strings is more apt to award your consulting firm with other consulting contracts.

Stan proceeds to tell you about your new assignment. "I want you to take the next two months off from active consulting work and develop a viable marketing plan that will allow Personal Dynamics to expand nationally to compete head-to-head with the Arthur Andersens of the worlds."

In his book, *The Road Ahead*, Bill Gates writes of "friction-free capitalism," a type of marketplace that will be ushered in by innovative alliances rather than traditional acquisitions or mergers. Over the next several months, driven by a vision of finding innovative ways to share both fixed-cost and market benefits with business enterprises around the world, you engineer 35 strategic alliances. The alliances are cost and market-sharing arrangements with personal-coaching businesses just like yours all over the country and include everything from the sharing of office space, joint marketing activities, to the codevelopment of new program offerings.

You hire Karen King to head up the administration of Personal Dynamics. Karen was born in Britain, raised in Russia, Indonesia, and Japan. She works closely with you to expand the alliance into western Europe and the far east. A few years earlier, and this would have been a cost-prohibitive option. All of this is now economically feasible with the relatively cheap access to videoconferencing, e-mail, and the Internet. The partners throughout the organization are deeply affected and motivated by your enthusiasm and vision. As news of your success spreads worldwide, more and more doors open up for strategic alliances, which enable Personal Dynamics to become known as one of the most forward-looking companies in the personal-consulting arena.

By the end of the year, Personal Dynamics closes 10 more alliances as a result of your efforts, all outside the United States. It reports an 86-percent growth in sales with a corresponding 79-percent growth in profits. Stan Lee calls you into his office for an emergency meeting two days before Christmas. As you walk into his office, you find the office filled with well-wishers all shouting "surprise surprise" at the same time, with banners displaying you as the "partner of the year." You wonder if things could get any better than this. They do when Stan hands you a $50,000 bonus check for your work and simultaneously announces that you have been appointed to participate on the Senior Advisory Board of the partnership.

As you drive home that evening, your methodical mind starts to assess what all of this means to your bottom line. No sooner is your car parked in the garage than you find yourself sitting in front of your PC updating the numbers on your net-worth spreadsheet. A smile crosses your face when you hit the key to recalculate your year-end net worth.

Third Year Financial Summary

Beginning Year Net Worth	$268,000
Plus: Third Year Revenues	$100,000
Less: Business and Living Expenses	$45,000
Third Year Net Worth	$323,000

As you wind down after the celebration, you realize that you may have underestimated the long-term ripple effects of what you have accomplished. The new year's eve party gives you plenty of opportunity to celebrate what has been a very good year. But the pressure is on when Stan Lee tells you he wants you to continue in your magical role of further growing the size of the firm. You thought you had exploited just about every option you could think of last year. In many respects, it might be prudent for the firm to stick with and refine the proven coaching concepts before advancing on to new endeavors. That would certainly be the safest route to take. On the other hand, personal family coaching is a budding but growing business. If Personal Dynamics were to move into family coaching, a whole new market would open itself up to the firm.

1. If you believe that sticking with proven personal-coaching strategies is the best approach to take, turn to Chapter 65.

2. If you believe that expanding the business to include family-coaching strategies is the best approach to take, turn to Chapter 66.

CHAPTER 45

REMAINING SOLO

Confident in your abilities to provide a broad spectrum of consulting and training services, you decide to be the sole employee of your company. You are four years into your start-up program and with the exception of the first year, your salary has always been in the six-digit figures. You realize you are eclipsing the traditional way to make money in this industry by not hiring as many bodies as you can to leverage earnings on head count, but you doggedly hang on to the idea of working by yourself.

First Interstate has been your anchor client. In fact, it is your only client, which begins to bother you for obvious reasons. If you lose the bank, you are temporarily out of business. Some careful nurturing and cultivation of key First Interstate executives and department heads opens the back door for you. You convince them that they really don't need you on a full-time basis anymore since much of your bank training material has been recorded on CD-ROMs, video, and audiotape. You diplomatically tell them that it would be in their best interest to reduce your hours by as much as 50 percent.

Reluctantly, they agree and offer to pay you on a full-time basis for six months or until you can find other clients to absorb the bank's cutback in hours. You graciously accept their generous offer and immediately begin searching to expand your client base. Bank of America has been after you for months to conduct part-time training sessions at its customer research facility but you beg off on the offer.

You believe your long-term interests would be better served if you diversified into another industry. However, the task of finding other suitable clients takes you longer than you had expected. Three months later, you sign lucrative contracts with Allied Signal and CompUSA.

To make sure you're doing the right thing, you take a week off to refine your strategic long-term plan. In your mind, you outline where you want to be in 5 years. Over the next 5 years, you'll make in excess of $3 million after taxes and will have more business than you can personally handle. At that time in your life, you can choose to retire, continue working on a part-time basis, or continue working full time. Whatever choice you make, it will not be influenced by money because you will have made enough of the stuff to cover your lifestyle for the rest of your life. It's not a bad position to be in, particularly when you like what you are doing anyway.

One of the reasons why you have become so successful is that you've learned to meet the training needs of your clients. You have specialized in training individuals so their knowledge and skills match their current and future job requirements. Since everybody is interested in advancement, you show them what they must know to qualify for a higher and more responsible position. You do this in both on- and off-the-job settings where individuals have the opportunity to interact with others outside of confining work environments.

Initially, all of your training programs are directed at hand-picked managers that Senior Management determined were worthy of attending your sessions. However, over time, you are able to convince them that your management-training programs could be closely integrated with the daily work of nonmanagement employees. This becomes a popular idea in view of the fact that your clients are currently experimenting with self-directed work teams where employees are expected to manage themselves. Your self-directed team-management program shows them how to master basic management principles to do their jobs more effectively with less direct supervision.

On occasion, you provide morale-improving seminars, a very sensitive subject at CompUSA. Helen Haden, its Vice President of Human Resources, is quick to remind you that its morale index is one of the best in the industry. To break the ice, you call Helen's attention to the fact that employees experience all kinds of feelings about their employment situation. They have feelings about their job, their supervisor or manager, the organization for which they work, their chances for advancement, and a number of other related issues. Their morale and overall level of job satisfaction directly influences employee productivity and voluntary turnover. The downsizing mania that occurred in the first half of the 1990s propagated a deterioration of employee morale, regardless of whether they were directly involved in a company that was undergoing downsizing activities or not. A general mistrust of corporate America developed. Helen reluctantly agrees with the premise of your position and allows you to conduct a "pilot" series of motivational seminars, which she personally monitors.

Against this backdrop, you developed and conducted several motivational seminars that showed employees how to improve and update their knowledge, skills, and abilities so that they can avoid the downsizing ax. In the process, you raised their self-esteem and prompted the view that top management cares about them or they wouldn't be attending your seminars. One of the senior managers would, on your insistence, address the group to reinforce the "I care about you" spirit of the seminar. The voluntary turnover rate of employees who attend your seminars is measured and compared to the voluntary turnover of employees who had not attended your seminars. To your delight, the turnover rate was half that of the other employees, a selling point that made your morale-boosting seminars extremely popular at CompUSA.

At the end of your fourth year, you are astounded by the sheer number of popular topics you have become proficient at teaching. The *Wall Street Journal* runs a front-page article about your training accomplishments, complete with an artist's sketch of you. Several business reporters dog you for interviews over the next several weeks, and although the media attention distracts you from your incredibly busy schedule, you love every minute of it. And, of course, the money you are making working for yourself is not bad. Your year-end financial statement reflects a favorable increase in your net worth.

Fourth Year Financial Summary

Beginning Year Net Worth	$270,000
Plus: Fourth Year Revenues	$168,000
Less: Business and Living Expenses	$96,800
Fourth Year Net Worth	$341,200

By the end of the fifth year, First Interstate, Allied Signal, and CompUSA continue to bombard you with new, unique, and challenging training requests. At one point, you considered adding a fourth client to your list but you don't know how you would work it in unless you started working on the weekends again, which you vow is not going to happen. Your financial position improves in the fifth year as a result of an eight percent rate increase you announce at the beginning of the year.

Fifth Year Financial Summary

Beginning Year Net Worth	$341,200
Plus: Fifth Year Revenues	$181,000
Less: Business and Living Expenses	$146,300
Fifth Year Net Worth	$375,900

This is the end of this path of play. If you would like to see how well you did in comparison to the alternative start-up paths you could have taken, turn to Chapter 77.

1. If you would like to see how well you would have done if you had brokered trainers, turn to Chapter 46.

2. If you would like to try another start-up path where you take action now, turn to Chapter 2.

3. If you would like to try another start-up path where you can conduct analysis before you take action, turn to Chapter 3.

CHAPTER 46

BROKERING TRAINERS

After reading more than a dozen books on building a training business, attending several training-development seminars, and your own experience at First Interstate Bank, Allied Signal, and CompUSA, you decide that brokering trainers could be the key to growing and diversifying your business. All the literature, your own thinking, and discussions with experts in the field convince you that brokering trainers is the only way to assure you've got the major needs of the market covered. In fact, Judy Stevens, Vice President of Development at Allied Signal, caused you to rethink your whole staffing strategy when she asked you to provide advanced cellular wafer training for its new multibillion dollar "chip" facility in Chandler, Arizona. You had to turn the request down because you weren't qualified to conduct the training sessions and worse yet, you could not provide Judy with an alternate trainer. You flat out did not know anybody who specialized in cellular training; you just never had to look for one before. In addition to Allied Signal, other clients, including First Interstate Bank and CompUSA, requested training specialties that you could not provide. Each time you said "I can't help you," you felt as if you had shot yourself in the foot one more time. At some point, your clients are going to wake up and realize you don't have the training depth to meet all their needs. If that happens, you'll be back teaching accounting basics at the local junior college, if you're lucky.

You firmly believe that adding a strategic core of trainers who would be willing to let you broker their training programs would create a "win-win" situation. You'd have a captive network of trainers you could rely on to meet client-training needs that are beyond your scope of expertise. Your trainers could spend more of their time concentrating on training assignments and less on marketing their services since that would be your function, for a fee of course.

However, when you introduce the idea to several of your colleagues, it's greeted with a total lack of enthusiasm. They fear that if they were to subscribe to a brokering service they would, over time, lose their direct contact with the market. The exception is Doug Hoagland of Hoagland Associates who applauds the idea and identifies the major problems you will need to overcome to sell the concept:

1. Show the short-term and long-term economic benefits of your proposal to potential subscribers.

2. Offer some kind of program guarantee with an "easy-out clause" for subscribers who may become dissatisfied with your program for any reason.

3. Identify strict parameters you will use to control the endeavor to negate potential subscriber concerns.

Several weeks later with the help of your friend Doug, you hammer out answers to the difficult issues he identified. Once again, you attempt to solicit your colleagues to attend a three-hour meeting on brokering trainers. Again, you receive a cold reception and mixed responses: "Not interested" or "I'll think about it" or "I'll call you, don't call me." To your surprise, Doug, who is well-respected by the tri-county chapter of the American Society of Training and Development (ASTD), persuades the members to attend your three-hour session at the Hilton Tuesday evening.

Tuesday evening arrives and you have a full conference room of, judging from the looks on their faces, doubtful prospects. Many have already told you they will leave in the first half-hour if they feel there is no substance in your offer. If there was ever a time to fine-tune all of your public-speaking skills, now is the time to do it! Although you thought you would never get this far, you heartily accept the challenge that lies before you.

You begin your presentation by showing the group what they already know. According to training industry standards published by

ASTD, 25 nonreimbursed marketing hours are spent per training consultant to close one 16-hour training session. The average hourly fee per session is $75. The adjusted hourly fee, which includes 25 hours of nonreimbursed marketing expense, is $48, which you show from an overhead projector:

- Fee from 16-hour training session is $1,200 (16 hours × $75 = $1,200)

- Adjusted actual billing rate per 16-hour training session is $48 ($1,200 / 16 training hours + 25 marketing hours)

Your bait-and-hook approach follows: "I propose to broker your services at 25 percent of what you are spending now to do the same thing. If I am wrong, it will cost you nothing to participate in the program. If I am right, you'll end up with a surplus of 25 hours per training session that you can either apply to your personal time off, which we all need, or to another billable training session. Let's assume for a moment that my assumption is right to see what effect it would have on your billable rate:

- Fee from 16-hour training session is $1,200 at $75 per hour (16 hours × $75 = $1,200)

- Marketing cost of obtaining program is $300 (25% × $1,200)

- Actual billing rate with broker support is $56 ($1,200 fees − $300 broker fee) / (16 hours)

"As you can see from my calculations, your effective billing rate increases from $48 to $56 per hour and you gain an additional 25 hours to use for whatever you want." In a bold attempt to qualify how well you think you are doing so far, you announce to the group that you're one-half hour into the session. "If there is anyone who would like to take this opportunity to leave, feel free to do so now before I continue." Nobody leaves! Armed with a fresh shot of adrenaline, you continue with the guarantee part of your program. "If you sign up for my program, you are in effect hiring me as your broker. I therefore work for you and you can fire me at any time for whatever reason. In this regard, I have a proposed employment contract for you to review, which Doug Hoagland is handing out now. I invite you to show it to your attorney to verify the fact that you have the option to cancel the contract at any time."

"You also have the option to identify strict parameters within the contract that you want me to comply with, such as not representing your services to named accounts and clients. The client-confidentiality clause, which is in the last paragraph of the contract, is backed with my $1,000,000 personal bond. You also have the option to modify the contract whenever you choose. Now, are you ready to do business with me?"

At the close of the meeting, 35 attendees agree to meet with you to sign contracts. Follow-up conversations with the rest of the participants pulls in another 20 interested prospects. Over the next two months, you talk to 55 trainers and sign up 25 to participate in your brokerage program. You diplomatically reject the application of 30 trainers who are either new in the industry, lack a proven track record, or have questionable reputations.

You kick your trainer brokerage program off in the second half of the year. The optimistic number that you presented in your presentation holds as you begin to discover the economics of brokering trainers for a fee. Your year-end financial statement looks great:

Fourth Year Financial Summary

Beginning Year Net Worth	$270,000
Plus: Fourth Year Revenues	$300,000
Less: Business and Living Expenses	$245,000
Fourth Year Net Worth	$325,000

It takes a disproportionate amount of time to schedule face-to-face meetings with decision makers, ones who can commit to training programs that meet the needs of their companies. During the course of the conversation with most major accounts, a wide range of training needs are always uncovered. The fact that you now have a set of trainers who can meet most of those needs has opened up a whole new and lucrative market for you. If you are not able to fulfill the training contract yourself, you can now fill it with one of your associates and earn a commission in the process. What a lucrative position to be in!

In fact, your broker-training program is becoming so lucrative, you wonder if you should consider expanding your local broker-trainer network to a national broker-trainer network. If you decide to go national, you realize that the job will require your full-time attention, taking you away from the training that you love doing. And, the additional travel time and hours could be a real killer. On the other side of the coin, the potential money you can make brokering train-ers nationally is exciting if you can successfully build and control a national network. However, if you keep the network small, it will be a lot easier to control and it too could be very profitable.

1. If you believe that you have a better chance of marketing your trainers through a small local network, turn to Chapter 67.

2. If you believe that you have a better chance of marketing your trainers through a large national network, turn to Chapter 68.

CHAPTER 47

STICKING WITH HOUSES

You have learned how to find and negotiate properties at zero down. It's now time to use your knowledge of real estate and your creative abilities to accelerate your dream of becoming financially independent in five years. You believe the opportunities are there if you invest in houses.

Your financial plan is based on acquiring single-family residences because they are in the greatest supply and the easiest for the small investor to buy. You have decided to keep your current job for the time being and devote Saturdays to look for real-estate investments. Your target market is homes in the $125,000 price range that can be purchased for $115,000 with a $5,000 or less down payment. This will take some looking but as long as you keep your current job, time is on your side.

When you find the right property, you commit to yourself that you'll buy it even if you have to borrow the down payment. As soon as you rent the property, you'll start looking for another property to buy. One of the keys to your financial plan is your ability to rent every house you purchase for enough money to cover all expenses including the mortgage, property taxes, and insurance. Over the next 12 months, you purchase 4 houses that fit into your financial plan. It's Sunday morning and as you relax beside your pool, your mind drifts back to business. With a scratch pad in hand, you calculate your projected equity position based upon a 10-percent appreciation rate for your houses:

	House #1	House #2	House #3	House #4	Total
Purchase Price	$105,250	$99,800	$99,500	$102,300	$406,850
Market Value	$115,700	$118,200	$110,600	$120,100	$464,600
Loans	$109,900	$112,300	$105,100	$114,100	$441,400
Equity	$5,800	$5,900	$5,500	$6,000	$23,200

After a dive into the pool to celebrate your attractive equity position, you find yourself left with several nagging questions. At this point in your investment program, you're clearing just enough money to cover expenses. You've maxed-out your available cash reserves and can't buy any more houses. How can you propagate your investment plan to make $500,000 over the next five years, which will afford you the opportunity to quit your current job, and invest in real estate full time if you choose? As you think through your dilemma, refinancing appears to be the way to go when you review your financial statement:

Fourth Year Financial Summary

Beginning Year Net Worth	$293,400
Plus: Fourth Year Rental Revenues	$33,600
Plus: Equity on Houses	$23,200
Less: Business Expense	$30,240
Fourth Year Net Worth	$319,960

In your early attempts to find the highest possible loans on your houses, you run into a brick wall. Curb appeal, or in the case of your properties, the lack of curb appeal, causes problems. One of the bank appraisers tells you the reason why you did not get the refinancing you requested was because of poor curb appeal. Your personal inspection of the properties verifies what he was talking about. The interior and exterior of all your houses need painting along with yard maintenance, new carpeting, and drapes. Before you proceed with any attempts to refinance your other houses, you decide to invest $5,000 to refurbish one of your houses. Your timing is perfect since the current tenants have just moved out and you are interviewing renters who want to move in as soon as possible.

Since your aim is to get the highest appraisal possible for your cosmetic dollar, you hire two college students who are anxious to make money over their spring break and have done home maintenance work during their summer vacations. You take a week off from work to help them out and to supervise the work. In a week's time, the three of you are able to paint the interior and exterior of the house, add new carpet and shape the landscape for $4,800. You ask the bank's appraiser to appraise the property for a second time and to your delight, he recommends that the property be refinanced for $125,000, a number that the bank accepts.

Because of the improved curb appeal, you increase the rent of the property by $100 a month and encounter no problems finding a qualified renter. The increase in rent will cover your $4,800 investment in 4 years, which represents an 18 percent return on your investment. Based upon your existing $125,000 loan, your net proceeds from the new loan are $20,000, which does not have to be reported to the IRS since you have not sold the property. The increase in rent is more than sufficient to cover your new mortgage payment and you can use the extra money to purchase additional houses.

You spend the next six months refurbishing and refinancing your other three homes. The program is working so well that you decide to accelerate your investment campaign and acquire five additional houses. By the end of the year you have managed to acquire 10 homes and this time, as you relax by the pool at The Grand Hawaiian in Maui, you redraw your revised equity statement and financial statement:

Fifth Year Financial Summary

Beginning Year Net Worth	$319,960
Plus: Fifth Year Rental Revenues	$53,600
Plus: Equity on Houses	$43,200
Less: Business Expense	$30,360
Fifth Year Net Worth	$386,400

This time when you dive into the pool, it really feels good and you stop thinking about your accelerated equity position. Tomorrow, you are going marlin fishing off the coast of Kapalie. You have successfully completed a start-up decision-making track, but you can keep playing the game by choosing one or more of the options below.

1. If you want to compare how the results of your last five years of start-up decision-making strategies stack up against the other positive outcomes, turn to Chapter 77.

2. If you wish to find out what would have happened had you chosen the alternative of financing marketing campaigns for equity, turn to Chapter 71.

3. If you want to discover the outcomes of other choices on the track, turn to Chapter 48. Return to Chapter 5 if you want to start the track from the beginning.

4. If you would like to pursue other start-up decision-making opportunities, turn to either Chapter 2 or 3.

CHAPTER 48

MOVING TO LARGER PROJECTS

You pore through the classified ads of the newspaper marking all possible real estate finds with a red felt-tip pen. Although you have decided to invest in larger real-estate properties, you aren't sure which offers are good deals. You snap the cap back on your pen and are about to toss the newspaper into the fireplace when one ad heading catches your eye: Conversion Opportunity! As you read on, the ad is for an apartment that can be converted into an office building. It's an idea that had never crossed your mind. Why would anyone want to convert an apartment into an office building?

A quick phone call to your real-estate agent Cheri Dengel gives you the answer—money! Cheri explains, "Office space on a square-foot basis rents for approximately twice what a square foot in an apartment rents for and tenant turnover is significantly less in offices than for apartments. Most office space is leased for longer terms than apartments and office-lease agreements often include annual rental-escalation clauses. Businesses tend to pay their monthly rents on time and many prefer to prepay rents once each quarter. You're always chasing late rent checks with apartment renters." Cheri concludes her remarks by asking if you would like to see the property tomorrow morning. You agree to meet her at the apartment at 10 A.M.

The apartment turns out to be a beautiful twenty-unit building in the center of town. It's a classic brick building with stately white balconies in an excellent location, directly across from the county courthouse. However, the interior needs work. Every wall needs painting and the carpeting desperately needs to be replaced, which you would have to do anyway if you converted the building to office space.

There are approximately 7,000 square feet on each of the three floors and plenty of parking space. The city clerk tells you one parking space is required for every 500 square feet of office space. With 20,000 square feet of anticipated office space, you need 40 spaces. There are 30 spaces available but if you removed a planter area on the east side of the building, you'll have room for 10 additional spaces. The property is already zoned for a professional office building. The city planner tells you there would be no problem with your proposed conversion, but that you would have to submit your plans to the city council for approval.

You next determine if there is an adequate market for office space. On a whim, you call one of the county commissioners and find out they need extra space for their county offices. She tells you whom to see and exactly what you need to do to get a lease commitment from the county. You make several cold calls on tenants in an office building a couple of blocks from where the apartment is located. One of the tenants wants to sign a lease with you for an entire floor (7,000 square feet). Others also expressed interest and you politely tell them you are in the preliminary planning stage and will get back to them by the end of the month. Signed leases from future tenants would give you added borrowing power at the bank.

The next item on your checklist is costs. You hire a local architect to make a quick study of the kinds of improvements that would have to be made to convert the apartment to an office. His cost estimate is $300,000 for the complete conversion. Can you get a $300,000 loan from the bank? Would it lend you the money? What would the building be worth after the conversion? Rents for similar office spaces are $10 per square foot per year. At that rate, you would earn $200,000 of gross income ($10 * 20,000 sq. ft.). You estimate that net income would be 60 percent of gross or $120,000.

Before you buy the apartment and spend an additional $300,000 on construction costs, you want to make sure the office conversion will be worth the investment. You call Cheri to get her advice. Cheri explains how to use the capitalization rate or "cap rate" to estimate the market value of commercial property. "As a general rule, the higher the cap rate the higher the price of a property. Most investors look for cap rates of 10 percent or higher to prequalify solid investment opportunities. Low cap rates are an indication that one of three things is wrong: Rents are too low, or operating and overhead expenses are too high, or the price of the property is out of line with reality." Cheri shows you how to how to determine the value of the office building based upon its cap rate:

Cap Rate = Annual Net Operating Income / Sales Price + Any Capital Improvements

= $120,000 / $450,000 + $300,000

= 16%

Market Value = Annual Net Operating Income / Capitalization Rate

= $136,000 / 16%

= $850,000

Based on Cheri's calculation, you would turn a $450,000 apartment building into a completely refurbished office building worth $850,000, which would be $100,000 more than what you would be investing into the property. You estimate that the apartment would generate about $40,000 a year, far short of the $120,000 anticipated from the office-building option. The appraisal ordered by the bank put the value of the apartment at $460,000 and estimated that the office version would be worth at least $900,000. The loan officer encourages you to charge $12 per foot for rent instead of $10, which was your original plan.

After having completed the capitalization analysis, you believe that $450,000 is a fair price for the property. You purchase the apartment, convert it to an office building and take the loan officer's advice by increasing rents to $12 per foot, which proves to be a very profitable decision.

Fourth Year Financial Summary

Beginning Year Net Worth	$293,400
Plus: Fourth Year Revenues	$120,000
Less: Business and Living Expenses	$98,700
Fourth Year Net Worth	$314,700

Your accountant gives you an added bonus when he informs you that you can take a 20-percent tax credit on the money spent rehabilitating the building. That's 20 percent of $300,000 or $60,000 in tax savings that you hadn't counted on in your fifth year. The completed office conversion project and unplanned tax deduction have a very favorable impact on your net worth in the fifth year:

Fifth Year Financial Summary

Beginning Year Net Worth	$314,700
Plus: Fifth Year Revenues	$132,500
Less: Business Expense	$77,600
Fifth Year Net Worth	$369,600

You have successfully completed a start-up decision-making track, but you can keep playing the game by choosing one or more of the options below.

1. If you want to compare how the results of your last five years of start-up decision-making strategies stack up against the other positive outcomes, turn to Chapter 77.

2. If you wish to find out what would have happened had you chosen the alternative of sticking with houses, turn to Chapter 47.

3. If you would like to pursue other start-up decision-making opportunities, turn to either Chapter 2 or 3.

CHAPTER 49

MOVING TO A NEW BUILDING

WITH MORE SPACE

When you announce your decision to move to a new building with more space, your employees react with enthusiasm. They are tired of tripping over the stacks of boxes filled with printed forms waiting for delivery. As you assess your need for more space, you believe the 1,500 square feet that you currently have is not adequate for your store. It is the minimum amount of floor space that the facility engineers at Mail Boxes Etc. (MBE) suggest you need to accommodate an adequate customer-service area, rental mailboxes, and a back-end production area for packaging, printing, and metering. The problem that confronts you is that you're using 350 square feet of your production area to store boxes of printed forms awaiting customer delivery. Quick math tells you that you'll need at least 1,850 (1,500 + 350) square feet just to accommodate your current operation. You may want to add an additional 250 square feet to accommodate future growth.

Sally Mercer, one of MBE's facility engineers, agrees to meet you in the store this morning to review your space situation. As is typical of facility engineers, she shows up at the precise time and wastes no time getting right to the subject. "Explain to me again what it is you want to do and precisely why you want to do it." Before you can answer, she raises her voice, making it clear that she wants specific answers to all her questions. "Moving any business is risky stuff and although I may sound like a hard-nose, I want to make sure you have thoroughly thought about all of your options."

After waiting a few seconds for the walls to stop vibrating, you calmly explain why you need additional storage space. You assure Sally that you have spent several weeks of painstaking research and analysis to uncover every option possible. You hand Sally a table that shows the options you believe would work along with the cost of the option, the advantages, and the disadvantages:

Option Description	Annual Cost	Advantages	Disadvantages
Lease offsite storage space and remain in current location	$4,200	Least expensive option	Requires transportation to and from offsite location
Stay in current location and add 350 square feet	$7,800	Minimum disruption to current business	Second most costly option
Move to industrial location at lower rent	$5,100	Location may also attract commercial accounts	Disruption to existing business
Move to larger location in strip mall with lower rent and lower traffic	$7,100	Reduces current overhead	Lower traffic
Move to larger location in strip mall at higher rent and higher traffic	$9,400	Potentially more business from higher traffic	Higher overhead

After studying your table for several minutes, Sally looks up and says; "There is a sixth option that you haven't considered. Let's go through each of your options first before I introduce you to the sixth option. What about the first option?"

Somewhat off balance, you proceed to explain the rationale behind the option to lease offsite storage space and remain in your current location. "There's a ministorage facility less than a quarter mile from the store. As you can see from the table, it is the least expensive alternative, but there are some hidden costs. Here's how the program would work: All of our completed printing material would be transported from our retail location to the ministorage area where our couriers would pick up the boxes for customer delivery. The logistic problems include extra runs that would have to be made from the main store to the storage area, and the lack of driver supervision at the storage area."

"The second option of staying at the current location and adding 350 square feet of space would minimize the disruption to my business. It's a viable option because one of the stores in the complex is going out of business and it occupies space that is exactly 350 square feet more than what I am currently leasing. Mr. Hennesy, the center owner, is willing to lease the space to me. As you can see on the table, it is one of the more expensive options. Using high-traffic retail space to store boxes is not very economical. If I need more space at some future date, Hennesy tells me I'm out of luck since all of the remaining tenants are represented by solid business ventures."

"If I move to an industrial location, I can get all the additional space I need at a lower rent. However, if I do that, I'll lose my walk-in traffic that currently accounts for 25 percent of my volume. Can I replace that business with new industrial clients? My gut tells me I probably can but for some reason, that isn't good enough because if I can't, I'm out of business."

"There are several larger locations that are available in strip malls that offer lower rent and correspondingly, lower traffic. I can get the additional 350 to 500 square feet I need and pay what I'm paying now for rent. However, based on observation of three possible sites, they all offer walk-in traffic that is considerably less than what I'm enjoying now. That could change over time since these sites are relatively new. There is one site that offers considerably more customer traffic than what I am experiencing now at a higher monthly rent."

You ask Sally for her opinion on which of the five options would be best for you. When she bluntly tells you she doesn't like any of them, you are frustrated and irritated at the same time. "Do you have a better idea?" When she says, "As a matter of fact, I do," you sit back to listen.

"First off, I would not move from your current location. You've built up a client base that you can't afford to lose just because you need a lousy 350 square feet of space. There are ways of adding space to your existing facility at a minimum cost. Let me show you some examples of modular wall-to-wall storage and display racks that not only look attractive, but will allow you to increase your current storage space by more than the 350 square feet."

As you pore through the modular storage examples Sally shows you, you admit that they represent a very efficient alternative. The total cost of the modular storage units would be $4,600, or about what you were planning on spending each year to rent the additional space you need. When you review the favorable impact the modular storage decision has on your financial statement, you quickly endorse Sally's recommendation.

Fourth Year Financial Summary

Beginning Year Net Worth	$305,300
Plus: Fourth Year Revenues	$460,000
Less: Business and Living Expenses	$424,000
Fourth Year Net Worth	$341,300

1. If you believe it would be in your best interest to acquire corporate shipping accounts, turn to Chapter 69.

2. If you believe it would be in your best interest to focus on residential customers, turn to Chapter 70.

CHAPTER 50

ADDING DELIVERY TRUCKS

Acting on your intuition, you decide to add delivery trucks to bolster your promising Mail Boxes Etc. (MBE) delivery service and take solace in the fact that none of your competition has pursued such a course. You hope it is because you know something they don't know rather than vice versa. You spend significant resources and several months developing a companywide delivery system that is capable of servicing your entire metropolitan market. Customer orders will be picked up and delivered the same day. A fleet of three panel trucks is needed to cover the delivery routes. Each truck will be fully utilized and will be on the road a minimum of eight hours a day. You'll need three full-time drivers and judging from your classified help-wanted ad, there are plenty of people who are willing to take the job at minimum wage. After carefully projecting the anticipated additional profit you will gain, you decide to implement the program:

Estimated Annual Gross Profits from Delivery Program

Additional Gross Sales	$93,000
Expenses	
Truck Lease Expenses	$9,000
Truck Maintenance Expenses	$3,600
Insurance	$4,250
Gasoline and Oil	$18,000

Driver Salaries and Payroll Taxes	$32,290
Total Cost of Delivery Program	$67,140
Annual Gross Profits	$25,860

Initially, your delivery program is successful. Your sales and cost estimates are right on, which allows you to sit back and enjoy the profits. Two months into the program, one of your drivers runs a red light, hitting a Ford Thunderbird. Fortunately, nobody was hurt, but both the Thunderbird and your truck were totaled. Your insurance agent tells you to anticipate a 25-percent increase in rates on your next statement. Your driver, whom you thought was not hurt, claims he has constant headaches as a result of the accident and files for long-term disability. Federal OSHA investigators are taking up a disproportionate amount of your time investigating the circumstances behind the accident.

No sooner do you find a replacement for your injured driver than one of your other drivers quits. You and your store manager are forced to make several delivery runs to placate incoming calls from irate customers, which forces you to add a person to cover the front of the store when you're making deliveries. Your delivery-related sales base begins to erode due to service disruptions. One valuable lesson you have learned from all of this is that customers are not very forgiving. If you disrupt the service you promised them, they will stop doing business with you and it is very difficult to earn their business back. At the end of the year, you review your financial position and discover you are worth less today than you were a year ago:

Fourth Year Financial Summary

Beginning Year Net Worth	$305,000
Plus: Fourth Year Revenues	$295,000
Less: Business and Living Expenses	$300,700
Fourth Year Net Worth	$299,300

Anxious to get your MBE franchise back on stable ground, you cancel your delivery program. You believe there are easier ways to make a living and sell the franchise for a loss. In retrospect, you wish you had stayed with the "tried and true" MBE program and left the experimenting with delivery services to others. Looking back on where you have been, would you alter your decisions in order to create a different future for yourself?

1. If you wish to find out what would have happened had you chosen the alternative of moving to a new building with more space, turn to Chapter 49.

2. If you would like to select another business venture to start-up, return to Chapter 2.

3. If you would like to conduct more analysis before you start-up another business, turn to Chapter 3.

If you're still feeling the sting of defeat and believe you could have made your last strategic choice work in real life, you may be right. After all, this is just a game. However, if you return to your last strategic decision and select the other alternative (Chapter 49), you will learn why the authors consider it a better choice. In real life, you probably would have kept the franchise since it was making money for you.

CHAPTER 51

MERGING WITH AN ESTABLISHED

SOFTWARE COMPANY

According to *PC Magazine*, the software-development industry is moving at the speed of light. The shelf-life of a newly released software application is six months at best before it is either replaced with an upgrade or rendered obsolete by a competitive product. To meet that kind of a production cycle, SWAT programmer teams are called upon to start and complete retail-ready computer applications in two to three months. Unfortunately, you don't have the technical contacts or the financial wherewithall to be a serious player in the software-development game. You've got two options: (1) shut your current operation down or (2) merge with a larger and more established company. After a number of phone calls that tapped every contact in your network, you managed to solicit some interest from Jim Nelsen, president of AutoLogic, a well-respected and growing multimedia software development company. Jim has agreed to meet with you tomorrow morning in his office.

As you walk into Jim's office the next morning, you're taken back by the physical size of the man. You guess he probably played college football or perhaps even pro ball. Before joining AutoLogic as its President three years ago, he was the Chief Information Officer at Hewlett Packard, a position not to be taken lightly. Word had it that he could get the personal ear of Walt Hewlett any time he wanted it!

In keeping with his physical size and strength, Jim introduces himself and aggressively shakes your hand. "I'm a Theory X man and

I believe AutoLogic is a Theory X organization. It's my job to make sure AutoLogic gets its worth out of everyone who works here. If we decide to acquire your firm, what will you bring to our table? I want more than just a bunch of potatoes; I want meat." You start to laugh before you realize the man is serious. Jim's Vice President of Operations Judy Crawford walks into the office with a "Sorry I'm late" explanation. Jim explains Judy's presence: "You met Judy last week when you were here to learn more about AutoLogic. For obvious reasons, I have asked her to sit in on our meeting. Why don't we get started by having you present your case for the acquisition."

After several weeks of painstaking research and analysis, you present your case for the acquisition. Jim seems to be particularly interested in the company's most recent product innovations, the development of college-level course material on multimedia CD-ROMs. You explain in considerable detail how your educational CD products are supplemented with "stand-alone" hard-bound books, which helps ease the electronic media transition into what had traditionally been an educational paper mill. As a footnote to your presentation, you review your current research projects, which include the development of state-by-state travelogues on CDs.

At this point in the discussion, Judy Crawford raises a question you anticipated but hoped wouldn't come up. "Explain to me why we should acquire your firm when it would be a lot cheaper to just make employment offers to your employees, offers that they could not refuse?" Before you can answer the question, she raises her voice, making it clear she is just stating a question and not a position. You begin with a carefully planned response. "Judy, as you know, I have employed ten of the best CD-ROM developers in the industry. They are fully capable of going from product conception to product release in 90 days. Microsoft employs teams of fifteen to accomplish the same thing in 180 days. Our product-development activity in the upper-educational arena is innovative and we have established a name for ourselves. I met with my team this morning before I left for this meeting and we openly discussed the option that you are suggesting. The team voted unanimously that it would not accept employment offers from AutoLogic. It would have to be an "all or none" acqusition offer. If you would like to confirm what I just said, you can talk to my employees who are waiting for me in AutoLogic's main lobby.

The silence in the room is so thick, you could cut it with a knife. After waiting for what seemed like an eternity in time, Judy tells you that won't be necessary. You conclude your remarks by insisting that the acquisition would be an excellent fit with AutoLogic's niche CD marketing objectives. Jim Nelsen, apparently satisfied with your arguments, changes the subject with a discussion on where to go to lunch. You end up at a steak house that serves the best prime rib in town.

In the end, AutoLogic approves your acquisition proposal for a $1.3 million direct buyout to you and lucrative two-year employment contracts for each of your employees. Your name is excluded from the employment contract. Over the next several months, you work hard to finalize the acqusition. Your legal counsel Steve Regan and AutoLogic's Judy Crawford prove invaluable in pulling everything together. At one point the whole deal comes close to unwinding because you can't come up with the employment contract terms AutoLogic's board of directors wants in the deal. With you out of the picture, your software team is nervous about its long-term future at AutoLogic. The problem instantly goes away when the board suddenly agrees to add you as AutoLogic's Vice President at a salary level that favorably affects your financial statement:

Fourth Year Financial Summary

Beginning Year Net Worth	$338,900
Plus: Fourth Year Revenues	$260,000
Less: Business and Living Expenses	$213,000
Fourth Year Net Worth	$385,000

By the end of your fifth year, AutoLogic substantially broadens the scope and depth of your educational product line. Total sales jump to $10.8 million, and profits on the line climb to 42 percent. You receive the coveted *Entrepreneur of the Year* award from *Inc. Magazine*. The year-end issue of *Forbes* publishes a cover story praising you and AutoLogic for commercial innovation in advanced education. Over the Christmas holiday, you find yourself extremely grateful for all that has happened as a result of your hard work. Your success is reflected in your financial statement:

Fifth Year Financial Summary

Beginning Year Net Worth	$385,000
Plus: Fifth Year Revenues	$290,000
Less: Business and Living Expenses	$257,100
Fifth Year Net Worth	$417,900

In five short years, you manage to catapult yourself into the ranks of a millionaire. Thanks to an early focus on an untapped market, the acquisition of a dynamite staff, the development of breakthrough product lines, and the early recognition of the need for a strategic acquisition to accelerate your start-up momentum, you made it. This brings you to the successful conclusion of this decision-making track. You can continue applying your entrepreneurial skill by choosing one or more of the alternatives that follow.

1. If you want to compare how the results of your start-up decision making in this track stack up against other track outcomes, turn to Chapter 77.

2. If you want to review the outcome alternative of obtaining a small business administration loan, turn to Chapter 52.

3. If you would like to review the outcomes of the other choices you could have made, turn to Chapter 51.

4. If you want to play a whole new track, turn to Chapter 1.

CHAPTER 52

GETTING AN SBA LOAN

You initially find out about Small Business Administration (SBA) loans by talking to people you meet at various business events, chamber of commerce meetings, and association meetings. Gloria Fields, the Regional Director of the SBA, does a good job at defining the agency's mission, charter, and loan program when you visit her office. She tells you, "The SBA was started in 1953 to help small businesses start, grow, and prosper. Included in that pledge was a loan program to make low-interest and long-term loans available to businesses that would otherwise have a hard time finding capital. In its 40 years, the SBA loan program has helped over a million small businesses get the money they need to develop products, hire employees, purchase equipment, and to make capital improvements."

You know several small business owners who were able to get SBA funding after they were rejected by other lending institutions. Gloria explains, "The agency focuses less on the business owner's collateral and more on repayment ability. Loans are distributed as either direct loans or through loan-guarantee programs administered by local banks." Initially, you were under the impression that SBA loans were simply money going straight from the government's coffers to small businesses. Gloria tells you this rarely happens. Direct loans are a small percent of the SBA loan programs and are awarded to applicants who are unable to secure a bank loan or an SBA-guaranteed loan. The SBA's most active lending arena is the guaranteed-loan program. Based on a working partnership with local banks and other lending institutions, the program guarantees small business loans issued by qualified lenders.

You learn that business owners gain significant advantages from SBA-guaranteed loans, such as longer terms and lower interest rates. At least 50 percent of traditional business loans by banks are for less than one year. The average maturity for most SBA loans is between five and seven years. Because payments are amortized over a longer period of time, they are smaller, more manageable, and help build relationships between small business owners and bankers. After reviewing your financial statement, Gloria tells you which SBA loan programs are available and how to apply.

There is no central clearinghouse of information on SBA loans. You learned that certain businesses, such as magazines, newspapers, religious bookstores, most live entertainment, nonprofit businesses, and multilevel marketing ventures are not eligible for SBA loans. You can't use an SBA loan to make speculative investments or to pay off nonbusiness-related debt. The SBA also imposes certain qualification limits on annual revenues and number of employees. You meet the basic requirements and start the application process, which involves a considerable amount of paper work. Gloria asks you to prepare a cash-flow projection showing how the loan will be paid back. Both the bank and the SBA want to see a detailed analysis of your business with cash-flow numbers and market-research data to back up your sales projections. In addition, you prepare a detailed description of your business backed up with a 5-year strategic business plan, including:

- Employee capability summary covering the qualifications of every key management and nonmanagement employee.

- Capital requirements showing planned purchases, dates, and amounts with justification rationale for each purchase.

- Your personal financial statement supported by three years of tax returns.

- Detailed financial plan and cash-flow analysis by month for the next three years.

You complete the entire application process in 60 days; it normally takes 90 to 120 days. Fortunately, there were no complications or incomplete information in your submissions package. Thirty days after you submitted your application, Gloria calls you to tell you the good news. "Your request for a $500 thousand SBA loan is approved. When would it be convenient for you to come down to sign the loan documents?" You're on your way!

Over the next several months, you use the money from the loan to develop Treasure Quest, a CD-ROM mystery with a $1 million grand prize. The program involves a linguistics professor who leaves a mystery in his will, knowing that his students will learn in their efforts to solve the mystery. Treasure Quest receives public-relations notoriety when the media touts it as a nonviolent educational family game.

Shortly after its release, Treasure Quest is chosen as Software Product of the Year. You are very pleased with the caliber of people you have been able to hire as a result of the SBA loan and you believe you can match your people against the best Silicon Valley team. Treasure Quest ranks No. 39 in *PC Data*'s April list of top-selling CD-ROMs, despite its late March release date. You are encouraged by steadily rising sales that are happening without the benefit of early exposure in computer-game magazines. By the end of your fifth year, you have accumulated a sufficient reserve of capital to easily retire the SBA loan and increase your net worth by more than $20,000:

Fourth Year Financial Summary

Beginning Year Net Worth	$385,000
Plus: Fourth Year Revenues	$275,400
Less: Business and Living Expenses	$250,900
Fourth Year Net Worth	$409,500

You have successfully completed a start-up decision-making track, but you can keep playing the game by choosing one or more of the options below.

1. If you want to compare how the results of your last five years of start-up decision-making strategies stack up against the other positive outcomes, turn to Chapter 77.

2. If you wish to find out what would have happened had you chosen the alternative path of merging with an established software company, turn to Chapter 51.

3. If you want to discover the outcomes of other choices on the track, turn to Chapter 36. Return to Chapter 19 if you want to start the track from the beginning.

4. If you would like to pursue other start-up decision-making opportunities, turn to either Chapter 2 or 3.

CHAPTER 53

BUYING A LARGER MOTEL

Noting that it is not out of the question, considering the convention-al wisdom of economies of scale, you have decided to buy a larger motel. Having sold your small motel, you can reflect on the fact that you made some money, learned a lot, and had fun doing it all at the same time. You pore through the classified ads of the newspaper, marking all possible motel-for-sale listings you can find with a red pen. Although you have decided to invest in a larger motel, you aren't sure which offers are good deals. You snap the cap back on your pen and are about to toss the newspaper into the trash when one ad head-ing catches your eye. As you read on, the ad is for a forty-unit motel on the west side of town, just off the Interstate. Is it a good buy?

A quick phone call to your real-estate agent Cheri Dengel gives you some buyer's issues to consider. Cheri tells you, "In the motel business, occupancy rate translates directly into income and your bot-tom line. The number of units in any motel you're considering are not important if you don't have the right occupancy rate. For example, a 50-unit motel with a 50-percent occupancy rate is worth the same as a 25-unit motel that operates at a 100-percent occupancy rate." Cheri concludes her remarks by asking if you would like to see the property tomorrow morning. You agree to meet her at the motel at 10 A.M.

The motel turns out to be a beautiful 40-unit building in the cen-ter of Billings' business district just off the Interstate. It's a classic brick building complete with an enclosed pool area directly across the street from a county park. Cheri tells you that the first item on your check-list should be to verify the occupancy numbers. With the owner's per-mission, you hire a CPA to audit the motel's registration records. One week later and your accountant presents you with a table that shows the average occupancy rates over the past three years:

AVERAGE OCCUPANCY RATE FOR PROPOSED MOTEL

	Year 3	Year 2	Current Year
Occupancy Rate	66%	72%	77%
Percent of Change	0	6%	5%
Increase in Tourism	0	7%	6%

The occupancy numbers are relatively easy to understand. The motel's occupancy has increased about 5 percent per year, which is consistent with the increase in tourism. The numbers are also consis-tent with the occupancy rates of the other motels in the area.

Before you buy the motel, you want to make sure the price is right. Cheri explains how to use the capitalization rate or "cap rate" to estimate the market value of commercial property. "As a general rule, the higher the cap rate the higher the price of a property. Most investors look for cap rates of 10 percent or higher to prequalify solid investment opportunities. Low cap rates are an indication that one of three things is wrong: Room rates are too low, operating expenses are too high, or the price of the motel is out of line with reality."

You estimate that the motel would generate about $60,000 a year of net operating income. The appraisal ordered by the bank put the value of the motel at $450,000, or the sales price. The loan officer believes the room rates are $12 below the market average for compa-rable motel rooms in Billings. Cheri shows you how to determine the value of the motel based upon its cap rate:

Cap Rate = Annual Net Operating Income / Sales Price
= $60,000 / $450,000
= 13%

Market Value = Annual Net Operating Income / Capitalization Rate
= $60,000 / 13%
= $461,538

After having completed the capitalization analysis, you believe that $450,000 is a fair price for the motel and purchase the property.

You take the loan officer's advice and increase room rates by $12 a room, which proves to be a very profitable decision. Your net income in the first year of operation exceeds $75,000.

Fourth Year Financial Summary

Beginning Year Net Worth	$325,600
Plus: Fourth Year Revenues	$300,000
Less: Business and Living Expenses	$250,500
Fourth Year Net Worth	$375,100

Your accountant gives you an added bonus when he informs you that you can take a 20-percent tax credit on the money spent rehabilitating the building. That's 20 percent of $50,000, or $10,000 in tax savings that you hadn't counted on in your fifth year. You also quickly discover the added benefits of running a larger motel. Many of your fixed costs remain the same even though you're running a larger unit. Only one reservations clerk is required for a small or large motel. The cost for the security patrol service is the same as it was for your smaller motel and you are able to save money on supplies by ordering larger quantities. Economies of scale and the unplanned tax deduction have a very favorable impact on your net worth in the fifth year:

Fifth Year Financial Summary

Beginning Year Net Worth	$375,100
Plus: Fifth Year Revenues	$304,700
Less: Business and Living Expenses	$274,500
Fifth Year Net Worth	$405,300

You have successfully completed a start-up decision-making track, but you can keep playing the game by choosing one or more of the options below.

1. If you want to compare how the results of your last five years of start-up decision-making strategies stack up against the other positive outcomes, turn to Chapter 77.

2. If you wish to find out what would have happened had you chosen the alternative of sticking with houses, turn to Chapter 47.

3. If you would like to pursue other start-up decision-making opportunities, turn to either Chapter 2 or 3.

CHAPTER 54

CREATING A LIMITED PARTNERSHIP TO BUY A LODGE

With the motel sale behind you, all of your attention is focused on buying a lodge. However, the specification for the lodge you want does not match the funds you cleared from the motel deal. In fact, you are $200,000 short of where you need to be. After racking your brain for days looking for financial alternatives, the idea of forming a limited partnership to buy a lodge intrigues you.

From what you have read, a limited partnership is a business owned by two or more individuals where some of the partners have limited liability. The most common reason limited partnerships are formed is to raise capital. Partner contributions may include cash, property, the performance of services, or some combination thereof. Limited partnerships can also raise capital by selling additional limited partnership interests. You know there must be at least one general partner who is personally responsible for all the partnership's liability, which is the position you want. The limited partnership you have in mind would include yourself as the general partner who manages the day-to-day operation of the lodge and a group of limited partners who would not exercise control over the general operations of the lodge. They invest capital into the partnership in return for a share of the profits (or losses) and would only be personally liable for an amount up to the extent of their investment. You list several advantages and disadvantages of limited partnerships:

Advantages	*Disadvantages*
Limited liability of limited partners	Unlimited general partner liability
General partner controls the business	Limited partners must trust general partner
Additional source of financing	Must comply with state regulations
Limited partners not taxed in most states	Set-up costs more than general partnership

Your accountant tells you that unlike a general partnership, a limited partnership agreement must be drawn up and filed with the state. For this reason, they are more complex to set up than general partnership agreements. You plan to use a fictitious name for the partnership and are therefore required to file a doing-business-as (DATA-BASEA) form with the county clerk.

To solicit interest in your limited partnership idea, you place a classified ad in the business-opportunity section of the Billings paper. With the exception of one phone call and one crank letter, your response to the ad is zero. The phone call was from an older gentleman who wanted to know what limited partnerships were, and the crank letter accused you of promoting "another investment rip-off scheme." Discouraged and wondering what you should do next, you call Ben France, a friend and owner of three McDonalds restaurants in Billings. Ben answers the phone and as you proceed to explain your dilemma, he cuts in, "You're out of breath so you got to be through right?"

Ben takes your silent response as a "yes" and proceeds with what initially sounds like the lecture you gave your teenage daughter about the sins of smoking. "My friend, you have forgotten about where you are. You are in Montana and not in the state of California. We do business here the old-fashioned way. In California, for example, they'll do business with anything that crawls. If you are not from Montana, which you are not, and you want Montanans to support your investment venture, then you are barking up the wrong tree if you think a simple ad placed in the local paper will generate the response you need. Montanans flat out won't trust you and they simply won't respond! Do you understand what I am talking about?" You are beginning to understand where Ben is coming from. Montana is an intensely proud state with a local business culture that is difficult for outsiders to crack. Subdued, you ask, "What do you recommend I do?"

"In my opinion, you've got two options. You can either try to solicit investors from outside the state or you can try to tap into Montana's business network. If you decide to go with outsiders, you'll run the risk of polarizing your lodge from any local patronization. There is money in this state but the residents want assurance they are spending it on locally owned businesses. You bypass this problem by soliciting Montana investors. Which way do you want to go?" Your response: "Obviously, I would like to pursue the second option, but you just told me an outsider can't crack into the Montana network." Ben jumps in with "I never said can't, just difficult."

"Here's what you need to do. You've got to cultivate interest in your lodge with at least one well-respected Montana businessperson. If he or she will back the project either as a limited or full partner, you stand a good chance of getting the rest of the limited partners you need." You thank Ben for his direct advice and hang up the phone. Over the next several months, you devote your full attention to cultivating Montana's business communities by attending countless chamber of commerce, Elks Club, Rotary, Kiwanis and even the Montana Cattlemen's Association meetings. In the third month, you strike pay dirt at, of all places, the 4th of July Cattlemen's Barbecue. Tim Fraser, a third-generation Montana cattle rancher from Butte, approaches you with your first real offer. He and ten other ranchers met privately and are willing to invest $500,000 in your limited partnership under one condition. The partnership agreement must include a statement which would allow the limited partners to approve any construction that could adversely affect the environment and land surrounding the location of the lodge. You quickly accept his offer and conditions.

Over the next several weeks, you have a number of conversations and a meeting with Tim Fraser and the other ranchers to develop a formal limited-partnership agreement that meets everyone's expectations. You tell them, "The lodge can be completed in six months, and if you can achieve an average occupancy rate greater than 55 percent, we'll all make money. Most states, including Montana, require limited-partnership agreements to be filed with the state. During the course of one of your meetings, you cover several important partnership-agreement issues including:

- Name, purpose, domicile, and duration of the partnership.

- Role and authority of each partner clearly defined.

- Financial contributions and obligations of each partner, identifying how much of the business each partner owns.

- Business-expense guidelines documented, showing how expenses will be processed.

- Documents the accounting books and financial records that will be maintained to run the business.

- Identifies how profits and losses will be allocated between the partners.

- Redefines salary schedules of all partners.

- Succession and buy-out options are clearly identified.

- Arbitration and the settlements of dispute procedures are defined.

- Absence and disability policies for the partners are defined.

With the partnership agreement in place, you proceed with the construction of the lodge, which takes six months to complete. Fortunately, you're able to open the doors just before the start of the summer season. By the end of your fourth year, the operation of the lodge is in full swing. You and your limited partners enjoy double-digit profits, which translate into a nice increase in your net worth.

Fourth Year Financial Summary

Beginning Year Net Worth	$325,600
Plus: Fourth Year Revenues	$340,000
Less: Business and Living Expenses	$280,500
Fourth Year Net Worth	$385,100

Thanks to a well-coordinated advertising and public-relations program, your occupancy rate jumps to 78 percent in the fourth year, well above your 55 percent break-even point. Your partners provide you with an added bonus when they agree to distribute 10 thousand lodge brochures at the National Stock Show in Denver. It's the biggest stock show in the world and the response to the brochure exceeds your wildest expectations. Summer and fall bookings remain at 100 percent, which further propagates the growth in your net worth:

Fifth Year Financial Summary

Beginning Year Net Worth	$385,100
Plus: Fifth Year Revenues	$440,000
Less: Business and Living Expenses	$424,000
Fifth Year Net Worth	$401,100

You have successfully completed a start-up decision-making track, but you can keep playing the game by choosing one or more of the options that follow.

1. If you want to compare how the results of your last five years of start-up decision-making strategies stack up against the other positive outcomes, turn to Chapter 77.

2. If you wish to find out what would have happened had you chosen the alternative of buying a larger motel, turn to Chapter 52.

3. If you want to discover the outcomes of other choices on the track, turn to Chapters 35 or 36. Return to Chapter 9 if you want to start the track from the beginning.

4. If you would like to pursue other start-up decision-making opportunities, turn to either Chapter 2 or 3.

CHAPTER 55

OFFERING TRADITIONAL

MARKETING CONSULTING

SERVICES

It has long been an axiom of American business that when sales or profits decline, the first order of business is to go back to the marketing basics. You've had several market-strategy meetings with your partners in an attempt to bolster Computech's sagging consulting sales. So far, you have not encountered any hint of disgruntlement when you proposed concentrating on traditional marketing-consulting services. The program you have in mind was carefully analyzed to make sure it did not adversely impact the short-term or long-term goals and objectives of Computech's objective to specialize in marketing. Everybody understands how the program would improve profitability.

Kathy Simon is particularly excited about the possibility of concentrating on the traditional marketing-service side of the consulting business. You have asked Kathy to recommend a specific set of marketing services to offer. Two weeks later, Kathy walks into your office, hands you a folder, and proceeds to explain her thoughts on the program. "Many new businesses fail because owners neglect to obtain sufficient information to accurately analyze their market. Having good hunches about what will sell is a valuable entrepreneurial quality. However, before you risk personal resources on a new venture, you need to get an objective picture of the prospective market."

"We can help our clients most by offering consulting services in the traditional marketing areas. For example, market analysis is the orderly, objective process of gathering and evaluating information about potential customers. We'll show our clients how to determine who their customers are, where they come from, and how to appeal to their needs. Market analysis also evaluates the factors that will influence the size and profitability of a market to help them prepare accurate sales forecasts. Market analysis then serves as the foundation for their strategic business plans, which is particularly important to our clients who are looking for outside investors."

You know this is important because investors require solid marketing information before they will consider backing a new venture. Whether small businesses need outside investors or not, the market analysis will help them understand customer needs and wants. It therefore becomes an ongoing process they can use to adjust to changes in the marketplace. Kathy tells you, "In my opinion, market-analysis consulting should be an easy sell." You agree!

"The next traditional consulting service we should offer is market research, the process used to gather information needed to complete the market analysis. Our research-consulting effort should focus on understanding customer needs and wants. It may involve asking prospective customers questions, researching existing customer data, utilizing questionnaire surveys, and collecting and interpreting customer data. Research findings should identify potential new customers and answer important marketing questions for our clients, such as what do your customers like and dislike? How can their needs be satisfied?" Kathy summarizes the four steps that are required to complete a market-research consulting assignment:

1. *Target Market Identification* is the research process by which we define the target market for our clients. Who are their primary customers?

2. *Market Information* involves the research processes employed to find the marketing information that is already available to answer target market questions.

3. *Research Programs* are used to obtain additional marketing information that is not readily available to complete the market analysis.

4. *Data Analysis* is where we analyze the information collected from all sources and formulate our conclusions in a market-strategy plan.

She tells you, "The last steps in the research process are the most critical. We should focus on the information our clients must have to make critical marketing decisions and to answer that most basic of all questions: Is there a viable target market for their products and services?"

You thank Kathy for her excellent job pulling together all of the salient components of a traditional marketing program. You spend the next several months working with the general partners to make sure everyone is on the same page relative to traditional marketing consulting. When you announce the availability of traditional marketing consulting to your client base, everybody seems to just yawn! As you approach the end of your fourth year, the demand for traditional marketing consulting is minimal. The slow start is reflected in the minimum gain you realize in your financial statement:

Fourth Year Financial Summary

Beginning Year Net Worth	$315,000
Plus: Fourth Year Revenues	$224,000
Less: Business and Living Expenses	$192,000
Fourth Year Net Worth	$347,400

As you enter into the new year, traditional marketing consulting begins to gather some momentum. However, you soon realize that every one of your competitors offers traditional marketing programs. To remain competitive, you reduce your fees to attract more clients, which helps improve your financial performance in the fifth year.

Fifth Year Financial Summary

Beginning Year Net Worth	$347,400
Plus: Fifth Year Revenues	$238,000
Less: Business and Living Expenses	$197,000
Fifth Year Net Worth	$388,400

You have successfully completed a start-up decision-making track, but you can keep playing the game by choosing one or more of the options that follow.

1. If you want to compare how the results of your last five years of start-up decision-making strategies stack up against the other positive outcomes, turn to Chapter 77.

2. If you wish to find out what would have happened had you chosen the alternative of offering results-based services, turn to Chapter 56.

3. If you want to discover the outcomes of other choices on the track, turn to Chapter 40. Return to Chapter 10 if you want to start the track from the beginning.

4. If you would like to pursue other start-up decision-making opportunities, turn to either Chapter 2 or 3.

CHAPTER 56

OFFERING RESULTS-BASED

SERVICES

In a world of accelerating change and intense competition, tangible results are the only thing that counts. You commit to specializing in results-based services that when implemented, will allow your clients to introduce new services that are designed to achieve specific results, which can be quantifiably measured. You have always considered yourself an action-oriented entrepreneur, able to run circles around your competitors, and since your sense of expediency has always helped, you feel especially well-qualified to specialize in programs that are based on results.

As you probe deeper into results-based services, you contact Tom Hopkins, an old friend at the Fielding Institute who tells you why the old assumptions about customer service and customer behavior no longer hold true. He sends you *Increasing Market Share Using Results-Based Services* by Valarie Henning and Sal Willow, two of his colleagues at the Institute. You read a few pages to whet your appetite. Customer demand has become astoundingly sensitive to the quality of services they receive, with price playing a distant second role. According to the article, the company who can predict customer-service expectations and responds immediately will quickly control the most profitable segments of the service industry. The rest of the competitors will get whatever is left over.

After reading the full Henning and Willow paper, you are more convinced than ever that you made the right decision to specialize in results-based service programs. You contact Valarie Henning and ask if she would be willing to introduce the subject to your consulting team. Better they hear it from an independent outsider, an expert in the field, than from you first. She agrees to meet with your team next week to discuss what she has learned about results-based services. In the first of two sessions, Valarie emphasized that developing and implementing service programs with predictable results is not easy. She explains why the program demands the complete focus of senior management: "Improving responsiveness depends on a complete shift of emphasis from price to results. Most organizations traditionally focus on financial measurement to justify service costs and rely on questionnaires to measure overall customer satisfaction. Anticipated performance results are rarely included in the measurements. For results-based services to work, quantifiable measurements must become the predominant element in a company's culture."

Valarie spends her second session showing your team several examples to illustrate how results-based services work. "Results-based service companies will install elaborate customer feedback mechanisms such as repetitive surveys to qualify the results they are achieving from their service offerings. If the responses fit within certain pre-established guidelines (e.g., 98+ satisfaction rating), no action is taken. However, if the results from the survey fall below an acceptable level, immediate action is taken to reconcile the situation." You thank Valarie for her excellent explanation of what results-based services is all about.

Despite the difficulties involved in understanding the complexities of results-based services, your consulting team respects your enthusiasm for introducing the program into Computech's catalog of offerings. They pledge their full support in learning all they can about results-based services. During the ensuing months, you become frustrated at what appears to be the inordinate amount of time it takes to get your staff ready to offer results-based services to your clients.

However, by the end of the year, everybody is ready to launch the program. It could not have happened at a better time. Consulting dollars in most companies dry up at the end of the year, but the financial faucet turns back on after New Year's Day. Anxious to see how receptive your clients are to results-based services, you mount a public-relations campaign that targets your top-20 clients. Your campaign is an instant success, and exceeds even your most optimistic of expectations. Every one of your major clients said they were intrigued by the concept of results-based services, which causes some immediate scheduling problems as you attempt to cover the surge in consulting assignments. When you review your financial situation, it looks like this will be a very good year.

Fourth Year Financial Summary

Beginning Year Net Worth	$325,000
Plus: Fourth Year Revenues	$224,000
Less: Business and Living Expenses	$192,000
Fourth Year Net Worth	$357,400

Several of your clients approach you and ask if your company would be interested in trading consulting services for equity in their companies. When you asked what form the equity would take, they tell you they would be willing to trade common stock shares for consulting services. The idea intrigues you. However, you are also considering devoting your entire attention to developing sophisticated measuring techniques to augment your highly sucessful results-based service program.

1. If you believe that exchanging consulting services for equity is the best strategy to take, turn to Chapter 71.

2. If you believe that developing measurement techniques is the best strategy to take, turn to Chapter 72.

CHAPTER 57

FOCUSING ON PERSONAL

PRODUCTIVITY IMPROVEMENTS

You decide to focus on enhancing your own productivity as the best way to set an example for others in the organization. Over the weekend, you read everything you can get your hands on about productivity starting with Hamel and Prahalad's *The Competitive Future*, Champy's *Reengineering Management*, John Naisbitt's *Global Paradox*, and numerous other books. However, one question sticks with you as you lie in bed that night waiting for sleep: "What's the most important thing I can do as the senior partner of Computech?" As you ponder the question, you recall a book you read years ago by Ken Schatz called *Managing by Influence*. The author used the simple analogy of a lever to illustrate his main point. The longer the handle, the more weight you can move. As Archimedes put it, "Give me a long enough lever and a place to stand, and I can move the world." This line of thinking raises yet another question: "What can you do to achieve the greatest impact on the most people inside and outside Computech?" Unable to sleep Sunday night, you go into your study and place a blank sheet of paper in the middle of your desk. On it you begin capturing your basic strengths and weaknesses as well as options for improving your strengths and eliminating your weaknesses.

Over the next few weeks, while keeping a close eye on your consulting assignments and financial performance, you continue considering your talents and capabilities. You are very project-oriented, you like developing new ideas, new thrusts, and new directions more than you enjoy implementing, executing, and developing concrete systems that crank out tangible results. In other words, you are a highly conceptual person, though you have also demonstrated a knack for orchestrating your ideas and concepts in a way that enables more practical, execution-oriented people to carry them out.

Your colleagues over the years have often characterized you as more of a leader than a manager, the sort of person who designs levers others can pull, though one of your clients, Bill Faragut, sought your services because he thought he saw in you what he described as "a unique combination of management and leadership skills." As he put it, "I liked the way you led my company's productivity retreat. You know how to develop managers." You have also gained a reputation for formulating sound strategies and building strong cultures, another plus in Faragut's mind. Still, most of your experience in that regard stems from consulting projects, not from hands-on involvement in a company.

In the past you have been able to step back from a complex business problem and grasp its essence. That ability underscores your basic intuitive nature. You thrive on the challenge of change, although you tend to let external conditions prompt your actions more than you let your own internal vision drive them. Those traits made you an effective consultant, but can you translate those into positive attributes at Computech?

This assessment proves you can look at yourself objectively. You think you know yourself and can stay in touch with who you are, with sufficient humility to examine your strengths and your weaknesses dispassionately. Over the years, this trait has helped you capitalize on your strengths and minimize the adverse effect of your weaknesses by associating with people who possess complementary capabilities.

With these thoughts in mind, you begin identifying the alternative tracks you might pursue at Computech to maximize your own productivity. Eventually, you crystallize your thinking around three basic options: (1) create a strong overall vision and strategic theme for Computech that can guide the firm toward prosperous futures; (2) develop strong strategies and cultures in each partner or (3) train each partner to think strategically. Which option will most powerfully leverage your own talents and capabilities? Which will be most consistent with the resources available within Computech? Which will provide the greatest value to Computech's clients? In short, which option will maximize my own productivity? Your chart of options is based on an analysis of your own strengths and weaknesses:

- Create a compelling overall vision and strategic theme for Computech that can guide the company to future prosperity.

- Provide integrity and continuity by combining functions and activities where appropriate.

- Develop strong strategies and cultures.

- Allow each partner to grow at his or her own pace to maximize strengths and capabilities.

- Train each of the partners to think strategically and give them the opportunity to become intimately involved with the development and training of Computech's client base.

As you stare at the chart, you keep coming back to the basic issue of leverage. Which options will most effectively deploy your talents and capabilities and, thereby, maximize your contributions to Computech? Your ultimate choice must take into account the needs of your partners, the long-range goals of the whole company, and the satisfaction of Computech's clients. Of course, it must also account for your own personal needs and goals, which include both your success as a leader and the financial rewards that success will garner. Content that you have laid the groundwork for a wise decision, you look forward to a relaxing weekend.

When you awake Monday morning, however, you find that the decision has not made itself, as you had hoped it would. Now, you simply must pick a course of action. What will you do? Your indecision about what to do causes some confusion within the ranks of Computech. Your projected personal financial statement for your fourth start-up year is as flat as Computech's sales.

Fourth Year Financial Summary

Beginning Year Net Worth	$210,000
Plus: Fourth Year Revenues	$150,000
Less: Business and Living Expenses	$150,000
Fourth Year Net Worth	$210,000

As you celebrate the start of your fifth start-up year, you continue to push several productivity programs that you are convinced will help Computech grow in the ensuing months. Nobody takes your program seriously and although they politely attend all of your meetings and seminars on the subject, you learn to recognize they are just paying you "lip service." Although Computech's financial performance in the fifth year was better than its fourth year, profits are up and you realize only a nice gain on your net worth position.

Fifth Year Financial Summary

Beginning Year Net Worth	$210,000
Plus: Fifth Year Revenues	$150,000
Less: Business and Living Expenses	$70,000
Fifth Year Net Worth	$290,000

You have successfully completed a start-up decision-making track, but you can keep playing the game by choosing one or more of the options that follow.

1. If you want to compare how the results of your last five years of start-up decision-making strategies stack up against the other positive outcomes, turn to Chapter 77.

2. If you wish to find out what would have happened had you chosen the alternative of developing new training approaches, turn to Chapter 58.

3. If you want to discover the outcomes of other choices on the track, turn to Chapter 39. Return to Chapter 10 if you want to start the track from the beginning.

4. If you would like to pursue other start-up decision-making opportunities, turn to either Chapter 2 or 3.

CHAPTER 58

DEVELOPING A NEW APPROACH
TO TRAINING PEOPLE

Given your own major strength, your strategic-thinking ability, you decide to develop a new training approach, which will represent the most valuable self-deployment and personal-productivity track you can pursue in your tenure as Computech's senior partner. Strategic training and development will be the foundation of your program. You institute two vital elements: first, a revised business-planning process and, second, a rigorous schedule of strategy sessions, plan reviews, and one-on-one interviews aimed at strengthening the strategic logic of your clients. You will also show them how to constantly think of the fundamental strategic and economic variables that are active in their businesses. You expect the business-planning process to bring more rigorous disciplined thinking as well as more creativity to bear on management decision making.

You launch your new business-planning training session with a set of guidelines that asks thought-provoking questions designed to guide the thinking of your clients as they develop business plans, a prerequisite to the session. You also conduct intense strategy sessions to formally kick off the business-planning process and help your clients stretch their strategic-thinking capabilities earlier in the process.

In each initial strategy session, you and your clients play The Strategy Game, an "interactive business simulation designed to test and improve strategic decision making." This simulation loosens up the group and prepares them for the real thing. The experience turns out even better than you hoped as the 20 executives and managers in one of your first sessions quickly expand their "bandwidth" to more effectively weigh alternatives and implications when making decisions. While the game requires decision making in a binary mode (i.e., a player picks one of only two choices at any given decision point), you make it clear to everyone that in a real-life situation, a full range of choices will crop up every day. You encourage your clients to expand and strengthen their decision making so that they can avoid making inappropriate, premature, incomplete, or half-baked decisions, thereby substantially improving productivity in the long run.

As you watch the level of strategic thinking rise even within Computech, you're pleased that your training and development efforts seem to be taking hold among your partners. However, you also begin to see a deterioration in operation efficiencies and effectiveness as some of your clients become overly preoccupied with strategic thinking and planning at the expense of operation considerations. Though you had anticipated this possibility when you launched your strategic-thinking program, you didn't recognize the full extent of the problem until the end of your fourth year, when revenues from the training session barely covered expenses. As a result, you realize only a modest improvement in your net worth.

Fourth Year Financial Summary

Beginning Year Net Worth	$310,000
Plus: Third Year Revenues	$175,000
Less: Business and Living Expenses	$170,000
Fourth Year Net Worth	$315,000

Given these disappointing results, you try shifting your emphasis to operational issues to boost client acceptance of the program, hoping that your earlier attention to strategic issues has taken hold and will remain strong. Unfortunately, several of your clients see the operational shift as pressure for short-term revenue gains, and they begin questioning your earlier emphasis on strategic thinking. Perhaps, they tell you, we wasted too much time in your strategic-training sessions. You fight this perception for several months while at the same time attempting to shore up operational effectiveness and results, but you make little headway convincing Computech's partners that strategic-training sessions will make the primary difference in the firm's future revenue growth.

By the end of your fifth year as Computech's senior partner, your performance is given a mixed review by the general partners. Although sales reach $14 million, profits remain flat. In light of your performance, you request a formal evaluation from Computech's partners to determine where your new approach to training stands in the organization.

To get a preliminary reading, you conduct an interview with each partner to find out where they stand. Sean Harrison says, "Getting sidetracked away from a focus on operations has simply convinced me that too much strategic thinking creates more problems than it solves." Mildred Hally suggests, "You need to provide more structure for the planning, integrating it with operations so that strategic thinking and positioning don't stand alone, so that the overall structure fits into a complete business process." Al Roberts echoes Mildred's concerns when he adds that "the business-planning process you instituted works, but it needs to be modified to include operations, financial, and human-resource planning as well. We simply can't take our eyes off operations." David Ziggler disagrees, saying, "I think you shifted away from your emphasis on strategic thinking too soon. You should stick to your guns because the program is working." Janice Harrison sides with Ziggler, offering, "I think the system of business planning and strategy sessions was brilliant. It changed my whole way of thinking about what kinds of training programs we should be offering to get a firmer hold on how we create value for our clients. Don't get bogged down in operation minutia. That's what got us in hot water in the first place." Mike Ferrante offers yet another view when he says, "The only concern I have right now stems from the reality that our clients feel confused. They're getting mixed signals about strategic thinking and operation effectiveness, and that's paralyzing them." Finally, Lisa McDonald summarizes her view of the situation: "You've made a definite impact on strategic-thinking training, but now we need to blend strategic and operation training to improve Computech's bottom line and give our clients a sense of consistency."

With this input from your partners, you look forward to developing your next wave of new training approaches at Computech. Most of your partners believe your strategic-training program will be a success. It just needs more time to translate into the bottom line, which is appropriate when you review the limited growth you have experienced in your financial statement.

Fifth Year Financial Summary

Beginning Year Net Worth	$315,000
Plus: Fifth Year Revenues	$233,000
Less: Business and Living Expenses	$165,800
Fifth Year Net Worth	$382,200

You have successfully completed a start-up decision-making track, but you can keep playing the game by choosing one or more of the options that follow.

1. If you want to compare how the results of your last five years of start-up decision-making strategies stack up against the other positive outcomes, turn to Chapter 77.

2. If you wish to find out what would have happened had you chosen the alternative of financing marketing campaigns for equity, turn to Chapter 71.

3. If you want to discover the outcomes of other choices on the track, turn to Chapters 39 or 40. Return to Chapter 10 if you want to start the track from the beginning.

4. If you would like to pursue other start-up decision-making opportunities, turn to either Chapter 2 or 3.

CHAPTER 59

JOINT-VENTURING ON A NEW

LODGE

The old man and godfather of business management sure knew what he was talking about! Back in your college days, Peter Drucker was your idol and he still is today. It seemed like every business management book you were required to read was either written or endorsed by Drucker. You remember a passage in one of his books that talked about joint-venturing. He wrote, "In today's environment, joint-venturing is a strategic business tool that you must be able to use effectively if you want to become a successful entrepreneur. You should not be misled by the analogy, often drawn, between strategic partnerships and marriages. Unlike marriage, today's strategic partnerships are not based on the notion of mutual attraction. They are rooted in cold necessity. No entrepreneur makes a strategic alliance with another unless they have to in order to achieve their strategic objectives more effectively, at a lower cost or with less risk than if they acted alone. The partnership therefore becomes a mechanism by which they can achieve a competitive advantage. They use it as a weapon in the continuous battle for the market they want to control." Drucker wrote that statement 25 years ago and in your opinion, he's more "right-on" today than he was then.

You have canvassed every available lodge in Montana and have come to the stark conclusion that if they are for sale, it's because they are about to fall down or they are situated in some mosquito-infested meadow that only the greenest of tourists will visit once, with no chance of a repeat visit. However, a number of outstanding land parcels are available at decent prices that would be perfect locations for new lodges. The local Montana bankers appear to be almost over-anxious to lend you the money for a new lodge, and why not? They stand to gain on any venture that brings tourists and new employees into their respective communities.

However, the Trojan Horse needs to be fed while it's growing up. It takes time to develop and build a new lodge. You talk to several local contractors and learn it's a six-to-nine month project to build a lodge, barring unforeseen weather events. You ask one of the contractors, what's an unforeseen weather event? "Well, you see in Montana, when you build anything at the 8,000 foot level where you want your lodge, winter can come early and it can stay late. I've seen it snow in August, freeze the lakes until May, and dump a wet snow on you in June just for spite. Now, that's the exception but bad Montana weather can, and in all probability, will delay any construction project." As Tony rocks back on his cowboy boots and lets loose with a wad of chewing tobacco, you carefully contemplate what he has just told you. The new lodge that you are contemplating building would be a "money maker" based on your construction estimates and your own financial projections:

Annual Financial Projection From New Lodge

Construction Cost for New Lodge	$539,000
Plus: Cost of Land	$160,000
Total Acquisition Cost	$704,000
Estimated Net Sales	$405,000
Less: Operating Costs	$324,000
Total Gross Profit	$81,000

Your best-case scenario on a new lodge would be six months construction time before it would be ready to produce any revenue. Based upon what you have learned, your cash requirements would be:

CASH REQUIREMENTS DURING 6-MONTH CONSTRUCTION PERIOD

	Month 1	Month 2	Month 3	Month 4	Month 5	Month 6
Purchase of Land	$160,000	0	0	0	0	0
Construction Costs	$100,000	$75,000	$80,000	$85,000	$105,000	$94,000
Living Expenses	$35,000	$35,000	$35,000	$35,000	$35,000	$35,000
Cash Required	$295,000	$110,000	$115,000	$120,000	$140,000	$129,000

To put everything into perspective, you review your financial statement and quickly realize you do not have a sufficient net worth to fund the construction of your lodge.

Fourth Year Financial Summary

Beginning Year Net Worth	$254,300
Plus: Fourth Year Revenues	$75,000
Less: Business and Living Expenses	$42,000
Fourth Year Net Worth	$287,300

You're an entrepreneur and you don't mind taking reasonable risks. If the lodge project could be completed in six months, and with a lot of luck, instantly draw a 75-percent occupancy rate, you could pull this project off on your own. However, given one small calculation error or misjudgment, and you could go out of business before you even got started. The analysis confirms your original conviction that you need partners to assure the total success of this project. Florence Harding, one of the lodge owners whom you had talked to about buying her "fixer upper" lodge, might be interested in a partnership. You heard she had received an offer from a major international corporation that was interested in buying her lodge as a company retreat. She has over twenty years of lodge-management experience and hopefully some money from the sale of her lodge that would make her a preferred joint-venture partner. You pick up the phone and call Florence.

Florence tells you she sold her lodge and is looking for something that's less strenuous to do over the next five to ten years, when she plans on retiring. When you ask her if she would be interested in joint-venturing a lodge with you, you hear nothing but silence on the other end of the phone. "Florence, are you still there?" you ask. "I'm here but I'm thinking. It depends on what you had in mind." You tell Florence about your idea of forming a general partnership where the lodge would be owned by two or more individuals. Like sole proprietorships, general partnerships are easy to form and are relatively free from government regulations. Most states, including Montana, do not require general partnerships to file formal partnership agreements, although it is recommended you file one. You tell Florence that general partnerships are formed for a number of reasons including the following:

- Allows partners to pool capital to start or buy a business, which may have been beyond the financial reach of the individual partners.

- Pools the partners' labor to share the workload and management of the business.

- Partnerships add strength to the business by combining individual skills that are strategic to the growth of the business.

Over the next several weeks, you have a number of conversations and meetings with Florence to further discuss your idea and her interest in forming a general partnership. Florence agrees to form a general partnership with you and a month later, the two of you reach an agreement on the elements of your partnership agreement, which include:

- Name, purpose, domicile, and duration of the partnership.

- Role and authority of each partner clearly defined.

- Financial contributions and obligations of each partner defined.

- Business-expense guidelines documented, showing how expenses will be processed.

- Identifies how much of the business each partner owns.

- Documents what accounting books and financial records will be maintained to run the business.

- Identifies how profits and losses will be allocated between the partners.

- Salary schedules of all partners are predefined.

- Succession and buy-out options are clearly identified.

- Arbitration and the settlement of disputes procedures are defined.

- Absence and disability policies for the partners are defined.

You realize that like sole proprietorships, each partner is personally liable for all business debts. If a partner incurs a debt on behalf of the partnership, all the partners are responsible. Knowing this, you believe Florence is a partner that you can trust. It takes six months to complete the construction of the new lodge. During that time, you and Florence agree to add two additional partners to bolster your working capital and to add levels of expertise you need to run the lodge. One of the partners is a CPA with a strong accounting background in the recreational industry. The other partner is a public relations expert, a credential that you believe will nicely supplement the lodge's advertising campaign.

The lodge opens just before the start of the summer season. Thanks to a well-coordinated advertising and public-relations program, your occupancy rate jumps to 78 percent, well above your 60 percent break-even point. By the end of your fifth year, the operation of your Montana lodge is in full swing and you realize a nice profit when you review your financial statement.

Fifth Year Financial Summary

Beginning Year Net Worth	$287,300
Plus: Fifth Year Revenues	$560,000
Less: Business and Living Expenses	$450,400
Fifth Year Net Worth	$396,900

You have successfully completed a start-up decision-making track, but you can keep playing the game by choosing one or more of the options that follow.

1. If you want to compare how the results of your last five years of start-up decision-making strategies stack up against the other positive outcomes, turn to Chapter 77.

2. If you wish to find out what would have happened had you chosen the alternative of financing marketing campaigns for equity, turn to Chapter 71.

3. If you want to discover the outcomes of other choices on the track, turn to Chapters 39 or 40. Return to Chapter 10 if you want to start the track from the beginning.

4. If you would like to pursue other start-up decision-making opportunities, turn to either Chapter 2 or 3.

CHAPTER 60

RAISING MORE MONEY

Up to this point, you have been working for the Timber Wolf Lodge, a five-star resort complex in northwestern Montana. However, your ultimate objective hasn't changed. You want to acquire and run your own lodge as soon as it's financially feasible. Fortunately, the opportunity to work for the Timber Wolf Lodge has provided you with some valuable insights on what it takes financially to run a successful lodge. You are well aware of the fact that if you are to succeed in this business, it is essential that you start off with adequate financing.

You review your financial plan with your accountant, Mike Esposito. Mike's guidance in the planning stages has been extremely helpful and he encourages you to answer several key questions in your plan:

1. How will you find the capital needed to launch your lodge venture?

2. Does your financial budget cover cash flow, profit, and income-statement projections for 3 to 5 years?

3. What is your break-even point and when will it occur?

As you prepare your financial plan, you know the amount of capital you need will depend upon the size and location of the lodge you buy or build. Personal living expenses must be taken into account until the lodge generates enough revenue to support you, which you

estimate will take about 6 months. You can cover living expenses with
personal savings and hope you'll have enough left over for start-up
costs. Just to be sure, you compile a list of anticipated start-up costs:

- Lease deposits
- Equipment and fixtures
- Inventory and materials
- Utility deposits
- Advertising and promotion expenses
- Remodeling and repairs
- Office supplies
- Insurance premiums
- Licenses and permits
- State, local, and federal taxes

Mike tells you to keep some capital in reserve for unexpected
contingencies and the daily operation of the lodge, which he calls
working capital. He explains, "Working capital is the financial fuel
that stokes the furnaces of your business. It's the capital that keeps
your business running. Employees must be paid and suppliers may
demand cash for your purchases. If you pay suppliers on delivery, then
you'll need more working capital. As a rule of thumb, working capital
should be equal to six months of anticipated sales." You prepare a
three-year cash flow projection to make sure you have sufficient
working capital.

SIX-MONTH CASH-FLOW PROJECTION

	Month 1	Month 2	Month 3	Month 4	Month 5	Month 6
Beginning Cash Balance	97,500	82,000	67,800	54,900	38,100	22,600
Plus: Net Lodge Sales	97,500	104,000	110,500	91,000	97,500	104,000
Less: Operating Expenses	78,000	83,200	88,400	72,800	78,000	83,200
Less: Living Expenses	35,000	35,000	35,000	35,000	35,000	35,000
Total Available Cash	82,000	67,800	54,900	38,100	22,600	8,400

Based on your cash-flow projection, you'll almost be out of
money by the sixth month. You ask Mike for his advice on steps you
can take to minimize your cash requirements. "There are several fun-

damental cash-flow rules you can apply to your business. First, when-ever possible, ask your customers to pay you in advance for reserva-tions. Ask your vendors to allow you to pay them as late as possible. Vendors want to grow and may be willing to extend liberal payment terms to your lodge. The premise is that every dollar collected in the morning that isn't needed for expenses until tonight is yours to use all day. The challenge is to determine when payments are due and make sure you have the cash to meet them."

What about bank loans? Mike tells you, "The two biggest mis-takes you don't want to make when applying for a loan are not being adequately prepared and not shopping around for the right bank. Banks focus heavily on cash-flow lending rather than straight asset-based lending because they want to know where you will get the cash to pay them back. Be prepared to show them detailed cash-flow state-ments and financial projections covering the next 3 years. You'll also need to present detailed marketing strategies that lend credence to your sales projections. Here are some questions you must be prepared to answer in detail from your banker or any potential investor:"

1. "How much money do you want?" The days of answering with "How much will you lend me?" are gone. Be as exact as possible and don't forget to add a little extra for contingencies.

2. "What are you going to do with the money we loan you?" There are only three things to do with a loan. You can buy new assets, pay off old debts, or pay for operating expenses. Never say you're just going to use the money for working capital.

3. "Why is this loan good for your lodge?" You may regard all banks as heartless money machines but they want to know how their financial support will help your business. Be pre-pared to discuss in detail what their money will do for your lodge.

4. "Why don't you have enough of your own money to cover your financial needs?" Bankers will attempt to find out if an internal management problem is to blame for your financial need. Have a well-thought-out answer to this question.

5. "When will you pay our loan back?" This is where your cash-flow projections will help you formulate a repayment time frame.

6. "How will you repay the loan?" This isn't the time to be vague. Use your financial projections and business plan to convince the banker of the long-term profitability of your business and your ability to repay the loan.

You thank Mike for his valuable input and admit to him that you were not aware of how involved the loan-application process is for a small business. You have a week of vacation time coming and wisely decide to take time off to prepare cash-flow and financial projections that Mike suggested. To make sure you have the best chance of getting the money you need, you schedule back-to-back meetings with the First National Bank of Montana and the Small Business Administration (SBA) in Bozeman. Three days later, you complete your cash-flow statement and a three-year financial projection. All of your numbers are based on a lodge you are contemplating buying for $750,000 with a 20-percent down payment.

The next morning, you walk into First National Bank for your 9 A.M. meeting with Harold Smith, the bank's loan officer. You explain to Harold that you want to purchase a lodge for $750,000 and need a loan of $600,000 to finance the transaction. After what seems to be a long silence, Harold tells you what you don't want to hear.

"Unless you are an established business person with a good credit rating and a sizable bank account, we may not be able to lend you money to buy your lodge. We typically expect you to have at least 30 percent of the down payment you need, and quite honestly, are more willing to supply financing after your business is established. We look for borrowers with good credit ratings, experience in the business they propose to enter, and business plans that demonstrate an ability to repay the loans. Interest rates and repayment schedules will vary from bank to bank. Although you have a good credit rating and can demonstrate some experience at running the Timber Wolf Lodge, you don't have the money to make a 30-percent down payment. If you pull the money you need out of your projected cash flow, you won't have sufficient working capital to keep the lodge running. We might be able to offer you a credit line six months after you get started." You think to yourself; "By that time it will be too late. I need the money now." As politely as you can, you thank Harold for his time, shake his clammy hand, and quickly exit his office.

Perhaps your afternoon meeting with Gloria Fields, the Regional Administrator for the Small Business Administration in Bozeman, will prove to be more fruitful. It's not, when you learn that direct loans are only a small percent of the SBA's loan programs. You hear that direct loans are given to applicants unable to secure a bank loan or an SBA-guaranteed loan. The SBA's most active lending arena is the Guaranteed Loan Program. Based on a working partnership with local banks and other lending institutions, the program guarantees small business loans issued by qualified lenders.

Gloria tells you, "Business owners gain significant advantages from SBA-guaranteed loans, such as longer terms. At least 50 percent of traditional business loans by banks are for less than one year. The average maturity for most working capital SBA loans is between five and seven years. Because payments are amortized over a longer period of time, they are smaller and more manageable. Another advantage is that applying for an SBA-guaranteed loan helps build the relationship between bankers and business owners."

You also learn that the entire process can take as little as 60 days, depending on the bank's backlog and your own preparation. Any complications or incomplete information takes additional time. Gloria tells you, "It's not easy to get financing through the SBA. In summary, the SBA exists solely to support and make loans to small businesses. Like banks, the SBA may limit the loan amount to 50 percent of the capital needed. In some cases, we will consider ventures with less capitalization if we are convinced of the favorable prospects of your business. The 50-percent requirement won't fit your immediate needs. As I understand your request, you were planning on putting 20 percent, or $150,000, down to secure a loan for $600,000. Unfortunately, that is outside of SBA's guidelines. We would need at least 50 percent down before we could do business with you. I'm sorry we were not able to help."

In the end, you realize there is no way your can qualify for the funds to acquire a lodge and have sufficient working capital to carry the venture for a safe period of time. You decide to continue working for the Timber Wolf Lodge. It's not what you wanted but at least you are working for someone else, doing what you ultimately want to do, and increasing your net worth at a modest rate.

Fourth Year Financial Summary

Beginning Year Net Worth	$254,300
Plus: Fourth Year Revenues	$90,000
Less: Business and Living Expenses	$65,000
Fourth Year Net Worth	$279,300

Looking back on where you have been, would you alter your decisions in order to create a different future for yourself?

1. If you would like to change your last strategic decision, return to Chapter 41.

2. If you would like to select another business venture to start-up, return to Chapter 2.

3. If you would like to conduct more analysis before you start-up another business, turn to Chapter 3.

If you're still feeling the sting of defeat and believe you could have made your last strategic choice work in real life, you may be right. After all, this is just a game. However, if you return to your last strategic decision and select the other alternative (Chapter 59), you will learn why the authors consider it a better choice.

CHAPTER 61

LOOKING FOR LODGES

IN THE EVENING

While you acknowledge that looking for a lodge in the evening will take much longer to find what you are looking for, you conclude that keeping your Cole & Weber job outweighs the downside. After all, you tell yourself, this will allow you to more fully utilize your time while you're still making a living. As the year unfolds, you find yourself spending a great deal of time in the local library scanning the classified sections of various Montana newspapers. You soon discover that very few lodges that are for sale appear in newspaper ads.

As Gil Amos, a real-estate agent in Helena, tells you, "Most lodges are sold by word-of-mouth in discretionary dealings. Lodge owners don't want to openly publicize the fact that they are selling their lodges. It's potentially bad for business. If guests see "For Sale" signs in the front lobby, they might suspect that something is wrong. The last thing owners want is a drop in their occupancy rates when they're trying to sell their lodge, for obvious reasons. It affects the asking price of the lodge." You ask Gil to contact you if a lodge in his area comes on the market and tell him to leave a message on your answering machine. You would prefer not to get personal calls at Cole & Weber since Mr. Weber frowns on the practice.

You revamp your search strategy and spend the next several months contacting real-estate agents throughout the state expressing your interest in buying a lodge. On several occasions, you receive messages from agents on your answering machine informing you about available lodges. When you play phone-tag to finally connect to the agent, you're told the lodge was either sold or taken off the market. Weekend trips halfway across the state to view lodges that are for sale become a slow arduous process. Montana is a big state, and you can easily spend a half-day traveling to a lodge. By the time you talk to the listing agent, view the property, collect important tourist facts from the local town, and drive back to Billings, a full day has been shot!

One agent tells you, "The best way to decide on a lodge is to find one you like that is not for sale and make an unsolicited offer. It may take a long time to get the property you want but that's the way it's done. You can't do this by phone since it requires face-to-face contact and negotiations. The lodge owner has to develop a trust in you before he or she will even consider your offer."

As you prepare for a New Year's Eve party to celebrate your fourth year in Montana, you mentally go over your New Year's resolution. Number one on your list is to stop wasting your time looking for lodges in the evening. You admit to yourself that the search process has dampened your desire to even find a lodge. You've got a good job at Cole & Weber and you have relocated to Montana, where you want to be. Maybe you should just leave things the way they are and work toward a retirement plan. As you review your financial statement, you are making some progress:

Fourth Year Financial Summary

Beginning Year Net Worth	$259,300
Plus: Fourth Year Revenues	$86,000
Less: Business and Living Expenses	$74,000
Fourth Year Net Worth	$271,300

If you can get a part-time job to supplement your Cole & Weber income, you might be able to save enough money to buy a cabin somewhere in Montana. It might not be a lodge but at least it would be a start. Looking back on where you have been, would you alter your decisions in order to create a different future for yourself?

1. If you would like to change your last strategic decision, return to Chapter 62.

2. If you would like to select another business venture to start-up, return to Chapter 2.

3. If you would like to conduct more analysis before you start-up another business, turn to Chapter 3.

If you're still feeling the sting of defeat and believe you could have made your last strategic choice work in real life, you may be right. After all, this is just a game. However, if you return to your last strategic decision and select the other alternative (Chapter 62), you will learn why the authors consider it a better choice.

CHAPTER 62

OBTAINING MAJOR MONTANA

LODGES AS CLIENTS

Your fourth year starts off on a very positive note when Mr. Weber, Cole & Weber's President, walks into your office unannounced and, without saying a word, hands you a sealed envelope. Reluctantly, you open the envelope and discover a $15,000 bonus check plus an invitation to become a partner in the agency. Instantly, your office is filled with Cole & Weber people all offering their congratulations. With a shaky hand, you thank Mr. Weber for what you acknowledge was a complete surprise.

Your partnership position sparks a new drive and level of enthusiasm that you hadn't felt since you took on this job. It was supposed to be just a temporary assignment that would allow you to learn something about advertising while you continued to search for a lodge. Mr. Weber has an uncanny ability to know personal things about his employees and you are no exception. Somehow, he found out about your interest in lodges and at the first partnership meeting you attended, asked you to launch a marketing campaign to obtain major lodges as clients. Before you can formally accept the offer, he tells you, "See Sue Redding in the research department. She has a complete file on Montana lodges, which advertising agencies represent them, and what types of ad campaigns they use."

Sue Redding is a feisty woman in her mid-thirties who loves her research job. She tells you she was a private investigator at one time, which you don't doubt. After spending several hours with Sue, you know everything you need to know to develop an effective advertising campaign for every lodge in Montana. You list key issues that Sue brings to your attention:

1. Ten Montana lodges control 80 percent of the lodge tourist trade. These are the prime accounts you should concentrate on closing.

2. All ten lodges are represented by small-town local ad agencies. Watch out for local loyalty issues.

3. The level of advertising is relatively unsophisticated. Although Montana's outback businesses shy away from city-slicker advertising tactics, don't let that fool you. These lodge owners like to make money.

4. If you do not earn the respect of lodge owners in the early stages of your business dealings, they will literally slam the door in your face. Be very careful not to insult their local customs and never wear a tie.

5. Lodge owners are not stupid people. They know how to play the "good ol' boy" dumb role with the best of them just to see if you know what they are talking about. Most of them have college degrees from Montana State or the University of Montana.

Sue tells you that the Lone Pine Lodge out of Butte will be the toughest account to crack. "We've been trying to get that account for the past 10 years and although we have come close, we have never connected. They're locked into a third-rate ad agency that's run by the General Manager's brother-in-law. This guy is so bad that I believe it's his only account." You decide to go for the brass ring and target Lone Pine as your first prize.

The four-hour drive from Billings to Butte takes you west on Interstate 10 through the Galatin National Forest into the Deerlodge National Forest that surrounds the town of Butte. Lone Pine Lodge is located at the base of Silver Bow, one of the better ski areas. Lone Pine's general manager, Jim Willard, was easy to get hold of and when you asked him to meet with you, he seemed almost too anxious to accommodate your request.

As you pull into the Lone Pine's parking lot, you are taken back by the physical size of the main building. The lodge has 150 prime suites with a fireplace in each suite. Huge basalt chimneys jut out from several locations on the roof to handle the smoke from the room fireplaces. The lobby is impressively appointed with cedar log walls tastefully adorned with northern artifacts, mounted elk, deer, moose, and antelope heads. The buffalo head over the main fireplace is almost as big as the fireplace itself. You must be easy to spot because Jim Willard walks up to you and casually asks if you like what you see. You shake his hand and tell him the lodge is utopia.

During the course of your breakfast meeting with Jim, he tells you what you already know. His brother-in-law Harold handles all of their advertising needs, which includes brochure designs, reprints, and the maintenance of a display ad in *Sunset Magazine*. When you learn that the lodge spends $250,000 for these limited advertising services, you can appreciate why Harold only needs one account to keep his agency alive. When you ask Jim if he is satisfied with the current level of services, there is a long pause before he responds. "Oh yes, we are very satisfied." There is something wrong with the tone of his response but you can't put your finger on the problem. You decide to push harder to find out more. "If things are going so well, why did you want to talk to me?" Jim responds with: "I just wanted to hear what you had to say. By the way, would you like to go for a horseback ride?" You haven't had a chance to say anything and apparently the man would rather go horseback riding than hear what you have to say. Patience overrides your impetuous nature to stay on a business track. You accept Jim's horseback riding offer and a half-hour later, you're riding a beautiful pinto gelding up a winding trail that leads into the Pioneer Mountains. During the course of the six-hour ride, you get to know Jim better as the two of you share your experiences, tell each other lots of jokes and in general, have a great time. The subject of advertising never enters into the conversation until you return from the ride and as you are about to steer your car down the mountain toward Billings, Jim asks you to recommend a competitive advertising program for Lone Pine. He tells you, "I'm not saying I am ready to switch ad agencies yet, but I'm willing to look at what you have to offer." You agree to meet with Jim next week in Cole & Weber's Billings's office.

One week later, you find yourself standing at the head of Cole & Weber's presentation room with Jim and his Business Manager Kori Baxter seated across from you. You introduce Jim to Mr. Weber and Sue Redding, who has worked with you diligently over the past week to prepare the presentation. You start off by showing Jim what you could accomplish if Cole & Weber was awarded a $250,000 annual advertising budget from the Lone Pine Lodge:

1. Target mailings to every Lone Star guest to encourage repeat business.

2. Complete revision of Lone Star's *Sunset Magazine* display ad that offers significant improvements over the current layout.

3. Selective ad campaigns in major metropolitan areas such as Denver, Chicago, and New York that have high-frequency visit rates to Montana.

4. Opening of a website on the Internet to attract national and international customers.

5. Total revamp of Lone Star's current black-and-white brochure to color.

6. Radio spot advertisements in Billings, Great Falls, and Bozeman to attract local guests.

You conclude your presentation by reminding Jim that your expanded program could be accomplished with Lone Pine's current advertising budget. When you ask Jim if he will give Cole & Weber an opportunity to earn his business, he asks if he can talk with you privately. In the confines of your office, Jim discloses to you that he has not been satisfied with the level of advertising service he's received from Harold for some time. "The contract's yours if you want it."

By the end of the year, three other major lodges switch their advertising programs over to Cole & Weber as a result of your efforts. Mr. Weber pulls you aside one Friday afternoon just as you are about to leave for a weekend trip to search for a cabin site and presents you with an interesting offer. "How would you like to establish an independent marketing firm for Cole & Weber that specializes in providing marketing and advertising services for national and international lodges?" You tell Mr. Weber you are very interested in his offer and ask if you can give him a firm answer on Monday. He agrees.

During your weekend search for a cabin site, you discover the Timber Wolf Lodge. It's exactly what you have been looking for and when you approach the owner, Steve Harding, to see if he would be interested in selling, he offers you an interesting counteroffer. "If you would be willing to provide your marketing and advertising expertise to get this lodge to full occupancy, I would be willing to offer you part ownership in the lodge. Are you interested in my offer?" You tell Steve you're interested and would like to meet with him on Monday to discuss the specifics. He agrees. Monday morning arrives sooner than you wanted. After reviewing your financial situation, you debate if you should call Steve or call Mr. Weber for an appointment.

Fourth Year Financial Summary

Beginning Year Net Worth	$259,300
Plus: Fourth Year Revenues	$98,000
Less: Business and Living Expenses	$52,300
Fourth Year Net Worth	$305,000

1. If you believe your personal interest would be better served by accepting Cole & Weber's offer to establish a marketing firm to service resort lodges, turn to Chapter 73.

2. If you believe your personal interest would be better served by accepting ownership in a new lodge in exchange for marketing services, turn to Chapter 74.

CHAPTER 63

CREATING A WEBSITE FOCUSED ON PERSONAL COACHING

It's Sunday morning and after a long sleepless night, you have decided to market your personal consulting business on the Internet. The fact that there are millions of worldwide websites beckoning Internet surfers from around the planet is a market opportunity that you cannot ignore. However, you are aware of the fact that many businesses who are marketing their products and services on the Internet have had disappointing results. You readily admit to yourself that you know blatantly little about what you need to do to set up an effective marketing campaign on the web. As you read the Sunday paper, your attention is drawn to a special section: *The Internet Marketplace*. It is as good a place to start as any. The comprehensive article summarizes several basic issues that you need to consider:

- Decide what you want your web presence to accomplish.

- Make sure your traditional advertising strategies complement your web marketing strategies.

- Dedicate a portion of your advertising budget to the web.

- Put yourself in the shoes of your target market and dream up the ideal website.

Patrick Conley, an Internet marketing strategist for Media Integrators out of Phoenix, was one of the commentators. You call Patrick to see if he would be willing to help get you started in the right direction and are pleasantly surprised with his enthusiasm for your project. He explains, "The web is currently dominated by product-marketing ventures; there's not much service stuff out there yet. Personal coaching is certainly a unique service offering. Although much of what I do involves technical personal coaching on how to effectively use the Internet, I'm not on the web yet! God help me if my clients ever find out. Developing a viable Internet marketing program for personal coaching would be a challenge to say the least. To be perfectly honest with you, I would definitely learn something in the process. Heck, I might even decide to do the same thing for my business. Why don't you attend my Internet Marketing seminar next Saturday, which will give you an opportunity to learn the lingo. That way, we can get started on the same page. Let's get together after the seminar and work out a program that hopefully makes sense to you. I charge $450 for the session but you can come as my guest at no charge."

You can't get the words out of your mouth fast enough to accept Patrick's generous offer. Saturday morning arrives and you settle into your front-row seat in the auditorium of the beautiful Phoenician Resort Hotel, the site of Patrick's seminar. You estimate the attendance to be in excess of 450 people. At $450 a "pop" Patrick must have something to say that everybody wants to hear. Assuming that they are not all guests like you, he's got to be making money on this event. A few minutes later, Patrick strolls up to the podium. You love his opening remarks: "Imagine someone handing you the key to a brand-new Ferrari. The leather seat fits you like a glove, the engine purrs like a tiger and you think to yourself, this baby can really fly. Nothing can stop you now; that is, if you only knew how to drive a stick shift. So there you sit in the world's most powerful car, stuck in neutral. That's how a lot of people feel when they get on the Internet, powerless and frustrated because they haven't yet learned how to use this powerful business tool."

"You can avoid this experience by finding an Internet consultant who knows how to do more than just get you connected. Find a consultant who understand your needs, has a flair for creativity, and the technical expertise to make it all come together. That is the only way you'll be able to get to where you want to go. For most companies, the Internet holds greater promise than just high technology. It can create a distinct competitive advantage for your business. Those that understand and use the Internet in the early stages of its conception will be on the competitive edge in the next century. Those that choose to sit on the sidelines will simply go out of business. The choice is yours."

"Do you remember the Clint Eastwood movie,*The Good, The Bad and the Ugly*? An example of an ugly page on the web was produced by a large do-it-yourself chain store, which blasted viewers with its financial success, community services, and company news about who got promoted. It was a total turn-off. Content is the most important element of a successful webpage. It's the biggest separator between the good, the bad, and the ugly site. I encourage my clients to offer dynamic information that's supplemented with first-class graphics and animation. Price list and order forms are a turn-off for most Internet shoppers. Many products and services are sold directly from the Internet. You can get a lot of sales leads that, if worked right, will turn into sales dollars. A good webpage is interactive and prompts viewers to fill out feedback forms or enter contests, while also providing weekly or monthly informational updates that encourage repeat visits. Websites that generate between 6,000 and 8,000 'hits' or 'visits' per month are considered successful pages. Visits to a site are automatically counted by computer host servers."

"To achieve that kind of traffic, your page should be fun, interesting, and informative to explore. If you have a good site, word-of-mouth referrals will spread the news quickly in the cyberspace community. Your page may even get featured in *What's New*, the news-review section of almost every Internet home page. Aesthetically pleasing websites use sharp, yet small graphics that don't take forever to download. Choose graphics and photographs that have some positive connection to your business. A successful webpage is linked to other heavily trafficked pages. This can be accomplished by asking the developer of a popular page for permission to link. Sites can also be listed in web search engines and the hundreds of web malls free of charge. The industry's biggest search engine is Yahoo, through which websites can be exposed to more than 5 million people per day. However, the exposure is not free. A full graphic link to your page can cost $5,000 a week. Are there any questions?" Someone asks; "How fast can you get on the WEB?"

"Before you jump on the Internet bandwagon, you should have a clear picture of what your company wants to establish with a web presence. Whom do you ideally want to visit your website? Do you want customer prospects to buy on their initial visit or just develop enough interest to give you a call? And that, ladies and gentlemen, concludes my portion of this seminar. Why don't we take a fifteen-minute break before the next speaker gets started."

Two weeks later, you meet with Pat in his Phoenix office and with his support, develop a web marketing strategy that precisely complements your global marketing strategy. The page layouts and presentation graphics are, in your biased opinion, better than anything out there on the web. Response to your web advertisement is initially slow but as you move toward the end of your fourth start-up year, the volume picks up. You close out the fourth quarter with a nice jump in sales, most of which is attributable to sales leads generated from the web. You realize a substantial increase in your personal financial position:

Fourth Year Financial Summary

Beginning Year Net Worth	$323,000
Plus: Fourth Year Revenues	$260,000
Less: Business and Living Expenses	$227,600
Fourth Year Net Worth	$355,400

As you move into your fifth year, your website seems to come alive. Inquiries about your personal coaching services exceed 6,000 hits a month. It becomes impossible for you to handle the inbound traffic. You turn to automation and purchase Dorlina's phone-fax software that allows you to automatically respond to websales inquiries by faxing back to the requester the information requested. You add a battery of telephone salespeople to handle "hot calls." There is no such thing as a "cold call" as you anxiously review your projected financial status:

Fifth Year Financial Summary

Beginning Year Net Worth	$355,400
Plus: Fifth Year Revenues	$285,000
Less: Business and Living Expenses	$247,300
Fifth Year Net Worth	$392,700

You have successfully completed a start-up decision-making track, but you can keep playing the game by choosing one or more of the options that follow.

1. If you want to compare how the results of your last five years of start-up decision-making strategies stack up against the other positive outcomes, turn to Chapter 77.

2. If you wish to find out what would have happened had you chosen the alternative of obtaining ownership in a resort lodge for marketing services, turn to Chapter 74.

3. If you want to discover the outcomes of other choices on the track, turn to Chapter 42. Return to Chapter 11 if you want to start the track from the beginning.

4. If you would like to pursue other start-up decision-making opportunities, turn to either Chapter 2 or 3.

CHAPTER 64

LAUNCHING A

PERSONAL COACHING

CABLE TV CHANNEL

You love the "Family Feud" game show. They walked off smiling, this family of five from Wylie, Texas, even though they've just lost a chance at $5,000 in cash. But first, the losing mom hugs Richard Dawson, host of ABC's "Family Feud," and tells him, "Seeing you was worth the trip." Even the losers go away happy.

The name "game show" conjures up gross images of self-degradation in the pursuit of money. It isn't very inspiring to see how one's fellow Americans will stoop for a trip to a class-C hotel in Puerto Rico. But "Family Feud" is not only the most humane game show on television, it's also the most popular. Feud is consistently the top-rated game show in the lucrative daytime market and is frequently the number 1 daytime show, beating even the mighty soaps. In a way, Feud is a nonfiction soap, because a single family may return for several consecutive days in its attempts to win the big prize.

You launch an aggressive effort to open a television series on personal coaching. But to be successful, you must first overcome a major hurdle: Find a television channel that will sponsor your show. You're convinced that if you can somehow capture the underlying theme of the "Family Feud" into a cable television personal coaching program, you'd have a winner. Instead of having "face-offs" between two families, you'd have "face-offs" between two management teams. Five members from each of the two competing management teams would try to guess the most popular answers to questions asked of

100 well-known executives in surveys conducted by mail. Questions could include: "Your Senior Vice President has just been accused of sexual harassment. What is the first thing you would do?" Or, "What is the most serious management problem you will have to confront tomorrow?"

The winner of the preliminary rounds goes on to the "fast-track" competition, which involves coming up with five quick answers to survey questions within one minute. "The morale index of your company just slipped to its lowest level in 25 years. What five immediate steps would you take to solve the problem?" As you continue to refine your personal coaching television show in your mind, you envision subjecting the various answers the teams give to an opinionated review by a panel of personal coaching experts. Viewers would not only have an entertaining opportunity to experience their peers attempting to solve tough management issues but would benefit from the expert advice of personal coaches participating on the panels.

You spend the better part of two months refining your ideas for a personal coaching cable television program. You even go so far as to rent a studio and, with the help of several friends, stage and videotape a mock show. The challenge will be to get a top television producer to view the video. If they see the video, you're convinced they will help you launch the program.

On a tip, you join the International Television Association (ITVA), the premier professional organization of television people, with over 10,000 members worldwide and 90 U.S. chapters. You run into Kelly Lange, a newscaster for ABC's Los Angeles-based station at one of the chapter meetings. When you explain your show idea to Kelly, she offers you some valid criticism. "Look, you've got lots of boring shows out there along with misery-and-tragedy shows. If you want a winner, produce a show that allows people to laugh and learn at the same time. Otherwise, you're just asking too much of viewers who've been hassled all day long to come home and watch your show rehash what they have already been through during the couse of the day. I like your personal coaching game-show idea but you've got to put some chuckles in it! If you can figure out how to add elements of humor to your script, I'll get our Producer to take a look at your video."

You know Kelly is right. The target audience for your personal coaching TV series would be executives and managers. In order to get them to watch the series after a long hard day at the office, you've got to offer quality education on personal coaching framed in a highly entertaining environment. Laughter is one of the best therapeutic remedies for work stress there is. How do you create healthy laughter in the work place? You create another minivideo series around the theme of laughter to help demonstrate how personal coaching can be effectively used to reduce work-related pressures. When Kelly views your newest video, she tells you the program will sell and arranges for a one-hour meeting with you and her producer, Alan Gant.

Your meeting with Alan is a memorable event. He starts the meeting off by telling you, "There is an unwritten rule in the cable-television industry for first-time participants. You have got to pay your dues first before we will even let you get to first base. I like your personal coaching program idea and the way you have shaped it around the success profile of "Family Feud." I'll produce the program as long as you are willing to accept an advisory position on the program. That does not mean that you will be in the show itself. We'll see about that if and when you pass the screen test. Are you with me?"

You accept Alan's offer as the program's Technical Advisor and suddenly find yourself working 12 to 16 hours a day to help launch the "Corporate Feud," the name that has been selected for the series. Richard Dawson hosts the first show that pits IBM managers against a management team from AT&T. The theme, reengineering, is a subject that both organizations are seasoned experts on since they wrote the book on downsizing. The mix of questions asked of the respective management teams is both challenging and entertaining at the same time. You pass your screen test and are one of three personal coaches on the panel who render an opinion of the positions taken by the corporate teams.

Initially, the television audience for the "Corporate Feud" is relatively small, but as the show gathers momentum, viewer interest increases substantially. Name recognition begins to set in as you start receiving hundreds of personal letters and telephone calls requesting more information about your personal coaching services. Before the year is over, you're the keynote speaker at the American Management Association's annual conference and several other major conferences. You selectively add clients to your list and your personal finances reflect the favorable increase in your income:

Fourth Year Financial Summary

Beginning Year Net Worth	$323,000
Plus: Fourth Year Revenues	$265,000
Less: Business and Living Expenses	$227,600
Fourth Year Net Worth	$360,400

As you contemplate your next strategic move, you consider the idea of joint-venturing a personal coaching program with one of the major broadcasting networks. Under the current program arrangement, you are receiving what amounts to a wage for your efforts. In a joint-venture arrangement, you would have an opportunity to share in the profits of the program as well. You're also intrigued with the sudden surge of interest corporations are displaying for personal coaching. Maybe it's time to bolster your services to include customized coaching programs for corporations.

1. If you believe you would be better off joint-venturing a program with a major broadcasting network, turn to Chapter 75.

2. If you believe you would be better off offering customized coaching programs to corporations, turn to Chapter 76.

CHAPTER 65

STICKING WITH PROVEN

PERSONAL COACHING

APPROACHES

When you announce your decision to stick with proven personal coaching approaches, the general partnership reacts with enthusiasm. Because of your earlier success at growing the partnership, they've come to respect you and will therefore support any decision you make. You know that sticking with proven personal coaching approaches does not mean that everyone can sit back and rest on their laurels. You can't continue to do the same old thing in this marketplace and stay in business for very long. You need to learn how to do it better and better.

To implement the new thrust on proven personal coaching approaches, you spend several hours with each Personal Dynamics partner to discuss what can be done to improve upon personal coaching, the core business of the firm. When you complete the one-on-one interviews with all the partners, you have an impressive list of what each believes he or she can do to improve the firm's coaching service. Everyone commits their support to improving upon the overall level of service with one important exception. Stan Lee expresses mild concern that this undertaking could turn into a costly distraction at a time when Personal Dynamics needs strong earnings growth. Committed to the program, you push forward to assure its success.

You hire a consulting group to independently monitor your success along the way. With the help of your consultant, you identify four major changes that must be made to improve upon the current level

of personal coaching: future needs of leadership, individual qualification assessment, personality typing, and revised client-satisfaction
testing. By the middle of the year, Personal Dynamics sales have fall-
en off substantially as everybody struggles to adopt to the new
improvement criteria while at the same time, supporting full-time
agendas of consulting hours. Something has to give and unfortunately, it's the firm's billable hours.

Predictably, you begin to receive pressure from Stan Lee and the
general partners to back off and return things to their normal level.
They keep reminding you that the time-consuming adjustments to
style are distracting them from focusing on the immediate needs of
their clients. By the end of the fourth year, Personal Dynamics' sales
remain flat. Year-end bonuses and salary increases are thin, although
you manage to increase your net worth thanks to your frugal savings
program.

Fourth Year Financial Summary

Beginning Year Net Worth	$323,000
Plus: Fourth Year Revenues	$140,000
Less: Business and Living Expenses	$118,000
Fourth Year Net Worth	$345,000

During the next several months, you devote most of your attention to improving upon Personal Dynamics' personal consulting
delivery program while Stan Lee attends to the sales and profit problems. In desperation, a consulting-discount program is announced in
the hopes of stopping declining sales. While customers respond
favorably to the discount program, at least temporarily halting the
sales decline, Personal Dynamics profits suffer accordingly.

You argue that this year's reduction in profits constitutes only a
short-term setback, which will be offset by a long-term increase in
sales and profits once clients believe in Personal Dynamics' ability to
deliver superior service, but nobody's listening. Just a few short
months ago, you were Personal Dynamic's hero. Now, you're the
company leper!

Lee asks you to consider disbanding your personal coaching
innovation program. Though you argue vehemently against such a
course of action, Lee's concerns about your judgment and strategic
decision-making ability deepen. As the fiscal year comes to a close,
you realize that you are not "in the shoe" for any kind of bonus. When

Lee tells you that you will not receive a raise in salary this year, your objection is met with the stark reality of the situation as Lee informs you of your options. "Take it or resign." As you quietly review where you are financially, you decide to stay where you are, lick your wounds, and hopefully move ahead.

Fifth Year Financial Summary

Beginning Year Net Worth	$345,000
Plus: Fifth Year Revenues	$140,000
Less: Business and Living Expenses	$105,000
Fifth Year Net Worth	$380,000

In retrospect, you wish you had considered expanding your personal consulting market to include family coaching. You have successfully completed a start-up decision-making track, but you can keep playing the game by choosing one or more of the options that follow.

1. If you want to compare how the results of your last five years of start-up decision-making strategies stack up against the other positive outcomes, turn to Chapter 77.

2. If you wish to find out what would have happened had you chosen the alternative of expanding into family coaching, turn to Chapter 66.

3. If you want to discover the outcomes of other choices on the track, turn to Chapter 43 or Chapter 12 if you want to start the track from the beginning.

4. If you would like to pursue other start-up decision-making opportunities, turn to either Chapter 2 or 3.

CHAPTER 66

EXPANDING TO INCLUDE FAMILY

COACHING

Acting on your intuition, you decide to focus on broadening the scope of the partnership's core services to include family coaching. You take some solace in the fact that none of your competitors is pursuing family coaching. Because of your earlier success at growing the partnership, the general partnership supports your decision with enthusiasm and you move quickly to get the entire organization thinking in terms of what's required to launch a family coaching program.

You spend significant resources and several months developing a set of family coaching programs that are designed to meet most of the critical needs of American families. Your core-competence programs include single-parent coaching, adolescence drug-problem resolution, parent mentoring, and family financial planning. Every partner agrees to attend your core-competency seminar to kick off the program.

At the start of the program, you outline the purpose of establishing core competence in family coaching to the partners: "First, core competence provides potential access to a wider market. Second, core competence makes a significant contribution to the perceived customer benefits derived from the family coaching program. Finally, once a core of competence has been established within the partnership, it becomes difficult for the competition to imitate our programs."

It was exactly six months ago when you first introduced the idea of adding family coaching to the partnership's service offering. While you expect your efforts to pay off eventually, midyear revenue from the program represents only 1 percent of total revenue. When you pick up on rumors circulating among the partnership that a vote is about to be called to cancel your family coaching business, you begin to wonder if you should start looking for another job.

However, being the tenacious entrepreneur that you are, you decide not to give up until you have at least found out what's wrong with the program and what can be done to salvage it. Recognizing the prudence of getting revenue out of the program, you immediately begin identifying client prospects that can be converted into customers in 60 to 90 days. Up to this point, your family coaching marketing program has been focused on individual families who have a need for the program. The problem of converting a family prospect into a client has been compounded by two issues. First, most families can't afford to pay for the program and secondly, after expressing interest in the program, they back off by saying "the problem personal coaching was going to solve has gone away."

You decide to introduce the concept of family coaching to your corporate clients and quickly develop a whole new level of interest. Jack Suhler, Vice President of Human Resources at Boeing, said it best when you first introduced him to the program. "There's not an employee in Boeing including myself who doesn't need coaching in at least one of your core programs. If we are honest with ourselves, we all have problems with our kids and if someone tells me family finances have never been a problem, they're lying. It might be easier for our employees to swallow the pill if they had the opportunity to attend group sessions in one of our classrooms after work. The sessions would be free to our employees. Boeing would even be willing to pay you directly for one-on-one counseling. Clearly, anything you can do to help resolve the personal problems of our employees, the better off Boeing is from a productivity standpoint."

The introduction of family coaching programs at Boeing is immediately successful. In your initial session, the classroom was filled to capacity and over 100 Boeing employees had to be turned away at the door. The problem is quickly solved by adding more sessions. To your delight, your partners applaud the success of the program and they assure you that they never had any doubts as to the viability of the program. You know better but your bonus check more than made up for the tough time you had getting this program started. Financially, you're in great shape.

Fourth Year Financial Summary

Beginning Year Net Worth	$323,000
Plus: Fourth Year Revenues	$120,000
Less: Business and Living Expenses	$68,000
Fourth Year Net Worth	$375,000

As you move into your fifth year of personal coaching, you reflect on what this line of business has done for you personally. By year-end, fifteen other corporations sign up for family coaching seminars and all adopt some form of payment reimbursement plan for one-on-one sessions. You feel good about yourself. It's a by-product one gets by helping others solve their problems. On occasion, you get depressed from listening to everybody's problems day in and day out, but you are able to overcome that obstacle. For the second year in a row, your annual compensation jumps 20 percent thanks to the steady flow of revenue from family coaching.

Fifth Year Financial Summary

Beginning Year Net Worth	$375,000
Plus: Fifth Year Revenues	$124,600
Less: Business and Living Expenses	$96,400
Fifth Year Net Worth	$403,200

You have successfully completed a start-up decision-making track, but you can keep playing the game by choosing one or more of the options below.

1. If you want to compare how the results of your last five years of start-up decision-making strategies stack up against the other positive outcomes, turn to Chapter 77.

2. If you wish to find out what would have happened had you chosen the alternative of expanding into family coaching, turn to Chapter 65.

3. If you want to discover the outcomes of other choices on the track, turn to Chapter 65 or Chapter 12 if you want to start the track from the beginning.

4. If you would like to pursue other start-up decision-making opportunities, turn to either Chapter 2 or 3.

CHAPTER 67

KEEPING THE NETWORK SMALL

You like having full control over everything you do and have therefore decided to keep your marketing network small. You learn that networking is a structured process you go through to build a word-of-mouth business base. Many of your close business associates have used networks to help them in their personal and professional lives. They formed coalitions because they knew sooner or later their welfare might depend on the willingness of others to help. Alan Cox's book *The Achiever's Profile* helps you understand from a historical perspective how networking got started. While the practice of networking isn't new, its widespread use and sophistication have changed significantly in recent years. During the late 70s and 80s, structured networking became a popular method of promoting one's business. Established networks were formed to communicate positive information about members' businesses and to generate referrals.

In your home town, local area networking is becoming a powerful marketing technique people use to formally and informally build their businesses. Your own networking system has evolved into coalitions of business professionals who, through mutual support systems, help you and you in turn help them do more business. *The Strategic Business Alliance* was one of the networking groups you helped form. It's made up of 20 team members from different product and service companies, including a CPA firm, law firm, insurance company, and computer chip manufacturing company. The group meets twice a month for about two hours. In that two hours' time, you receive information on a minimum of 3 to 5 prequalified prospects who are interested in your training and consulting services.

It's been exactly one year today since you first introduced your broker-training program at the Hilton and it has turned out to be a smashing success. By applying what you have learned about networks, you develop a small network of available trainers, who have agreed to allow you to represent their services. Your head count to twenty-five trainers is all you have time to track in your network. Each one is a training specialist in his or her own right. You know every trainer whom you represent personally and can attest to their excellent training qualifications. That's important when you are out in the field representing their individual qualifications. If something goes wrong and the client gets upset, you are the one they go after for misrepresentation. You know they are not really your trainers; you just represent them as an independent contractor. But, as far as your clients are concerned, they are your trainers.

Because you have managed to keep your network of trainers small, you have not encountered any client complaints. However, your program is not without its drawbacks. Your small network of trainers prevents you from fulfilling all of your client's training needs. It's like leaving money on the table, which drives you crazy. Inevitably, they will identify a training need that you can't cover. You simply don't represent anybody who has the talent to meet their needs. Your excuse: "Sorry, I can't help you in that area" inevitably generates one of those "I'll just have to find someone who can help me" responses that send shivers down your back. You've just invited your competition to come into your client base and gain a foothold.

In spite of all that you have accomplished networking with and brokering trainers, you have to constantly fight to keep the competition away from your clients. Ten of your best clients including First Interstate Bank have already signed exclusive contracts with national training firms who offer a wider spectrum of training programs than you can at this time. As you review your financial spreadsheet, you realize that your decision to keep your network small has cost you money.

Fifth Year Financial Summary

Beginning Year Net Worth	$325,000
Plus: Fifth Year Revenues	$389,000
Less: Business and Living Expenses	$340,200
Fifth Year Net Worth	$373,800

In retrospect, you wish you had considered expanding your brokerage program nationally to increase your depth of training talent. You have successfully completed a start-up decision-making track, but you can keep playing the game by choosing one or more of the options that follow.

1. If you want to compare how the results of your last five years of start-up decision-making strategies stack up against the other positive outcomes, turn to Chapter 77.

2. If you wish to find out what would have happened had you chosen the alternative of expanding into family coaching, turn to Chapter 66.

3. If you want to discover the outcomes of other choices on the track, turn to Chapter 43. Return to Chapter 12 if you want to start the track from the beginning.

4. If you would like to pursue other start-up decision-making opportunities, turn to either Chapter 2 or 3.

CHAPTER 68

DEVELOPING A NATIONAL NETWORK

As you pore through your autographed copy of Ivan Misner's *The World's Best Known Marketing Secrets*, you are intrigued by the word-of-mouth marketing theme of the book. Ivan founded *Business Network International* in 1985, a highly successful international networking organization that boasts over a million members today. You're convinced more than ever that developing a national network for your consulting and training business will be paramount to its success.

You're interested in developing a national network to expand your sphere of influence with people who can help build your business. Your national network would include people you know either very well or as casual acquaintances. To evaluate your sphere of influence, you take an inventory of the people you already know by asking yourself, "Whom do I know and who knows me?" You include everyone with whom you interact or might interact with professionally or personally, including:

- Clients

- Business associates

- Vendors and creditors

- Present and previous employees

- Friends and family members

- Previous managers

As you go through your *Act One* contact software database program, address book, and business-card box, you analyze your relationship with each person and ask yourself, "How well do I know these people?" In the process, you determine which individuals are strong contacts, close associates with whom you can actively network. You create a second category of casual contacts or individuals with whom you will network on a passive basis. Whatever is left over, such as people with whom you have lost contact or have a limited relationship, are discarded.

You realize it's important to have both strong and casual contacts, but for different reasons. Strong contacts are usually personal friends, close family members, partners, preferred clients, and close business associates. They are people that you can actively network to help you build your business. They tend to belong to closed circles of influence, which typically don't change and as a result, they tend to offer the same leads again and again.

Casual contacts, which are made up of acquaintances, ex-colleagues, suppliers, and previous customers are the people whom you passively network. As you review your list, you realize that you have many more casual contacts than strong contacts. This doesn't surprise you since it is much more difficult and time consuming to establish a long-term relationship. Casual contacts are used to assist you in seeking out and finding new clients. They provide you with new business leads that are outside your circles of influence. By successfully using your passive contacts, you vastly increase your networking range and discover that strong contacts provide a better quality connection into your network, while casual contacts provide a greater quantity of connections.

The process of developing your company's national network continues with a concerted effort to develop connections with other business professionals. Your friend Jerry Simons, a well-respected consultant, tells you that most businesspeople are "cave dwellers" who spend their days going from cave to cave. In the morning, they enter their office cave where they stay until it's time to go home. The next day they do it all over again. These are the same people who say, "Gee, I wonder why I'm not getting any referrals." You realize that just showing up for work is not going to build your referral business. Will Rogers said it best: "You might be on the right track, but if you're just sitting there, you're going to get run over!" You know Jerry is right. In fact, you secretly admit to yourself that in the past, you've been a cave dweller. Not anymore!

You are determined not to let it happen this time. To break out of the cave-dwelling mentality, you begin by evaluating the time you're spending in your cave. For starters, you make a commitment to allocate a specific amount of time to call both your casual and strong contacts each day. Something in your inner mind says, "Why not start today?" "Not today!" "I'll start tomorrow." You think to yourself, "I can't believe I'm having this conversation with myself. Tomorrow is the best excuse there is for call reluctance."

Since you have a network list, why not take the next hour and start making calls? You call Dan Corbin, the first strong contact on your list. You worked for Dan ten years ago and have kept in touch with him through Christmas cards and an occasional "how are you doing" call once every six months or so. It turns out that Dan is doing quite well as the Chief Financial Officer for Ralston Purina.

Dan answers his private line, "Good morning, this is Dan Corbin. What can I do for you?" After a friendly "How are you doing, Dan?" introduction, you get right down to business. Dan's a busy man with a limited attention span. He knows you are in the training business but he doesn't know anything about what you have been doing. You explain how you intend to expand your network of clients and trainers nationally and tell him about some of the exciting programs you already have in place. "Quite frankly, Dan, I could use your help in kicking this program off. A name-brand company like Ralston Purina with its corporate headquarters in the midwest would really help me anchor a market in a geographical region of the country that I have not penetrated." To your delight, Dan asks you to outline a seminar series for his MIS Department. "Why not come out here, spend a couple of days at our expense, and talk to my people before you recommend a program?" You thank Dan for his time and tell him you'll see him next week.

You work the trainer side of your national network by attending National Trainers Association regional meetings. By the spring of your fifth year, you double your broker training force from 25 to 50. What's really exciting about your training team is that you can now cover just about any company's training needs. As your client base begins to stabilize, and you approach the end of your fifth year, you update your financial statement:

Fifth Year Financial Summary

Beginning Year Net Worth	$325,000
Plus: Fifth Year Revenues	$560,000
Less: Business and Living Expenses	$477,600
Fifth Year Net Worth	$407,400

It has been a very good year and, with the exception that you will be paying out a lot in Federal taxes this year to cover increased revenues, it all seems worth it! Tomorrow, you and your spouse leave on an extended Caribbean cruise. The captain schedules you to give a training session on nutrition in exchange for a permanent seat at the Captain's Dinner Table. Maybe you can write this trip off as a tax deduction. You pick up the phone and call your accountant.

1. This is the end of this path of play. If you would like to see how well you did in comparison to the alternative start-up paths you could have taken, turn to Chapter 75.

2. If you would like to try another start-up path where you take action now, turn to Chapter 2.

3. If you would like to try another start-up path where can conduct analysis before you take action, turn to Chapter 3.

CHAPTER 69

ACQUIRING CORPORATE

SHIPPING ACCOUNTS

Confident that expanding your service activities will become more and more important to the success of your Mail Boxes Etc. (MBE) franchise, you doggedly hang on to the idea of acquiring lucrative corporate shipping accounts. The question is how? There are 225 corporations in your market area who have an internal shipping department that is responsible for their national and international shipping functions. You decide to conduct telephone interviews of 50 randomly selected companies to learn more about their internal shipping operations. The questions you ask have been carefully worded to obtain the information you need to mount an effective marketing campaign:

1. How many full-time employees are in your shipping department?

2. Does your shipping department handle all of your shipping needs?

3. If your answer to question #2 was no, what shipping services are performed outside of your shipping department?

4. How do you know if you are paying the lowest shipping rates possible on everything you ship?

5. How many square feet does your shipping department occupy and what kind of shipping equipment do you own or lease?

6. How satisfied are you with the services from your shipping department?

Over the next two months, you call the companies on your list and carefully record their answers to your questions. Because this is a phone interview, you have the opportunity to probe for more information than you initially ask for. If the person you are interviewing tells you they are not satisfied with their shipping department, you always find out why. It's Thursday afternoon and you finish the last telephone interview. Tired and scratching your sore ear, you believe you have collected enough information to help you launch your corporate shipping program. Since tomorrow is Friday (TGIF), you reconcile yourself to the fact that you would be better off tabulating the results tonight, rather than waiting until tomorrow. Later that evening and with the help of your PC, you compile interesting statistics from your telephone interviews:

1. Average size of internal shipping department is three full-time employees. Twenty percent of the companies hire contract employees in their shipping departments.

2. On average, 80 percent of all shipping needs are satisfied through internal shipping departments. Most international shipments are contracted through freight forwarders, which represents about 20 percent of the annual shipping volume.

3. None of the people you interviewed knew if they were paying the lowest shipping rates possible on everything they shipped. Most indicated a real concern in this area.

4. The average shipping department occupies 1,000 square feet of prime office space and uses shipping equipment with an average value of $60,000. Most of the equipment is old and has subsequently been depreciated off the books.

5. Most of the people you talked to said they were neither satisfied nor dissatisfied with their shipping department. "They just do their thing and we hope they are doing it right" was a common answer you received when you asked this question.

6. The average annual shipping and postage expenses were $120,000 not counting material and labor costs. Direct mail represents $65,000 and 150,000 units per year. The remaining $55,000 covers 1,375 bulk national and international shipping units.

Working with the information you've collected, you begin to lay out a shipping program that you believe would be attractive to corporations. The challenge that confronts you is the old "how to save them money and improve their service at the same time" saw horse! If you can do all that, you've got a winning program. The average size of a shipping department (e.g., three people) is the first area you consider. You believe you can run the department with one person, in view of the fact that only 1,375 packages are shipped each year. Package shipping is the labor-intensive part of the job. Based upon your calculations, one person would have almost an hour to prepare each package (1,375 packages / 2,080 individual work hours per year = .66 hours).

The use of freight forwarders to handle international shipments can be an expensive proposition. They typically charge 15 percent of the gross shipping charges for their services. According to *Direct Mail Magazine,* the average shipping charge for an international shipment is $40. Based on average numbers, approximately $1,650 a year is spent on freight-forwarding services based on your calculations:

Freight Forwarding Fees = (Units shipped × average shipping charge per unit) × 15% freight forwarder fee

= (1,375 total units shipped per year × 20% international shipments × $40 average shipping charge) × 15%

= (275 units × $40) × 15%

= $1,650

The shipping program that you propose to offer corporations would include one MBE employee who would reside onsite to coordinate all shipping activities. His or her responsibilities would include the coordination and metering of direct-mail services and logging bulk items for national and international shipment. MBE would pick up bulk items once a day and deliver them to your retail store where they would be packaged, metered, and shipped. You thank yourself for having the foresight to have acquired space to accommodate additional future business. This process would eliminate the need to store bulky packing material and equipment at the corporate shipping center, which would reduce the amount of space you need by 50 percent or 500 square feet (1,000 square feet × .50 = 500 square feet). The cost-savings side of your shipping service package comes together in the following table:

ANNUAL CORPORATE SHIPPING
PROGRAM COST COMPARISONS

Item Description	Current Cost	Proposed Cost
Onsite Labor	$37,440	$12,355
Freight-Forwarding Charges	$1,650	$0
Office Space savings*	$6,000	$1,000
MBE Service charge**	N/A	$12,000
Total Program Costs	$45,090	$25,355

* 500 square feet of office space would be saved at an estimated cost of $12 per year per square foot.

** MBE service charges cover pick-up service, in-store packaging labor costs, and profits.

The cost side of your corporate shipping program comes together. On average, you can show a 43-percent savings. Each client would pay for actual shipping charges and packaging materials used. Up to this point, you have only addressed the cost-improvement side of your program. What about service improvements? MBE people are shipping specialists. Once each quarter, you hire an independent auditor to review your shipping records to validate all shipping charges. If you paid too much, reimbursement vouchers are sent to the appropriate shipping company. This same service would be extended to your corporate clients. You take on the full responsibility of supervising their shipping department so that their management can attend to more pressing corporate matters.

All of the advantages of your program are assembled in a quality brochure, which you use to kick off your marketing and sales program. By the end of your fifth year, ten corporations have contracted with you to use your service. Your corporate shipping program becomes a welcome source of recurring revenue that covers the seasonal fluctuations of your retail-mail business. Thanks to your ingenuity, your personal net worth takes a nice year-end jump.

Fifth Year Financial Summary

Beginning Year Net Worth	$341,300
Plus: Fifth Year Revenues	$460,000
Less: Business and Living Expenses	$423,300
Fifth Year Net Worth	$378,000

You have successfully completed a start-up decision-making track, but you can keep on playing the game by choosing one or more of the options that follow. If you want to compare how the results of your last five years of start-up decision-making strategies stack up against the other positive outcomes, turn to Chapter 77.

1. If you wish to find out what would have happened had you chosen the alternative of focusing on residential customers, turn to Chapter 70.

2. If you want to discover the outcomes of other choices on the track, turn to Chapter 34. Return to Chapter 6 if you want to start the track from the beginning.

3. If you would like to pursue other start-up decision-making opportunities, turn to either Chapter 2 or 3.

CHAPTER 70

FOCUSING ON RESIDENTIAL CUSTOMERS

The seasonal cycle of the mailing and shipping business is driving you crazy. Your cash-flow projections look like a roller coaster as people and their use of shipping services flow with the seasonal tide. That's the nature of the business and there is not a whole lot you can do about it. However, you are bent on increasing your sales volume so that your average net sales in an "off-season month" will, at minimum, cover your fixed cost. Adding more space helped you expand your Mail Boxes Etc. (MBE) franchise into the business sector of your market to offset part of your fixed costs. But your residential-customer business has remained relatively flat over the past year. Two years ago, it was increasing at a rate of 10 percent a month before it flattened out. You know why. Residential clients that were predisposed to using mailing services in your market area discovered where you were located and started using your services. Over time and through word-of-mouth, potential customers discovered your location and your new business base stabilized.

Perpetuating new business is a challenge to any retail businesses. The easy customers have already been discovered. They are the ones that, by habit, shop at your mall location on a recurring basis and build into their shopping agenda a service stop at your store. You have decided to focus on increasing your residential-customer business base.

On a busy Saturday morning, you find yourself standing in front of Albertsons, the official "anchor store" in your mall, talking to customers as they enter and exit the store. It doesn't take you long to discover that most of them still aren't aware of the fact that your MBE store is located in the mall complex. Your storefront sign is easily visible from the entrance into Albertsons and most of the people you talk to shop here at least once a week. Ninety percent of the shoppers live within three miles of the mall. Worse yet, when you ask them if they knew what services MBE offers, most said "they had no idea."

You have been in this business for over three years and have just discovered that a large block of your potential clients don't even know you exist or what services you offer. You find yourself trying to kick yourself in the backside as you drive home that evening. After two hours of lying awake in bed progressively building on your frustration level, you jump up and head to your den where your PC is waiting to help you. The decision-making software application you just purchased is about to get its first "Is it worth it?" test!

You bought this application for two reasons; it was relatively cheap ($49) and you were curious to find out how it could help you make strategic decisions. It doesn't take you long to realize that the software is based on a reasonably sophisticated relational-database structure. You respond to the application's opening question: "What do you want to do?" You respond with, "I want to increase sales." After responding to a series of questions that follow, like the type of sales you want to increase, specifics about customer profiles (i.e., residential, etc.) and demographic data, the program responds with a "Please wait while I determine the options that are available to you." A few minutes later and the screen displays a new message: "Three strategies have been discovered that will help you increase residential customer sales. Press any key to see what they are." You quickly press the return key and the options instantly appear on your screen:

1. Send a newsletter to households in the zip code where you do business to inform them of the types of services MBE offers.

2. Place a sign in front of the entrance of other mall stores that advertises your location and business features.

3. Send direct-mail coupons to households in the zip code where you do business, offering discounts to attract new customers.

All three ideas make sense and with the exception of the newsletter, are relatively simple to implement. You decide to implement all three strategies in the interest of discovering which one or combination works best. The next morning, you ask several store owners in your mall if they would allow you to place a sign in their window that announces MBE's location and service features. At first they are reluctant to give up part of their window space. When you offer to include their store ad in your first newsletter at no cost to them, they are more than willing to accommodate your request. After contacting three coupon-mailing services in your area, you settle on one company that appears to have more expertise in designing direct-mail coupons. You contact several of their customers to confirm their reputation.

The following month, all three programs are launched. Your storefront announcement signs have been printed up and placed in mall store windows. Coupon mailers are ready to go and after a lot of work using the desktop-publishing system on your PC, you create a first-class newsletter that covers all kinds of helpful mailing tips and money-saving coupons from the stores in your mall. It costs you $2,200 in postage, printing, and coupon service fees to launch the program.

Three days after the coupons and your newsletter are mailed, and your signs are in place, you realize a decided increase in customer walk-in traffic. You find yourself so busy handling the additional new business that you have little time to find out which one of your pro-motional programs attracted the new customers into your store. Over time, you invite customers to fill out a card that tells you what drew them into the store. It turns out that all three programs contributed equally well. Your sales figures increase by $6,200 for the month as compared to sales for the same month last year. By the end of your fifth year, you are covering all of your monthly fixed costs and realiz-ing a profit even in the slow seasonal months. Your year-end net worth shows the wisdom of your decision:

Fifth Year Financial Summary

Beginning Year Net Worth	$341,300
Plus: Fifth Year Revenues	$453,700
Less: Business and Living Expenses	$423,300
Fifth Year Net Worth	$371,700

You're convinced that the coupon-sign-newsletter program combination is working when many new customers become recurring customers. You continue with the same program through the end of the year. Your newsletter program is successful at not only drawing customers into MBE but into the other stores in the mall as well. You become the mall's direct-mail expert. Over time, the store owners compensate you for your newsletter service, which becomes a new profit-making venture for MBE.

You have successfully completed a start-up decision-making track, but you can keep on playing the game by choosing one or more of the options that follow.

1. If you want to compare how the results of your last five years of start-up decision-making strategies stack up against the other positive outcomes, turn to Chapter 77.

2. If you wish to find out what would have happened had you chosen the alternative of acquiring corporate shipping accounts, turn to Chapter 69.

3. If you want to discover the outcomes of other choices on the track, turn to Chapter 33. Return to Chapter 6 if you want to start the track from the beginning.

4. If you would like to pursue other start-up decision-making opportunities, turn to either Chapter 2 or 3.

CHAPTER 71

FINANCING MARKETING

CAMPAIGNS FOR EQUITY

Your search for clients who are willing to pay you to develop and implement their marketing programs has been a disaster. It has been two months since you mounted your own strategic-marketing campaign and you have not landed a single account. Your closest shot was Marshal Industries, a $1 billion semiconductor and electronics distribution company in Santa Clara, California.

When Susan Gore, its Vice President of Marketing, explained what was happening to the company, you could understand its reluctance to pay for any discretionary services. "We've lost over $750 million in two years. Last year, our gross sales were $2 billion. This year, we'll be lucky to reach $1.5 billion. The problem is the big guys like Intel are beating us with extreme cost-competitive tactics. They have destroyed our sales base and will force us out of business before the year is over. We've slashed all of our expenses to the point where we are rationing sheets of toilet paper to employees. That's supposed to be funny, but it is almost the truth."

"Most of our good sales and marketing people have left the company. We're left with people who are about to retire or can't find a job anywhere else. Here's the bottom line. We desperately need a firm like yours to help us implement a viable marketing program. However, with our dismal cash-flow situation, we've got no way to pay you."

You cut in. "Susan, there has got to be a way for us to salvage Marshal Industries. You guys have been in the business since the early

1980s and you're still producing one of the best IC chips in the industry. I've got a couple of ideas I want to check out before I get back to you."

That evening, you meet with Dan Ritter, one of your partners, and expound on the problems that confront Marshal Industries. Dan jumps in with a blasting statement: "Why are you wasting your time on Marshal Industries? You've been chasing marketing-consulting assignments for two months and if Marshal is the best you can come up with, you've got some serious problems. We're not running a giant consulting firm with unlimited resources that can afford to chase losers like Marshal Industries. Forget Marshal and get back into the business of finding viable clients who can afford our services."

Tempers flare as you challenge Dan to explain the specifics of his contributions over the last two months. You're quick to remind him that he spent a month in Hawaii attending a "boondoggle" seminar. The shouting accusations continue for a few more minutes when you both abruptly stop, look at each other, and when Dan starts laughing, you break out into an uncontrollable laugh too as you both realize how immature you must sound! You and Dan go back a long way and you have the ultimate degree of respect for the man.

Dan is the first to talk. "All right, partner, let's figure out a way to help Marshal and somehow make money at the same time. What's its stock trading for right now?" It closed at three points yesterday, a long way from its $26 high two years ago. "Does the company hold any trade stock?" You think so.

Dan proceeds to outline his master plan. "Computech has been trying to entice our clients to let us show them how to use the Internet to mount an aggressive marketing campaign. Up to this point, the interest level has been lukewarm at best. Go back to Marshal Industries and tell them we'll help them implement an Internet marketing campaign in exchange for shares of common stock. If we can get the company's sales curve moving in the right direction, we both win. Marshal stays in business, the stock we get will be worth something, and we have a good chance of getting other Internet marketing accounts if we can show success at Marshal Industries."

Your meeting with Susan the next morning to sound out the Internet marketing idea goes well. A meeting of Marshal's executive staff is hastily called to hear what you have to say about your Internet marketing program. You explain to them, "Building a world-class website isn't cheap and you would be one of the first distribution companies to launch a website." You show them the number of visits typical commercial websites are experiencing and explain how Computech would assist them in making their site unique to attract an even larger audience. And, most importantly, since Marshal does not have a lot of time, you point out that if you had management's backing, the site could be installed in three weeks. Marshal's executives unanimously agree to endorse your plan in exchange for 1,000 shares of common stock with a par value of $13 a share.

Marshal's World Wide Website pays off as it immediately begins garnering more than 1,000 sales leads per month. In the first three months after the site is installed, sales increased by $250 million, triggering new improvements to the site. Marshal's stock soars to $39 a share as the company adds an extremely popular industry newsletter complete with sound and video clips. You tell Dan, "They've blended many good aspects of advanced traditional marketing into an electronic media that is receiving rave reviews by the industry." Computech is inundated with calls from companies all over the world seeking Internet marketing-consultant services. To make sure you remain loyal to the company, Computech's general partners approve a 25-percent increase in your salary and grant you a $25,000 year-end bonus. The net-worth line on your year-end financial statement takes a big jump:

Fifth Year Financial Summary

Beginning Year Net Worth	$357,400
Plus: Fifth Year Revenues	$244,000
Less: Business and Living Expenses	$189,800
Fifth Year Net Worth	$411,600

You relish the success you have enjoyed at Computech when you stand up to make some ridiculous speech at your celebration luncheon. Computech has been good to you and as you peek around the corner, you can see the "early retirement door" just a few feet down the hall. You wonder who just opened the door!

You have successfully completed a start-up decision-making track, but you can keep on playing the game by choosing one or more of the options below.

1. If you want to compare how the results of your last five years of start-up decision-making strategies stack up against the other positive outcomes, turn to Chapter 77.

2. If you wish to find out what would have happened had you chosen the alternative of developing sophisticated measurement techniques, turn to Chapter 72.

3. If you would like to pursue other start-up decision-making opportunities, turn to either Chapter 2 or 3.

CHAPTER 72

DEVELOPING SOPHISTICATED

MEASUREMENT TECHNIQUES

You decide to develop sophisticated measuring techniques, which you plan to make available as a niche consulting service to your clients. After all, how can your clients really know if their results-based services are working if they have no yardstick against which to measure the results? With all the elements of results-based service strategies in place, you must now find a way to constantly gauge the impact of services. However, you know that finding the right yardstick could prove difficult since it involves measuring some rather qualitative variables, such as customer experiences as well as quantitative operational and product factors. Whatever measurement system you use to monitor customer satisfaction, it must be flexible enough to allow any of your consultants the ability to refine it or even replace it if the need arises.

Although you have a secret desire to personally author the new measurement system, you know its success will be significantly enhanced if you involve all of your partners in the development process. With their help, you develop a system based upon four principles:

- Let customers determine what is important to measure.

- Never stop adding new measurements or refining old ones.

- Make measurements a central part of operational management.

- Focus on measures that monitor customer expectations, uncovering unmet needs and discovering unique solutions.

After conducting numerous customer focus group sessions to determine what should be measured, the baseline criteria for your measurement system are complete. It includes benchmarking of competitors' services and replicating "best in the world" practices from premier organizations around the world. As the year comes to a close, consulting sales at Computech continue to accelerate, allowing you to make good on your promise that Computech's best years were yet to come. Computech records revenues of $3.5 million and gross profits of $520 thousand for the year, as shown in the accompanying financial statement.

SELECTED FINANCIAL INFORMATION FOR COMPUTECH
(DOLLARS IN THOUSANDS)

	Current Year
Operations	
Net Sales	$3,500
Cost of sales	27.2
Research and development	7.0
Marketing	21.0
General and administrative	8.8
Gross Profit	$520
Financial Position	
Current assets	$28.7
Current liabilities	14.9
Working capital	13.8
Other assets	8.6
Property and equipment	10.7
Total assets	48.1
Other Data	
Capital expenditures	$4.1
Depreciation	1.1
Return on sales	27%
Return on assets	49%
Number of employees	175

Tony Berger, one of the senior partners at Computech, believes that the significant increase in sales over the last year are a direct result of your efforts to develop sophisticated measuring techniques. In his words, "It very nicely complements our results-based consulting service." The numbers prompt Tony to encourage the general partnership to approve a 20-percent increase in your salary. Looking back, the measurement system you developed provided a concrete vehicle for moving Computech aggressively forward. With the new benchmarking, best practices, and other measurement programs in place, Computech's consulting team can confidently offer sound advice to their customer set. Tony tells you that this past year has been the most demanding of his career, yet he believes that the measurement system represents the best management tool created by any company in the consulting industry. Your success at Computech is nicely reflected in your own personal financial statement.

Fifth Year Financial Summary

Beginning Year Net Worth	$355,500
Plus: Fifth Year Revenues	$223,000
Less: Business and Living Expenses	$169,000
Fifth Year Net Worth	$409,500

As you review your four years with Computech, you know that both the tough times and rewarding times will serve you well in the future. You're convinced that long-term competitive advantages will go to service leaders and not service followers. You take great pride in the fact that you have started a service legacy that will keep Computech ahead of its most earnest competitors. Five years ago, you focused on affiliating with a consulting firm; then, as the years unfolded, you decided to remain somewhat independent when you linked up with a small group of independent consultants. You focused on marketing and stressed a narrow scope of services and implemented techniques to measure and monitor customer expectations. All of your efforts resulted in a twofold increase in sales from $1.75 to $3.5 million and a sevenfold increase in profits from $87,000 to $520,000.

You have successfully completed a start-up decision-making track, but you can keep playing the game by choosing one or more of the options that follow.

1. If you want to compare how the results of your last five years of start-up decision-making strategies stack up against the other positive outcomes, turn to Chapter 77.

2. If you wish to find out what would have happened had you chosen the alternative of financing marketing campaigns for equity, turn to Chapter 71.

3. If you want to discover the outcomes of other choices on the track, turn to Chapters 39 or 40. Return to Chapter 10 if you want to start the track from the beginning.

4. If you would like to pursue other start-up decision-making opportunities, turn to either Chapter 2 or 3.

CHAPTER 73

ESTABLISHING A MARKETING
FIRM TO SERVICE RESORT
LODGES

Mr. Weber is well aware of your desires to acquire and run your own Montana resort lodge. He has presented you with an interesting alternative and offer, which you have decided to accept. He asks you to set up a subsidiary company under the parent company of Cole & Weber that would specialize in providing marketing services for lodges in the United States and Canada. If all goes well, you will be free to expand the venture internationally. Cole & Weber's Board of Directors has allocated $10 million to back the new venture under the company name of Market Direct Inc. You have been named the company's President and CEO. Although your annual base salary is relatively low, a mere $95,000, bonuses and perks could amount to an additional $70,000 a year. Mr. Weber has given you one year to make this "start-up pup" fly.

Your initial start-up challenge is to quickly find two things you don't have, a competent staff and clients. Five thousand square feet of office space, complete with furniture, telephones, a computer system, faxes, and copy machines have been leased for Market Direct in a high-end industrial park next to Billings's Logan International Airport. Now, all you have to do is fill the space with business and employees.

You convince Mr. Weber that Cole & Weber should afford every employee the opportunity to transfer over to Market Direct so that you can focus your efforts on acquiring new accounts. You tell him you need 30 good men and women. He agrees to let you take 20 from the inside and tells you to get the rest from the outside. On the first day in which Cole & Weber posts the Market Direct "open positions" announcement, your phone rings off the hook with inquiries from interested employees. You immediately use one of your outside requisition chits to hire a top-notch executive secretary to help you handle the phone traffic.

You spend the next thirty days conducting comprehensive interviews with Cole & Weber employees to find their "best of breed" employees. In the end, you select fifteen of Cole & Weber's top Account Executives, three of their best media people and two of their best production people over the vocal objections of their Vice President, Cheryl Cole. You remind Cheryl, "A deal is a deal and the fact that Mr. Weber didn't inform you of the deal doesn't change anything." She quietly tells you, "If you slip up once, I'll have your heart for breakfast." Welcome back to the corporate world where the vampires are everywhere!

With your 20-member Cole & Weber transfer team in place, you call your good friend Steve Harding at the Timber Wolf Lodge and schedule a weekend retreat for your newly formed swat team. Unaware of your hidden agenda, when the team shows up at the lodge early Saturday morning, you announce the overnight horseback ride into the Pioneer Mountains to discuss Market Direct's corporate strategy. Without exception, everybody is legitimately excited about the program. After a delightful two-hour ride to the base camp on Lake Wilderness, and an absolutely fabulous barbecue, your team settles down in front of the campfire to hear what you have to say.

You proceed with what sounds like an admission of guilt. "As your new CEO, I must confess that I am deeply honored that the 20 of you have chosen to join Market Direct. And, as I told you during our interview sessions, we have just one short year to show that we can pull this thing off. To that end, I must confess that I have loaded the front end of the shotgun. Fifteen of you are salespeople because we desperately need new sales. We have only five production people to handle the work when it comes into the office. We all know that's the wrong mix. The proper mix is more like one salesperson to five production people. But I need sales first before I dare add any more production people. The risk I take is that you salespeople could quickly overload our production capacity and in the process, we would lose our quality control. That would be it! We'd be out of business. I need a solution to the problem and I need your help."

Your dilemma is met head-on with open and positive discussion amongst the group that continues into the early morning hours.

Somehow you have managed to form an empowered team. All of your salespeople vowed to form an alliance with your production team not to overload its capacity. If fact, many of the salespeople volunteered to offer help if they overloaded production. Countering, the production side of your team said they knew of contract people who could be pulled in on a moment's notice to handle the extra work.

Over the next several months, Market Direct's empowered team meets every customer's creative and production challenge with a degree of excellence that you have never experienced before. You concentrate your efforts on solidifying marketing accounts with Montana's 10 major lodges and 25 major lodges in the Canadian Rockies. By the end of your fifth year with Cole & Weber, your first-year gross sales exceed $10 million and net profits are $1.5 million. Cole & Weber's Board of Directors gives you an overwhelming vote of confidence that is anchored with a $150,000 bonus. All of this positive financial action is favorably reflected in your financial statement.

Fifth Year Financial Summary

Beginning Year Net Worth	$305,000
Plus: Fifth Year Salary and Bonuses	$165,000
Less: Business and Living Expenses	$75,200
Fifth Year Net Worth	$394,800

You have successfully completed a start-up decision-making track, but you can keep playing the game by choosing one or more of the options that follow.

1. If you want to compare how the results of your last five years of start-up decision-making strategies stack up against the other positive outcomes, turn to Chapter 77.

2. If you wish to find out what would have happened had you chosen the alternative of obtaining ownership in a resort lodge for marketing services, turn to Chapter 74.

3. If you want to discover the outcomes of other choices on the track, turn to Chapter 42. Return to Chapter 11 if you want to start the track from the beginning.

4. If you would like to pursue other start-up decision-making opportunities, turn to either Chapter 2 or 3.

CHAPTER 74

OBTAINING OWNERSHIP IN A
RESORT LODGE FOR MARKETING
SERVICES

The Timber Wolf Lodge is the largest and in your opinion, the most beautiful lodge in Montana. Your decision to work for a well-known lodge was a good one. The lodge is located on the north end of Canyon Ferry Lake surrounded by the beautiful Helena National Forest. All 172 suites in the lodge overlook the lake and offer majestic views of the bordering Rocky Mountains. Every conceivable recreational activity is offered, including superb rainbow and native cutthroat trout fishing and horseback riding, complete with breakfast and overnight rides, jeep rentals, mountain biking, and rental boats of every size and shape. Fall and winter activities include exotic snowmobile excursions into prime elk country, guided big and small game hunting, and some of the best skiing in the state.

With all of the sophisticated recreational services the lodge has to offer, you are perplexed when you discover the limited advertising program they have in place to attract visitors. Steve Harding, the lodge's general manager, spends a week with you venting his frustration as he shows you every facet of the lodge's operation.

He bluntly explains the situation in a way that clearly defines the problem. "We are spending in excess of $100,000 for a third-rate brochure and a bunch of national radio ads that quite frankly, just aren't working. Our inadequate ad campaign is costing us in excess of a half-million dollars a year in lost business. We have a 75-percent average occupancy rate, compared to an 88-percent rate for the

Montana lodge industry. If you can help us solve our problem, I'll offer you part interest in this place." Steve agrees to transfer the Timber Wolf account over to Cole & Weber as long as you are the Account Executive. You and Steve agree to review your progress at the end of six months. Although the whole deal sounds vague, you decide to assess the viability of Steve's offer as you work through Timber Wolf's occupancy problem.

You implement a national advertising campaign where you place short but effective television ads on the national travel stations complete with scenic videos and 1-800 reservation numbers that quickly become overloaded. By midyear, Timber Wolf's occupancy rate jumps to 91 percent, well above the lodge-industry average. Steve insists that you join him for a celebration party at the lodge with all expenses paid, including keys to the executive suite for you and your guest. During the course of the evening, you tell Steve of your intent to leave Cole & Weber. You assure him that the ad program you started will be well taken care of by your replacement. When he asks who that will be, you tell him the announcement has not yet been made. Steve snaps back with a: "I don't need someone else, I need you! Your advertising program proves beyond a doubt that we have got to continue to target our market if we are to remain competitive. Do you remember the equity position in the lodge that I promised you last January? If you will work for Timber Wolf on a full-time basis to further refine and improve our advertising program, I'll pay you a darn good salary and you can earn 25-percent ownership in the lodge over the next five years! In other words, for every year you're in the program, you'll earn 5 percent ownership up to 25 percent at the end of the fifth year. Will you accept my offer?"

He's taken aback when you politely decline his offer and aggressively asks you why. Over the past six months, you have gotten to know Steve reasonably well but because of the serious nature of your assignment, both of you have restricted your conversations to strictly business matters. With the success of the marketing program behind you, you tell Steve, "To be honest with you, I want to open my own lodge somewhere in Montana. I want to own the whole thing and run it myself."

Steve interjects with, "Do you really know what you are getting yourself into? Starting one of these puppies is not cheap. How much money do you have to invest?" When you tell him you have $225,000, he laughs! "I don't mean to make fun of you but you're going to need at least twice that much to start a successful lodge. I'll show you our books, which will tell you exactly what it cost to get the Timber Wolf off the ground and into a profitable state. If you are intent on starting a lodge on your own, you'll need a lot more money than $225,000 to get started."

"It takes years to build a client base and you know as well as I do that referrals are a big part of this business. The politics of building anything in Montana right now is tough. The governor said she will do everything she can to keep the state's population below a million. It's all there in this morning's paper. If you don't build, then good luck at finding one to buy. There are only five lodges besides the Timber Wolf worth owning and none of them is for sale. Even if they were, you'd need a million dollars to fund the deal." Almost out of breath, Steve stops talking for a moment and you tell him you will think about his generous offer and give him your answer in the morning.

Fifth Year Financial Summary

Beginning Year Net Worth	$305,000
Plus: Fifth Year Revenues	$98,000
Equity in Lodge	$50,000
Less: Business and Living Expenses	$39,300
Fifth Year Net Worth	$413,700

That evening, you review your year-end financial statement and although you are pleased with the progress you have made, you realize that Steve is probably correct in his assessment. You don't have the capital to buy or build your own lodge. At the very least, you would have to take in partners to finance the deal. In the end, you would still only be a part owner.

As you assess Steve's offer, you believe that the Timber Wolf Lodge is worth at least $1 million, based on what you have discovered in your search for a lodge. And, in your opinion, this lodge could be worth a lot more if the advertising program that you put in place is refined to further improve on the lodge's occupancy rates. You project what a 25-percent ownership in the lodge would do to your financial statement.

Projected Financial Summary with Lodge Included

Beginning Year Net Worth	$539,000
Plus: Fifth Year Revenues	$260,000
Less: Business and Living Expenses	$374,000
Fifth Year Net Worth	$425,000

As the old expression goes, "Never look a gift horse in the mouth." You can't wait to accept Steve's generous offer in the morning. You have successfully completed a start-up decision-making track, but you can keep playing the game by choosing one or more of the options that follow.

1. If you want to compare how the results of your last five years of start-up decision-making strategies stack up against the other positive outcomes, turn to Chapter 77.

2. If you wish to find out what would have happened had you chosen the alternative of establishing a marketing service firm for lodges, turn to Chapter 73.

3. If you want to discover the outcomes of other choices on the track, turn to Chapter 61. Return to Chapter 11 if you want to start the track from the beginning.

4. If you would like to pursue other start-up decision-making opportunities, turn to either Chapter 2 or 3.

CHAPTER 75

JOINT-VENTURING WITH TBN

The old man sure knew what he was talking about! Back in your college days, Peter Drucker was your idol and he still is today. It seemed like every management book you read was either written or endorsed by Drucker. One of his books talked about joint-venturing where he wrote, "In today's environment, joint-venturing is a strategic business tool that you must be able to use effectively if you want to become a successful entrepreneur. You should not be misled by the analogy, often drawn, between strategic partnerships and marriage. Unlike marriage, today's strategic partnerships are not based on the notion of mutual attraction. They are rooted in cold necessity. No entrepreneur makes a strategic alliance with another unless they have to in order to achieve their strategic objectives more effectively, at a lower cost or with less risk than if they acted alone. The partnership therefore becomes a mechanism by which you can achieve a competitive advantage. Use it as a weapon in the continuous battle for the market you want to control." Drucker wrote that statement 25 years ago and it coincides precisely with your thinking today.

You mount a major marketing campaign to solicit joint-venture interest from a major television network in your personal coaching program. Joining the National Association of Television Broadcasters helps you get started by helping you find the telephone numbers and names of "who's who" in the industry. Carefully worded letters supplemented with a brochure that outlines precisely what you want to do with your program are sent to every network executive in the country. Your follow-up telephone calls run into a fire wall when you attempt to get past the executive secretaries to discuss your ideas with the network executives. These people have been trained to filter out all incoming calls from unknowns and you can't blame them. They must get inundated with calls from every "get-rich-quick" scheme artist in the country.

Your current approach is not working. As you thumb through *Broadcast Magazine,* you are attracted to a full-page ad that announces the National Association of Television Broadcasters annual conference to be held in Salt Lake City next week. The impressive list of guest speakers includes such names as Ted Turner, Gary Steiner, and Tom Shales. If you could just get one minute of one of those people's attention, you would at least have a shot at getting your foot in the door. You put the paper down, make a few phone calls, and you're booked into the conference.

The conference proves to be one of the most astute strategic decisions you have ever made. All of the name-brand television executives are there in sports attire in the relaxed atmosphere of the conference setting. You sign up for the conference tennis tournament and discover that you have been paired-up with Ted Turner as your doubles partner. You get to know Ted reasonably well during the course of the match as you patiently avoid talking about your joint-venture idea. However, the opportunity presents itself when Ted invites you to attend a reception he's hosting later that evening. Reception parties are made to discuss business propositions.

That evening, you talk to Ted about your personal coaching program and your ideas about joint-venturing the program on Turner Broadcasting Network. Ted tells you, "Call my office next week, like Monday around 9 A.M., and tell my secretary I'm expecting your call." A week later, you call Ted. The conversation is short, but productive. He ask you to work out all of the details with Jack Ritter, one of his Senior Vice Presidents. "If it looks good to Jack, I'll sign the joint-venture agreement and we're off and running." You agree to meet Jack in Burbank, California the following week.

Your flight into Burbank was uneventful, which is the way you like it. Jack meets you at the gate and the two of you head out to Steamers, the best seafood restaurant in Malibu. During the course of your lunch, Jack is blunt when he tells you, "In the television business, you earn prime-time stripes one stripe at a time. We'll start your program off on secondary time and closely monitor your audience ratings. If your ratings go up, you can advance up the secondary time ladder into a prime-time slot. If your ratings go down or are simply not there, we'll shut the program down. That is the way it works in the cruel world of television. You get 10 percent of our net revenue from advertisers. Initially, it won't be much. Maybe $5,000 a show but, as you move closer to a prime-time spot, the advertising dollars go up exponentially. Do you still want to try a joint venture shot with TBN?"

Launching a personal coaching cable-television program gave you some new insights into the power of the television media. You realize that your program is not on prime time and in fact, it is on at the worst time, 6 A.M. in the morning! Even given the disadvantage of an ungodly early hour, the response you have received from the program has been outstanding. In some weeks, you receive over 500 pieces of mail from people who are interested in receiving more information about personal coaching. You had to stop giving out your business phone number and convert to an answering service because you could not accommodate all of the incoming calls.

Your entrepreneurial mind tells you this is good, but what would happen if you made it better? If you could figure out a way to get your program on prime time, it would really take off. You convince Jack Ritter to sponser celebrity coaching interviews, which initially include Ross Perot and Bill Gates. Viewer ratings jump 23 percent and *TV Guide* calls your program the Oprah Winfrey of the only personal coaching talk show on television. As you close out your fifth year with a review of your financial statement, you think to yourself, "This has been a very good year."

Fifth Year Financial Summary

Beginning Year Net Worth	$360,400
Plus: Fifth Year Revenues	$263,500
Less: Business and Living Expenses	$210,900
Fifth Year Net Worth	$413,000

You have successfully completed a start-up decision-making track, but you can keep playing the game by choosing one or more of the options that follow.

1. If you want to compare how the results of your last five years of start-up decision-making strategies stack up against the other positive outcomes, turn to Chapter 77.

2. If you want to discover the outcomes of other choices on the track, turn to Chapter 63. Return to Chapter 12 if you want to start the track from the beginning.

3. If you would like to pursue other start-up decision-making opportunities, turn to either Chapter 2 or 3.

CHAPTER 76

OFFERING CUSTOMIZED

COACHING PROGRAMS TO

CORPORATIONS

Comfortable with your personal coaching cable TV series, you begin focusing on customizing coaching programs for corporations as the most important element of your company's synthesis of best practices. Thanks to your TV series, you're receiving well over a hundred letters a week from companies all over the world who want to know more about personal coaching.

As one responding executive put it, "The role played by management to employees is the same role a coach plays to team players. The difference between these two professionals (manager and coach) is that coaches have had formal training on what they need to do to become a good coach. Personal coaching programs for managers are almost nonexistent."

You're convinced that for this program to be effective, it must synthesize the best contemporary management practices in corporate America. You contact Jean Farland, the executive editor for *Fortune* magazine, who interviewed you recently for an article on the future of personal coaching. She likes the idea of synthesizing the best management practices into personal coaching programs and agrees to open her files to you if you will, in turn, share the results with her. You agree and she sends you a large bundle of articles and research material *Fortune* magazine recently used as background for an extensive feature article on state-of-the-art organizational and management practices in the United States. The material pinpoints several best-of-breed management practices that are employed by highly successful companies.

As your synthesis project gathers momentum, you become more energized than ever as you anticipate incorporating exciting practices from other companies into personal coaching programs for corporations. Ninety days later and after much discussion with corporate executives from all over the country, you review the six best-in-the-world practices that become the nucleus of your corporate-coaching program:

1. General Electric's "workout session" will be used to show how to resolve problems in a single meeting without impeding the input, suggestions, and problem-solving ability of the people involved.

2. 3M's autonomy, which on the surface looks like disorganization and chaos, but in fact allows people throughout an organization to pursue a variety of experimental paths to keep 3M on the leading edge of technological developments.

3. CNN's ability to become a world-news powerhouse through controlled determination and energized employees is used to bolster energy coaching.

4. IBM's approach to new-product development, based on a deep commitment to basic research to remain a technical leader, will be the foundation of the technical part of your program.

5. Walmart's ability to provide superior service offers an excellent backdrop of relevant examples for customer service coaching.

6. McKinsey & Company, one of the most respected international consulting firms in the world, follows no formal policy or procedure system. Powerful on-the-job training programs replace the needs for policy and procedure manuals. You'll use the McKinsey system to augment your critical-thinking coaching sessions.

The mix represents an impressive array of practices, but you can't help wondering to yourself if you can really synthesize all of them into your personal coaching programs. Theoretically, it can be done, but how long it will actually take causes you some concern. As you mull over the issues, you keep telling yourself, "There's no turning back now."

Over the next six months, you actively network corporate prospects who are interested in your personal coaching programs. You show them how they can select any one or combination of the six best-in-the-world programs and, based upon their input to you in a series of interview sessions, you offer to customize a personal coaching program for their employees. Initially, your program gets off to a slow start, which is not unexpected for a new and unique program. You only hope that it's not too unique. Thanks in large part to your cable TV program, your credibility is already established and the program gathers momentum by the end of the year. As you peer over the horizon into next year, you suddenly realize that customized coaching commitments and your television program will absorb all of your time. As you review your year-end financial statement and the growth you have achieved in your net worth, you quickly conclude that you may be able to retire in three instead of five years.

Fifth Year Financial Summary

Beginning Year Net Worth	$360,400
Plus: Fifth Year Revenues	$252,500
Less: Business and Living Expenses	$222,300
Fifth Year Net Worth	$390,600

You have successfully completed a start-up decision-making track, but you can keep playing the game by choosing one or more of the options that follow.

1. If you want to compare how the results of your last five years of start-up decision-making strategies stack up against the other positive outcomes, turn to Chapter 77.

2. If you wish to find out what would have happened had you chosen the alternative of financing marketing campaigns for equity, turn to Chapter 71.

3. If you want to discover the outcomes of other choices on the track, turn to Chapter 63. Return to Chapter 12 if you want to start the track from the beginning.

4. If you would like to pursue other start-up decision-making opportunities, turn to either Chapter 2 or 3.

CHAPTER 77

A RANKING OF THE

SUCCESSFUL OUTCOMES

Your experience playing *Starting-Up* will be enhanced if you wait to read this chapter until after you have come to the end of all the decision-making tracks. Your experience to this point should have enhanced your productivity insight and decision-making ability. In developing *Starting-Up,* we intended more than anything else to broaden, deepen, and strengthen your entrepreneurial consciousness and competence. We also hope playing *Starting-Up* has entertained and inspired you through its virtual-reality challenges, dilemmas, and choices. There are 26 outcomes in the game, ranging from triumph to disaster. In order to compare the various outcomes, find the number of the chapter you just completed (which represents the end of a decision-making track) ranked on the following page according to your personal net worth at the end of five years. All outcomes, both positive and negative, are ranked, but only those that allowed you to complete five years show your earned net worth.

RANKING OF SUCCESSFUL OUTCOMES

Chapter	Title	Rank	Net Worth
29	Finding Associates to Build Project Teams	#17	$384,300
45	Remaining Solo	#21	$375,900
47	Sticking with Houses	#16	$368,400

48	Moving to Larger Projects	#24	$369,600
51	Merging with an Established Software Company	#1	$417,900
52	Getting an SBA Loan	#5	$409,500
53	Buying a Larger Motel	#7	$405,300
54	Creating a Limited Partnership to Buy a Lodge	#9	$401,100
55	Offering Traditional Marketing Services	#15	$388,500
57	Focusing on Personal-Productivity Improvements	#26	$290,000
58	Developing a New Approach to Training People	#18	$382,200
59	Joint-Venturing on a New Lodge	#11	$396,900
63	Creating a Website Focused on Personal Coaching	#13	$392,700
65	Sticking with Proven Personal Coaching Approaches	#19	$380,000
66	Expanding to Include Family Coaching	#8	$403,200
67	Keeping the Network Small	#22	$373,800
68	Developing a National Network	#6	$407,400
69	Acquiring Corporate Shipping Accounts	#20	$378,000
70	Focusing on Residential Customers	#23	#371,700
71	Financing Marketing Campaigns for Equity	#4	$411,600
72	Developing Sophisticated Measurment Techniques	#10	$409,500
73	Establishing a Marketing Firm to Service Resort Lodges	#12	$394,800
74	Obtaining Ownership in a Resort Lodge for Marketing Services	#2	$413,000
75	Joint-Venturing with TBN	#3	$413,700
76	Offering Customized Coaching Programs to Corporations	#14	$390,600

Now that you know how your initial choices in *Starting-Up* stack up, put your entrepreneurial consciousness and competence to the test again by choosing one of the options at the end of the chapter you just finished. When you reach the end of another decision-making track, you can return to this chapter to compare your results. Good Luck!

INDEX